WHAT DOES THE NEW EXECUTIVE WOMAN DO:

—When a company officer makes a pass at her?
—When she has to fire a man twenty years older than she?
—When her woman secretary treats her as a chum?
—When "all the boys" meet for drinks after work without ever inviting her?
—When she wants a job that has been classified as "a man's position"?

To weave a pattern of executive success, a woman must make countless choices and moves that can spell the difference between getting stuck and getting ahead. She needs all the help she can get to make them—and now at last this definitive guide to corporate success gives her all the advice she needs.

THE NEW EXECUTIVE WOMAN
A Guide to Business Success

MARCILLE GRAY WILLIAMS was, by the age of 23, president of her own advertising firm, with over $1,000,000 in annual billings. Subsequently she moved on to even more impressive business triumphs, and currently is a leading California advertising consultant, as well as a highly successful writer and lecturer.

MENTOR and SIGNET Books of Special Interest

☐ **ENTERPRISING WOMEN by Caroline Bird.** Women who have shaped American economic life from Abigail Adams to Sylvia Porter. "Illuminating . . . a pleasure to read."—*Kirkus Reviews* "For all of us who have been taught only half the economic history of the United States."—Gloria Steinem
(#MJ1485—$1.95)

☐ **BACK TO BUSINESS: A Woman's Guide to Reentering the Job Market by Lucia Mouat.** Guidelines for self-assessment, choosing your field, exploring job prospects, the art of the resume, and the interview . . . "Can double a woman's chances."—W. Willard Wirtz, former Secretary of Labor
(#J9304—$1.95)

☐ **YOUR CAREER: How to Plan It—Manage It—Change It by Richard H. Buskirk.** Whether you're in school, on your first job, or in a position that is dead-end or wrong-way, this remarkable and practical guide is for you. Filled with fascinating case histories, this book is meant not just to be read but to be used. Its goal is yours: the career and success you deserve.
(#MJ1537—$1.95)

☐ **HOW TO TURN YOUR IDEA INTO A MILLION DOLLARS by Don Kracke with Roger Honkanen.** Researching, patenting, negotiating, financing, manufacturing, marketing, presentations, distribution—everything you need to know to turn your new product, invention, technique, or gimmick into a gold mine. The fantastic step-by-step guide by one man who did it!
(#ME1787—$2.50)

☐ **HOW TO START AND MANAGE YOUR OWN BUSINESS by Gardiner G. Greene.** If you run a small business, you need all the help you can get—and this is the book that gives it all to you, with information on financial strategies, developing and marketing your product, contracting with the government, and everything else you need to know.
(#ME1929—$2.50)

Buy them at your local bookstore or use this convenient coupon for ordering.

THE NEW AMERICAN LIBRARY, INC.
P.O. Box 999, Bergenfield, New Jersey 07621

Please send me the SIGNET and MENTOR BOOKS I have checked above. I am enclosing $_____ (please add 50¢ to this order to cover postage and handling). Send check or money order—no cash or C.O.D.'s. Prices and numbers are subject to change without notice.

Name _____

Address _____

City _____ State _____ Zip Code _____
Allow 4-6 weeks for delivery.
This offer is subject to withdrawal without notice.

THE NEW EXECUTIVE WOMAN

A Guide to Business Success

by

Marcille Gray Williams

A MENTOR BOOK
NEW AMERICAN LIBRARY
TIMES MIRROR
NEW YORK AND SCARBOROUGH, ONTARIO
THE NEW ENGLISH LIBRARY LIMITED, LONDON

NAL BOOKS ARE AVAILABLE AT QUANTITY DISCOUNTS
WHEN USED TO PROMOTE PRODUCTS OR SERVICES. FOR
INFORMATION PLEASE WRITE TO PREMIUM MARKETING DIVISION,
THE NEW AMERICAN LIBRARY, INC., 1633 BROADWAY,
NEW YORK, NEW YORK 10019.

COPYRIGHT © 1977 BY MARCILLE GRAY WILLIAMS

All rights reserved.
For information address Chilton Book Company,
Chilton Way, Radnor, Pennsylvania 19089.

The excerpts on pages 44–45 from *Body Language* by Julius Fast
(Copyright © 1970 by Julius Fast)
are reprinted with the permission of the publishers,
M. Evans and Company, Inc., New York, N.Y. 10017.

This is an authorized reprint of a hardcover edition published by
Chilton Book Company and simultaneously in Canada by
Thomas Nelson & Sons, Ltd.

MENTOR TRADEMARK REG. U.S. PAT. OFF. AND FOREIGN COUNTRIES
REGISTERED TRADEMARK—MARCA REGISTRADA
HECHO EN CHICAGO, U.S.A.

SIGNET, SIGNET CLASSICS, MENTOR, PLUME, MERIDIAN AND NAL
BOOKS are published *in the United States* by
The New American Library, Inc.,
1633 Broadway, New York, New York 10019,
in Canada by The New American Library of Canada Limited,
81 Mack Avenue, Scarborough, Ontario M1L 1M8,
in the United Kingdom by The New English Library Limited,
Barnard's Inn, Holborn, London, EC1N 2JR, England

4   5   6   7   8   9   10   11   12

PRINTED IN THE UNITED STATES OF AMERICA

This book is dedicated to my Dad,
who taught me never to accept second best.

Acknowledgments

I am grateful to the wonderful women who candidly and conscientiously contributed to this book through their interviews, and helped make a dream become a reality. They are Barbara Allen, Gayla Black, Karen Bochman, Jo Conover, Diane Czernowski, Sylvia Dennen, Jane Voit Dowling, Margaret Drossel, Mary Gregg, Mary Jane Hewett, Beverly Kees, Linda Ketchum, Gloria Kraemer, Diane Levine, Priscilla List, Marsha McManus, Sunny Poulson, Charlotte Scott, Pat Zimmerman, Lorraine Zutell, and several other women who asked to remain nameless.

I would also like to thank Vic Drumm whose generous assistance helped me in the beginning and Bill Barbour for his sage advice.

My heartfelt love to my brothers and their wives, Gary and Ann, Gordy and Michale, Mother, Alma, and Dad, and my in-laws, Cecil and Fay Williams, who were all there when I needed them, and who each in their own way contributed to the effort.

Most of all, I would like to acknowledge my husband, Dennis, who provided both encouragement and feedback along the way, and who shared with me the pains and pleasures of writing a book.

Contents

Introduction

When I became a business executive a number of years ago, I found myself constantly confronted with situations and problems that I was not sure how to deal with. I, like most businesswomen, was without a role model to observe and emulate. I was in a continual quandary over exactly how I should behave and what was expected of me. Often I felt alone and confused, and I wished I knew how other women were coping with the myriad difficulties that were arising weekly.

I searched for a book to give me the answers, but none could be found that was truly relevant to my particular dilemma. None were written by authors engaged in a real business situation. Most were either pedantic or political, difficult to wade through, and of very little assistance to the striving woman executive.

So I took a break from my advertising career to write the book myself. I devoted months to analyzing my own experiences to determine what had worked for me, and why. I camped in the library doing extensive research, studying both feminist and antifeminist literature, books on business and books on sociology. I arranged interviews with women executives across the country and spent weeks on the road meeting with them. I did all the things an author does to prepare a book.

A funny thing happened to me on the way to writing this book. I had my consciousness raised.

When I started this book in 1976, I was what you might call a latent feminist. I believed in the essence of feminism all along, but I had failed to recognize it within myself. If anybody had asked me if I were a feminist, I would have said no. I arrogantly felt that I did not need the feminist movement for I had made it on my own. Frankly, I truly couldn't understand what all the fuss was about. I owned my own business. I was president of a professional association consisting mostly of men. I had a husband who fully supported my activities. I had achieved a high level of success at an early age. I failed to see how the women's movement helped me.

But, in fact, it was through the women's movement that I first realized that others actually felt I was inferior because I was female. I was fortunate to be blessed with parents who held the same expectations of me that they held for my brothers, and my supposed inferiority had never occurred to me. I was naive. I realize now that my own success was due to incredibly hard work and fortuitous timing. Even though I denied their assistance at the time, I was benefiting from the efforts of many women before me. Others had helped make my executive success possible, and I was taking the credit.

Recently I was reviewing some notes I had jotted down a year ago that were clearly antifeminist statements. The realization of my gradual transformation leaped before me, and I was amazed at the difference in my attitude. I'm not exactly sure when, but indeed I had my consciousness raised.

Originally, there had seemed to be such a fragmentation of purpose and such a lack of direction within the movement that I had failed to comprehend what the movement was all about. But now I have a better idea. The movement is about options. Consequently, it's too diverse to be cohesive. How could one expect lesbian and heterosexual, housewife and hardhat to be unified toward a single goal? The movement, in its bigness of heart and wideness of scope, attempts to encompass all, and by doing so, dilutes its effectiveness for any single cause.

There are many ideologies of the women's liberation movement with which I still tend to disagree. For example, I support both the concept and use of femininity, and many feminists would take issue with me on that. I believe in wearing make-up and skirts, and shaving legs. Many of my sisters would find that despicable. But although I still find myself having difficulty identifying with some feminists, I have an even harder time relating to the opposition. The women's movement, with all its frailties, has unlocked opportunities and alternatives for us that we never before considered. It has helped women gain access to management jobs and has arrested the rampant perpetuation of male chauvinism. For this we should give it our full, unconstrained support—that is, if the movement still exists.

"Where have all the feminists gone?" movement spokespeople ask. Witty *Esquire* columnist Nora Ephron said at a lecture I recently attended, "The women's movement consisted of a bunch of writers who ran off to start a magazine. There is no leadership." She, like many others, fears the movement is dying out.

I don't think it is. The spirit of feminism has been captured in the hearts of millions of Americans. Abortion laws and the treatment of rape victims have changed. Women's athletics are beginning to flourish. Women newscasters are cropping up across the country, and increasingly more businesswomen are succeeding.

I suspect that many of those women who had participated in consciousness raising groups and feminist political activities have now redirected their energies toward personal goals. Instead of attending a consciousness raising group, they are attending professional organizations, working long hours, going to school, or pursuing other activities to further their careers. They are not sitting around and talking about the movement, they are living it. Each is effecting individual change and is making her presence felt through her endeavors.

This book is not intended to be a political statement, but a practical guidebook and survival manual for the striving executive woman. And, despite my conversion to feminism, some may consider the advice in this book antifeminist. For example, I preach executive success through individualized effort—your goals should be personal ones if you wish to succeed in business. Feminists strive to meet political goals that are group objectives, such as ending discrimination against all women. *Psychology Today* defines the difference between feminists and antifeminists this way: "Feminists believe in group strategies, such as visible, organized protest, while antifeminists believe in individual strategies."

This book is bulging with advice on how you must succeed in business by individual tactics. Does this mean I'm antifeminist? I think not. Indeed, the feminist movement and the emergence of the new executive woman go hand in hand. But I may differ with the movement leaders over the useful application of the collective strength of the movement. Collective strength and group strategy, through labor organizing, are techniques well-suited to helping women in the blue collar and low-paying white-collar jobs, where the majority of workers are. This is one of the directions in which the movement is headed. Another fertile area for organizing woman is in "the Pink Collar Ghetto"—that group of women in typically female jobs that are low-paying: waitresses, beauticians, and sales-clerks, for example. In the March 1977 issue of *Ms. Magazine*, Gloria Steinem said, "The work revolution we need isn't the toleration of a few women in 'male' professions. It will begin with the rise of the pink collar worker." Focusing the emphasis here will help the greatest number of women.

This book is not addressed to women who wish to become welders or pipefitters, beauticians or waitresses, medical technicians or secretaries. It's written for the woman who is, or wants to become, a business executive. For that, she must get there on her own. Strategy to gain executive success, the kind with big salaries and equally big responsibilities, must be based on individual efforts.

The woman who survives as an executive will be the one who relies upon herself as an individual. Her true potential will be realized through her own capabilities and contributions, not through collectivism. To survive in the teeming corporate jungle, self-preservation comes first. She must set her priorities first to gain personal success, rather than to promote the good of the cause. Impassioned feminists believe that the choice is one or the other, that there is no in-between. I believe that there is some middle ground, and this position is imperative for the woman executive.

The executive woman can do more for the plight of others by performing well. She can alter the male chauvinist's perception of women by being different than he expects. She can pave the way for other women by demonstrating her worth. She can be career-oriented, and prove that other women can be also. She can make being a woman executive easier for others who follow after her.

But she can't accomplish all this if she doesn't have the job to begin with. Within the existing structure, the only way she is going to survive is if she looks out for herself first.

Following that philosophy doesn't necessarily mean that she is antifeminist. It just means she's smart, and understands the nature of business dynamics. The individualist approach to executive success that I offer is not just my opinion alone. It has, of course, worked for me. But the philosophy was continually reinforced through my conversations with many other executive women.

My intention when I interviewed these women was to collect their experiences and attitudes to lend the book insight and objectivity and to make it relevant to the widest group of people. So I chose women from a multitude of professions, mostly non-traditional (finance, scientific instrumentation, journalism, utilities, transportation, paper, chemicals, advertising, computers, publishing, and government). They were engineers, researchers, sales personnel, and managers with a variety of job titles. They were scattered across the nation in New York, Philadelphia, Chicago, Minneapolis, San Francisco, and Los Angeles. Their ages ranged from twenty-six to sixty, and most had been to college.

I went through unconventional channels to locate these women. I chose not to use the most obvious source—magazine articles on executive women who had made it to the top. The feminists claim that those women whose stories are spread throughout the media are non-typical women and that they are tokens. Although the women I interviewed were each special in their individual way, only one had been hyped by the media. They held a wide assortment of "regular" jobs, and none felt her position was token (although a few admitted that they formerly held token jobs). I deemed it important to seek the views of the "typical" woman executive, if there is such a thing, rather than the exception. Only then could I impart relevant information.

I had no intention of conducting "scientific" research, as my sample was based on variety rather than on statistical accuracy. But through these interviews, I found a pattern. I discovered the new executive woman. I discovered that her attitudes and philosophies were similar to mine. I found that the new executive woman is a unique blending of feminist and antifeminist. Like me, she considers herself a feminist, yet she prefers to attain corporate success through her own efforts. She is attempting to work with the system and is effecting change by becoming part of it. This is the attitude of the woman who is succeeding today.

The new executive woman is a feminist in principle, but she is an individualist in practice. She is not the stereotypical antifeminist career woman, nor is she the dedicated feminist who believes the system will never let her win and who believes she can succeed only through collective action. Her beliefs fall somewhere in between.

What distinguishes the new executive woman is her willingness to help other women. Most of the women with whom I talked had made a conscious effort to help other women. Quite frankly, a few had been burned in the process. Nevertheless, they displayed a positive attitude about it and indicated they would continue to help women in the future.

Now that's good news!

I wish each reader could have been with me to meet these wonderful women. They were intelligent and articulate, self-confident and charming. They made me proud to be a woman. I asked them frank, relevant questions about their lives and attitudes, their beliefs and aspirations. Their willingness to talk was magnificent. Their responses offer true insight into the real dilemmas facing today's executive woman.

The emergence of the new executive woman has brought forth a whole new set of problems, ones not easily remedied, and it is these problems that I cover in this book. I wish I had all the answers to give you. Unfortunately, life is not so simple. There are many complex areas where there are not true answers—just alternatives and compromises. But I've raised all the questions you are apt to encounter, and the subtle and not so subtle reasons behind them. I've made a diligent and conscientious effort to give the best advice I can in a way that will be meaningful to you. I've given a strategy for corporate success based on real-life experiences, one which has been proven to work. It can work for you.

M. G. W.
March 1977

❧ 1 ❧

Imagine Yourself a Success

This book is for the woman who wishes to become a business executive. It is also for the woman who has already started on a business career and wishes to increase her potential for success. If you fall into either category, this book will help you suceed.

A few years ago, no market would have existed for a book such as this, for the executive woman was a rare commodity. Happily, that situation has changed. Bright, capable women are entering the corporate scene, lighting up the horizon like city lights at dusk, casting a new glow on the entire community. These are the new women executives.

According to the U.S. Department of Labor's Women's Bureau, in 1977 5.9 million women held professional and technical jobs. Another 2.1 million were managers and administrators. *Business Week* estimates that women comprise 15 percent of all new entry-level managers. And although those statistics are low, they are a far cry from a few years ago. Progress is being made. Increasing opportunities exist.

It's not that the opportunities haven't always been there. A few existed for very special women, leaders who plunged forward on the corporate scene without the benefit of others to guide them. These women survived because they were incredibly strong. They were unafraid of loneliness and rejection because they faced it often. They were superior people surviving in a hostile environment. And these women possessed a special vision that allowed them to see themselves as executives. They believed that they could be a success.

To succeed in today's environment, which is more receptive to women, you still must possess these pioneering qualities. Most important of them all, you must imagine yourself a success, and believe that you can be. Your self-image is where it all starts.

A few years ago, women rarely thought of themselves as business executives. Of course, men didn't see us that way either. But before we can expect men to change their image of us, we first must change our own. Self-image is truly the launching pad for your career as an executive. You must believe that you can succeed, or you will evaporate in the corporate atmosphere. Being an executive demands extraordinary self-confidence from anybody, and the demands on you will be even greater. You must battle a chauvinistic society that is seemingly against you. You must create equality for yourself, and that starts only from within.

Self-confidence begins with seeing yourself intellectually equal to men. You don't have to arm wrestle in business, so intellectual equality is all that is required. You must believe that you are equal, because you are. Pardon me, if that seems obvious in these days of women's liberation, but many women, supposedly enlightened, still behave as if they were inferior. So before you consider embarking on an executive career, first examine yourself for any evidence of lagging self-confidence. Make sure *you* believe that you can suceed, that you can match wits with anyone, or at least give it a good try. To compete with men, you must first *believe* that you can compete with them. Make sure there's no area of self-doubt lurking in the cobwebs.

Once you feel yourself equal to men, you have a chance to be treated equally. Women who expect to be treated as equals eventually will. This expectation of equality should be inherent within your personality. Your demands will be met if you believe in yourself. You can receive equal status in the business world by accepting nothing less than totally equal treatment.

Okay, so now you are full of self-confidence and infused with a sense of equality. But do you see yourself as an executive? Before you can achieve an executive position, you must first be able to visualize yourself in it. Your goal must fit comfortably within your self-image. Sit back for a minute and try to imagine yourself as an executive. Or think of yourself as your boss's boss. Does it fit? Can you see yourself doing the job? Before anyone else will see you as an executive, you must first see yourself as one and feel confident that you can do the job. Unfortunately, this is easier said than done.

A female executive in Minneapolis was overlooked for promotions in her department because she was told a woman couldn't possibly handle them. She would nod her head in agreement. One day, she started asking why. It was then she started moving up the corporate ladder, but not until she made the first move. It took her years even to question the male establishment. Once she began to see herself in those jobs and to believe that she could handle them, she made her point to management. So her management began questioning an issue that they had taken for granted. They promoted her. Today, she supervises dozens of people.

You must be convinced that you have the capability to handle executive status, and can see yourself functioning in that role. No doubt, this need is much greater than would be necessary for a man in the same situation. Management seldom questions whether a man can supervise others or make tough, unemotional decisions. Men automatically receive the benefit of the doubt whereas women must constantly prove themselves.

Women tend not to rise to their level of incompetency in business, as suggested by the Peter Principle, because women are not automatically promoted as men are. That's why self-image is so critical to success. Possessing a good self-image will compensate for the lack of career-paving enjoyed by men. You will have to carve your own path. Instead of looking at your job as just a job, see it as a step in a career path. No matter what you're presently doing, somehow it prepares you for the next step. See where your job fits into the big picture, and then zero in on areas upon which you can expand.

It is vitally important that you see yourself as a professional, and behave as a professional behaves. For example, attend lectures and seminars. Read trade journals. Gain all the knowledge that you can about your field, whether or not it is pertinent to your particular job, for all the information that you can amass will help you build your career. You must develop a career-oriented personality before you will be taken seriously by business. Give yourself to your field. Only then do you begin to function as a professional. Unfortunately, this professional, career-oriented attitude is lacking in most women. But it has become second nature to the successful female executive who has integrated her self-image as a business executive with her identity as a woman. She believes that she is capable of being a success.

Desexed by Success?

There's a popular theory among psychologists that women fear success because it may force them to play an inappropriate sex role. Margaret Mead says, "In our society, men are desexed by failure, but women are desexed by success."

That may have been true a few years ago, but woman's role in our society is changing, and the old rules no longer apply. Today's corporate woman is not desexed by success. On the contrary, success can enhance her desirability in much the same way that a man's success would enhance his image. The single female executive finds that the number of available men decreases the higher she goes in business, but the quality of the men available to her increases. Success breeds self-confidence. The self-confident, self-actualized woman attracts men who boast the same qualities. If being desexed translates to being unattractive to the opposite sex, then Margaret Mead is wrong, at least in today's society. Your success may intimidate the blue collar worker, but a senior vice-president of a bank may find it exciting.

But more important than your relationship with men is your relationship with yourself. And there's nothing more comforting than the warmth of self-confidence. A successful career is marvelous for the ego, as any woman who has made it will tell you. Here's what one said about her life since she had enjoyed business success: "I can hardly believe that this person is really me. My self-image when I grew up had been really poor. Now I get complimentary letters from the president of the company. I can still hardly believe they're for me." Another woman said, "I have developed so much self-confidence it's like a whole new world has opened up to me. This job has meant so much to my personal growth. I've put a great deal of emphasis on it. I started getting such good feelings about myself that I had never received from anything else before."

If you even hinted that these women could be desexed by success, they would say you were crazy. To them, their personality has been enhanced by success. A wife of a famous Hollywood producer said she sat meekly by his side for years. She started a public relations business, and she swears that even her sex life has improved.

Despite the evidence that success is not desexing, many psychologists feel that some women throw road blocks in the way to their own success for fear of playing inappropriate sex roles. They claim that you can be doing everything on a conscious level to succeed, but you subconsciously set yourself up for failure because you've been conditioned to think of success in business as unfeminine and therefore undesirable.

I talked to an executive who said she didn't feel she had a fear of success syndrome until a friend pointed it out to her.

> He told me I was going through a "fear of success" syndrome because I was anxious about my job. He asked if I had grown up in a negative atmosphere, which I had. He asked me why I was putting myself under a lot of pressure with my job. We discussed it, and I discovered that I did fear success. He told me I could probably have work done before it's due. Then I could sit back and reward myself. Instead, I waited until the last minute, then rushed around trying to get the job done. That way, if it wasn't as good as it should have been, I could always say, "I didn't have time to do a decent job. I didn't have time to try." That way I prepared myself for failure.

So before you embark on a business career, you must resolve the conflict between your self-image as a woman

and your identity as an executive. Formerly, these were
virtually mutually exclusive roles, and somewhere down
deep in your psyche you may believe they still are, so examine your feelings closely.

You can happily and successfully integrate a business
career and personal life. What you lack, and what women
have lacked all along, are role models. Because there are
so few role models to look to for guidance, women are not
used to seeing themselves in positions of authority, especially in the business world. We need role models to follow—other women whom we admire and respect who
have chosen a business life and who have succeeded at it.
Role models are necessary for blacks or American Indians,
or any minority, including businesswomen. Many women
hamper their own progress because they don't see themselves in proper roles.

Men have always enjoyed the benefit of suitable role
models and will continue to have them. They had Brooks
Brothers tell them how to dress, and older men who taught
them how to act. All they have to do is sit back and observe how to behave, emulate the behavior, and they
would then be able to create an executive image for themselves. Some corporations actually dictate what the proper
image for their executives should be. In the old days at
IBM, for example, one always wore a dark suit, white
shirt, black shoes, and black socks. No provisions were
made for female executives. Many companies look for
tallness as a trait for executives, as tallness helps in gaining power over others. If a woman were as tall as the accepted standard, she'd be considered a freak. If she
dressed like an "executive" she would be deemed aberrant.
You get the picture.

Without the benefit of role models, many women would
continue to flounder around in business, getting nowhere
because we lacked models to emulate. This shouldn't be so
much of a problem anymore—this book is full of successful role models.

A Report from the Front

I journeyed across America in search of the new executive woman. I interviewed businesswomen holding non-tra-

ditional jobs from California to New York to develop a composite woman and to learn the secrets of her success so that I could share them with you. Through in-depth interviews with two dozen intelligent, exciting women, I discovered who the corporate women in American is, what she thinks about herself, her job, her family, and her life in general. I asked her how she directed employees and how she dressed, how she thwarted off passes and how she won at office politics, how she dealt with problems with her husband or her boss. I discovered the new executive woman.

The new executive woman is a different breed of woman from those in years past. She is neither the stereotype of the merciless, castrating lady tycoon (à la Joan Crawford), nor is she the dowdy spinster in oxfords who loyally toils her life away for the company and never questions why she is passed over for the top positions. The new executive woman is assertive and articulate, in the groove and on the move up the corporate ladder. She achieves a balance between executive qualities and femininity. She understands why men may discriminate against her, and without dwelling on it, she uses this knowledge to her advantage. She regards herself as an equal. As she destroys the myth of masculine superiority, she soothes the insecure male by reconfirming his masculinity.

The new executive woman survives power struggles because she is calm and objective. She develops an intelligent career strategy based on overcoming sexist assumptions. She's good at handling other people, and she has an especially pronounced way with men. She's always at ease in business and social situations. She's a master at applying subtle means to gain power, and no one intimidates her. Without being sexually suggestive, she uses body language to gain attention and hold interest, but she rarely becomes sexually involved with colleagues. Her home and family life are under control. This is a partial portrait of the new executive woman. The specifics will be dealt with throughout the rest of this book.

From my research, I developed a composite role model of today's successful woman executive that is the basis for most of the advice I give in this book. Although I have attempted to be definitive, sometimes I will present more than one alternative to the encounters you will face as a woman executive. You can decide which solution is more comfortable for you, or best applies to your situation.

I'm always amused by "how-to" books like this one that tell you exactly how to behave and mold an ideal personality model for you, and then tell you "most important, be yourself." Well, I'm going to say that too. Even though I will describe how to create an executive image for yourself, it's important that you remember to be yourself. You shouldn't create an image; you should deal with your own. But you can emphasize certain aspects of your personality that will help you become successful in business. There are certain qualities that you can work on improving within yourself to become career-oriented and success-oriented. And there are other parts of your personality that you should minimize, for they could obstruct your path.

Charles Revson of Revlon, Inc., once told an associate, "I can't make executives, they've got to make themselves." You must program yourself for success and live like it is going to happen. You must imagine that you can be a success. In fact, it's necessary that you make it yourself. Women executives are still too few and far between to be of much real help to one another, unless it's through an endeavor such as this book. At least now you have a direction toward which you can point, and some guidelines on what will be expected of you, and how you should behave.

As you read through the various chapters, visualize yourself in each situation presented, acting decisively and confidently, knowing exactly how to handle yourself, no matter what the situation. That way, when you do face an awkward dilemma, you'll already have worked out a solution. Then you can concentrate on dealing with the other person rather than focusing in on yourself.

There is no advice in this book, however, that can substitute for hard work and thorough job skills. In fact, most female executives think that it is still necessary to work harder than men in order to excel at business. Here is a typical response I received from a New York executive:

> Business expects more out of women. The standards are higher. I read an article on women in *Fortune* a few years ago in which I thought there was a terrific quote. It was from a man who was sitting

around listening to some women complain about discrimination in business. And at the end of it he said, "I see what the problem is. You want your share of mediocrity at the top." And I do think that is the real problem. There are a lot of mediocre men in high positions, and yet a mediocre woman would never be tolerated in that kind of situation. There is double standard about that.

But don't be too dismayed about this obstacle, which the male chauvinistic society has put in our way. You can overcome it by hard work and perseverance. Of course, men who succeed must work hard also. Business is tough—for anybody. I consoled a business associate one afternoon, a sales rep, who was experiencing difficulty reaching a prospect to buy his product. His management was pressuring him for results, and he was frustrated. I sympathized with him as I had encountered similar obstacles in sales and knew how discouraging they could be. He was amazed that I had experienced his same problem. Because I was a woman, he felt that I should have an *easier* time in business than he. His reasons were the growing popularity of the women's movement and the enactment of equal opportunity laws. Once I recovered from the short-sightedness of his comment, I enlightened him. Many men share his sentiments, unfortunately.

But although business at management levels is tough for anybody, especially women, today success is much easier for a woman than ever before. And the rewards far outweigh the difficulties for most women. A business career is total nourishment for the competitive, achievement-oriented personality. You have to be willing to work harder and longer, to be emotionally tough, and be willing to make sacrifices. But you can succeed—provided first you believe in yourself.

Your self-image is where it all starts. If you can see yourself as an executive, you've already reached the first rung of the ladder. You must be able to imagine yourself a success.

❦ 2 ❧

Dealing with Male Chauvinism

The phrase male chauvinism incites a highly charged emotional response from just about anyone who hears it. The
feminist seethes and the truck driver smiles, the liberal becomes defensive and the housewife looks befuddled. Yet
male chauvinism is more than a mere emotional response
like a bad temper that can be controlled. Its insidious
roots are ingrained in the very core of our society and
have been passed along for generations.

Male chauvinism has reached epidemic proportions
among those who constitute the establishment. The
women's liberation movement is attempting to stifle its existence by re-educating our society to a new way of thinking. But this new philosophy is in conflict with our very
culture. At best, this re-education is an ambitious under-
taking. The harder the movement pushes, the more society
seems to resist. Living in a dechauvinized society is still a
dream if one is to dwell among the establishment.

Nowhere are the establishment's conservative values
more ingrained and upheld than in the business world. Almost by definition, the business community consists of fis-
cally, and probably politically, conservative people.
Conservative politicians are friends of big business. And
the typical business person clings to the status quo. He's a
capitalist in the purest sense. He thinks and votes conservative.

The businessman is probably a male chauvinist. Because of their politically conservative nature, most businessmen feel threatened by the feminist movement. To them it represents the New Left, labor unions, the Third World, and other liberal causes. They see a threat to the structure of society as a threat to the structure of business. They fear changing a system that they are succeeding in.

Because of this, with the exception of the military, nowhere does male chauvinism flourish more than in business at executive levels. Despite the vast inroads that have been made, business still has a tremendous distance to go in eliminating chauvinist attitudes. The government can only legislate so much equality. But real change must come from within. Business as a private sector armors itself from government intrusion. When government gets too close, business draws under its shell like a frightened turtle and hires more lobbyists to fight its battles. As Ralph Nader found out, effecting change within the business system is a long and arduous process.

To succeed in today's corporate environment, you must accept male chauvinism as a fact of business life. It's not lurking around every corner waiting to shove you back into the kitchen as some feminists would have you believe. But it's there, and you must learn to deal with it.

Before you get too discouraged, I want to remind you that everybody experiences discrimination of some kind or other. Old or young, black or white, Jew or Catholic, you'll be the target of someone's prejudices for reasons perhaps not even known to you. Some of you will be discriminated against because you are a woman. Face it. But don't constantly search for discrimination or dwell on it when you discover it, for it can defeat you emotionally.

If you do dwell on it, you will become like some radical feminists, bitter and defensive, unable to deal with men at any level. I recently read a discussion about all the sex discrimination a woman faces in business. The author was obviously suffering from an overdose of feminism. The hatred and hostility she felt toward men was reflected in every word she wrote. Undoubtedly, it had permeated all aspects of her personality. I doubt that she, or many others like her, could succeed in a male-dominated environment whether they were being discriminated against or not.

Another danger of dwelling on discrimination is that you can become too emotionally involved with it, and you will be unable to discern the real obstacles in your path.

A secretary for one of my clients was always complaining to me about not getting ahead in her career. She blamed it on sex discrimination against her. But I had seen her in action. She displayed a negative attitude about her work, and considered most of it beneath her, including the typing she was hired to do. Despite a sometimes heavy workload, she was the first to leave in the evening, and the last to arrive in the morning. She would only do what she was asked, nothing more.

The idea that maybe something besides sex discrimination was to blame never occurred to her. One day I was talking to her boss over lunch. I asked him if he had ever discussed with her why she was overlooked for promotions. He shook his head sadly, and said, "Yes, several times I've talked with her. But each time I criticize her, or make suggestions on how she could be doing better, she retorts with, 'You're just saying that because you are a male chauvinist!' "

This woman, like many, used male chauvinism as an excuse for failure. It's such a nice, understandable thing to blame it on. And, in fact, male chauvinism could be a reason for failure, but only if a female executive or would-be executive has no understanding of male chauvinism and how it affects her success.

The way to succeed in a chauvinistic society, which business clearly is, is to understand male chauvinism. Business lives in a huge, structured environment. You must learn to cope and adapt to the environment, become part of it, and effect change from within. When you set your aspirations toward an executive position, you must fully understand what you're up against when you make the plunge. If you strive to become a woman executive, you are going against the grain of the society.

As long as you stay a secretary, or in a typically female position, and comply with the system, you will find the going comparatively easy. But venture out beyond the accepted ranks, and it's a lonely, tough world. As the new woman executive you'll be David with a sling-shot battling against a Goliath structure. You'll need all the pebbles of wisdom you can obtain.

So the first rule of survival is to learn all you can about how the business mind works, how the businessman thinks, and why he behaves the way he does. You need to know his attitudes about you and how they may block your career path. You need to know these things because only then can you counteract them. You can deal with the male chauvinist by outwitting him, by first knowing more about his inherent prejudices than he does.

My best advice is to assume that everyone is a male chauvinist, men and women alike. Assume that the people you meet in business have smatterings of these tendencies somewhere within their makeup. If he's a business person, he's probably a male chauvinist, almost by definition. Assume this is an obstacle you must overcome. Indeed, at some points in your career you will have to. Be prepared to deal with these eleven common male chauvinist misconceptions about businesswomen.

Eleven Common Male Chauvinist Misconceptions About Businesswomen

1. You really don't want an executive job (or a promotion).

This one comes first because it's so absolutely ridiculous yet so downright common. Many men feel that we really don't want all that responsibility that comes with executive jobs, even though we may say we do. Even in today's society many men feel women are just passing time in their jobs until some man offers to support them.

Indeed, this may be true for many women. Many women do take jobs in business until they get married, or just until their children are through college. These women will continue to exist. That is not your motivation, and you should let that be known. You must establish yourself as a woman different from the ones that your employer has been used to. You must establish the fact that you are seriously intent on pursuing a career. And you must keep reminding them.

As recently as 1965, *Harvard Business Review* conducted a study that concluded that top corporate executives believed that women really don't want more than just a mediocre job, that we really don't want responsibility.

Your ambition may be self-evident to you, but you're battling an assumption that's usually unspoken. No matter how high you climb on the corporate ladder, there will be someone who believes that you wish to climb no further. You'll have a difficult time being taken seriously, especially when you are younger. I married after owning my own business for a couple of years. One of my clients asked me in all seriousness if I was planning to stay home now that I was married. His question left me speechless.

2. There must be something wrong with you.

The male chauvinist juggles his perception of what a woman should be against his perception of you. Something doesn't quite fit. So instead of changing his perception of women, he decides there's something amiss with you—that you couldn't be a regular woman uttering Edith Bunker inanities and smelling like gingerbread and baby powder. He believes that most successful women are neurotics, or bitches, or both. The more successful you become, the more aberrant he deems your personality.

It's difficult for this kind of guy to give you credit, even when you blatantly deserve it. He refuses to accept the notion that a regular women, for Pete's sake, would want to compete in business.

This male chauvinist is murder if you get promoted over him, for then his need to find fault with you is even greater. He'll make sly comments behind your back, somehow demeaning your character. His favorite phrase is "All she needs to straighten her out is a good roll in the hay with a real man."

3. You can't travel (or relocate).

This is a vital area that you need to clear up early in your business life, because most executives do some traveling. You'll need to be mobile and perhaps even relocate at some point along your career climb. Upward mobility within large corporations often means geographic mobility also. But beyond that, you'll need to travel during your career, the degree depending on your particular job.

Management often assumes that you won't or can't travel, and you should let it be known that you can and will. A corporate exec on the East Coast said the first time she was scheduled to travel out of town, her boss asked her if she was sure she wanted to take the trip, that they could send someone else in her place. She discovered that her boss, without ever asking her, assumed that she didn't want to travel. He was surprised to hear of her desires.

A computer executive applied for a job opening in the Soviet Union which she was qualified to fill. Since she had been a Russian major in college, she possessed ideal qualifications for the job. The personnel department sent someone over to inform her about the difficulties facing a woman living in Moscow. She didn't get the job.

4. Men are forced to behave differently around you.

Men love the jungle aspects of corporation life. It makes them feel like real he-men fighting for survival amidst a hostile environment. The intrusion of women into this very private society threatens them. Somehow, they think we'll require them to behave differently. They believe that we will deny them some of their male rituals.

A friend of mine worked for a large company, and she applied for a job opening in another department. Although she had suitable qualifications, she was told that she would be working only with men. Their language might be too harsh. She would make them feel uncomfortable. Work might suffer because of it. She was told they just couldn't have a woman in that job for that would disrupt the status quo.

5. He can't take you to lunch (what will everyone else think).

Men, even though they may be bona fide business associates, may be fearful of being seen alone with you. A man's afraid of what others may think. He sees you as a sex object, so he projects his attitudes on others. He may be afraid to be seen alone with you in case his wife gets wind of it.

An associate told me that he stopped doing business with a lovely sales rep because she was too pretty. He was afraid if her company missed a delivery, his boss would come down on him, accusing him of only doing business with her firm because she was so attractive. She lost his business.

"He can't take you to lunch" is only one of the manifestations of this kind of "what will everyone else think" chauvinism. But I mention it because it is so common. In fact, many women are reluctant to be seen alone with a man for fear also of what everyone else will think.

An engineer in Minneapolis said she had this problem. "After I'd been on my job for about a year, I was having a frank discussion with my boss about some of the problems. I told him I couldn't work out my problems as easily as a man because I couldn't say, 'Hey, Bud, how about a drink after work?' or 'How about lunch?' like a man can. He said, 'Why can't you say those things to me?' and we discussed it. But you know, he had never asked me to lunch before, and I knew he frequently took out the other people on my level who were men. He asked me out to lunch for the first time."

If you are going to freely operate within the business structure, you must get over, and others around you must get over, the fear of being seen alone with you. You must overcome this objection if you are going to receive equal footing with men.

6. You're too emotional.

Being too emotional is a common complaint against women. Men fear that we are unable to make rational decisions because of it. They fear that during times of stress, we'll fold under the pressure. It's been known to happen.

Some women are indeed too emotional to be executives, but then so are many men. The problem is that men can get away with emotionality, whereas women just can't. Others expect us to be too emotional and will look for the signs of it within us. The only way to combat this common male misconception is by demonstrating your icy stability during times of stress. You will be considered too emotional until you prove otherwise, whereas men receive the benefit of the doubt.

I did some work for a company whose president was the most emotional person I've ever seen. Each time a minor annoyance would occur, he would rant and rave, and you could hear him bellowing throughout the entire building. It was unnerving and almost embarrassing to be at the firm on one of his bad days.

As the shouting became worse, employees began leaving and morale was declining. The president, an intelligent and resourceful man, became worried and finally called in an industrial psychologist to isolate the cause. After spending several days interviewing the employees, the psychologist came back to the president with the problem. It was being caused by the president himself. His inability to control his emotions was creating an unpleasant work environment for his employees. The only solution was for the president to learn to control his emotions, and he started making a diligent effort to do so.

That kind of behavior is intolerable in most situations, for either male or female. Both can be too emotional; it is not just a feminine trait.

7.   *You need protection.*

Especially if you are youngish, you'll get a lot of protection, whether you like it or not. Some men feel the need to father you and protect you from the harsh realities of life. Deal with this male chauvinist, but do it tenderly, because he could become your mentor. He's the kind that will.

One industrial executive told me about her boss trying to protect her. "My boss gets very upset," she said, "if he receives a memo with a copy to me that has four-letter words in it. I've tried to explain to him that I talk that way myself. Lots of women accept that kind of protection, but you just can't. You must give the impression that you can stand on your own two feet. People will get tired of protecting you and will start discounting you."

An older man may see you as a daughter figure and will treat you accordingly unless you stop him. A younger man will tend to treat you either like his wife or mother. Those are the two strongest impressions about women that he carries with him. Make it clear early in your career that you can fight your own battles, or you'll never be viewed as an equal.

8.   *You'll accept less salary or reduced benefits.*

This is another widespread misconception that women have allowed to propagate. Often, we'll accept less pay or benefits just for the opportunity to get the job. When you're first getting started, there may be some wisdom to that approach, just to get your foot in the door. But never accept less pay once you're established. Eventually you must demand equal pay in order for others to regard you as equal. Management views salary as an expense, and the more you cost, the more you're valued. These are the same guys that cherish status symbols. That's their way of thinking.

Legally you never have to accept less pay. But you may be forced to press the issue before you get results. A Midwestern executive recounted a story about her fight to receive equal salary.

> Pay scales used to be confidential in our company, but they decided to open them up. Since I was a manager, I received a packet of information indicating what all the salary ranges were. Since I didn't know my grade, I was curious, I called my boss to ask him. He told me that I was ungraded, that I was special. I accepted that at first, but then I began thinking about it. I called his secretary, and asked if she knew my grade. She told me. I checked it, and I was making considerably less than my grade minimum.
>
> At that point, my boss happened to be walking past my door. I called out to him in a friendly tone. Now most people would go home, get upset, or think about resigning. I probably would have too, except he just happened to be walking by. I asked him about the discrepancy between my grade and my salary. He kind of laughed and told me that the company had promoted me faster than any man in the department, and that I'd catch up.
>
> I told him that either he should lower my grade, or give me a higher salary. He said that the company couldn't give that big a raise. I retorted, "Why not? The president took a 72 percent increase last year. I won't accept those answers." So he told me to write a memo, and he'd discuss it with his boss. He took the memo to his superior who took one look at it and said to give me the raise. Now I am paid equivalent to my grade, but it took some fighting to get it.

In most corporations, unless you know someone in the personnel department, it's difficult to learn other people's salary, especially when you're new on the job. You'll probably have to discover it by using some ingenuity (which is a nice way of saying you may have to be sneaky). It's so important to be paid equally, I can't stress it too much.

Your pay indicates your value. You will never be valued equally until you are paid equally.

If you determine an inequity, deal with it calmly. Most people are aware of the legal ramifications of unequal salaries for women. They are aware you can sue. Don't threaten legal action unless you are serious about your intentions, for the law itself is threat enough for most situations. Don't risk getting a black mark after your name unnecessarily.

9. *You're out to usurp his masculinity and/or his job.*

When a businessman reaches middle age, he begins feeling threatened by younger men coming up through the ranks. He's afraid their education will better prepare them for today's world. They represent fresh ideas and youthful enthusiasm. The middle-aged executive is afraid they may take his job.

He harbors the same anxieties about you, only they are heightened. The male chauvinist believes that women are inferior. If a woman passes him by, or takes his job, his self-image worsens. He'll resent you. In fact, he may feel you're out to get him, that it's something personal. You may be a different type of woman than any he has known. He automatically assumes that you are a feminist. To him, that means you are out to usurp his masculinity. You pique his feelings of inadequacy. He harbors resentment against you.

Even if he's moving up, having a woman replace him can also be embarrassing to the male chauvinist. I've heard guys take ribbings about it. It's too bad men have to feel that way, but many do. There's really very little you can do about it except be aware that men may hold this subconscious attitude toward you.

10. *You have no authority.*

I've seen sales reps go over me, around me, and even under me to obtain a decision to buy their product. Other female executives have experienced this also. Even though you may have a title and all the trappings of an executive, some male chauvinists find it hard to believe that you have authority. They may pay lip service to you, but down deep they believe the actual decision lies with someone else. They regard you as a token.

If this happens to you, your tendency will be to be vindictive toward the offender for he has insulted you. And I can't say I really blame you. But try to avoid letting your emotions interfere with your business dealings. A few minor annoyances are the burden an executive woman must bear.

11.   *Your home responsibilities take precedence over your career.*

Management may overlook you for promotions, especially if you have children, because they feel you would have a difficult time juggling both a career and family. They have made the decisions for you. A recent survey of 1,500 *Harvard Business Review* subscribers concluded that "managers expect male employees to give top priority to their jobs when career demands and family obligations conflict. They expect female employees to sacrifice their careers to family responsibilities (Rosen, Benson, and Jerdee, Thomas, "Sex Stereotyping in the Executive Suite," *Harvard Business Review* vol. 52, no. 2 [March-April 1974], pp. 45-58).

Sandy works for a computer manufacturer in the Midwest. She had been with the firm for some time and had quickly progressed through the first few rungs of management, but suddenly it seemed her career had stopped. Twice she had been passed over for promotions in her department. The last time it happened, the job had been given to a man who had worked for her. She went to her boss to question why she had been overlooked for the job.

"Well, to be honest with you, Sandy," her boss told her, "this job requires you to travel. We didn't think your husband would allow you to do it."

"What do you mean, my husband would not *allow* me to travel?" she demanded. "What does he have to do with my job? And why didn't you come to me and ask me whether or not this was a problem for me?"

"We just assumed it was," her boss replied. "The next time a job opening comes up I promise we'll evaluate you in a new light."

Sandy told me she was assigned the next job opening which was a promotion, involving extensive travel, and she had been having a wonderful time trotting across the globe for her organization ever since. But she never would have gotten that job if she hadn't removed the sexist assumptions about her flexibility.

Methods for Dealing with Male Chauvinism

There are several theories about why men fear women in business. The most popular is that men possess unconscious insecurities and fear that women are indeed superior to them, and they don't want to give us an arena upon which to prove it. Perhaps there is some truth to that. But it seems to me, given the business mind, that if a man really believed that women are superior, he would find some way to turn that knowledge into profit for himself. Actually, there is little reason to suspect that either the male or female is intellectually superior (although, proportionally, our brains are larger than theirs).

We'll leave the heavy-duty analyzing to the sociologists, and not worry about who's superior, for it makes little difference to your success.

You need to be able to discern whether in a particular situation the male chauvinism is important enough to fight head-on, or whether it is a matter that you should just drop. Since there are many varying degrees of chauvinism, it becomes a matter of judgment. Unfortunately, the appropriateness of dealing with male chauvinism is not a clear-cut issue. You are continually making a choice, and it's a selfish one. Often, what you do to better your own future may not be in the best interest of women as a whole.

Here's an example of what I mean. One of my advertising accounts had just hired a new general manager. I was meeting him for the first time at a luncheon also attended by the client's ad manager. I had worked with him for some time. After the usual preliminary small talk, we began discussing the marketing of the company's products. Although they were highly technical and complex, I was very familiar with them. My knowledge of their products was an expected part of my job. But the more I talked, the more the new man didn't. He just sat there like Harpo Marx, staring and not saying a word.

Finally, the ad manager, sensing my dilemma, turned to his supervisor and said, "Marci may look like a girl, but deep-down she's not. She understands our products as well as I do."

Now, the ad manager and I had developed an excellent working relationship, and I knew he respected my business abilities. I had never felt any discrimination from him, his attitude had always been supportive. He had no concept of how offensive his comment was. He sincerely meant it as a compliment. In face, it did bridge the gap between the new man and me. The rest of the meeting progressed smoothly.

I let the comment drop. As an executive, I had no choice. As a woman, I felt annoyed. But my task that day was to instill confidence in our new client and keep his business with our firm, not to lecture him on the tenets of male chauvinism.

But herein lies the conflict you'll face. A concerned feminist would have taken issue with that slur, and justifiably so. But she might have also embarrassed the well-intentioned person who made it and widened the gap between her male associate and herself. Yet this is clearly self-defeating.

That's why judgment is so important. You'll frequently encounter these situations of divided loyalties between your professional and political self. How you handle them is your decision. But if you truly want to succeed in business, office politics will take precedence over sexual politics, at least for a while until you work into the structure.

Before you'll be given any serious consideration for advancement, you'll have to prove you're not "one of them," those radical labor union types who are attempting to destroy America. You need to prove that before corporate America will allow you to join the competition. But that doesn't mean you should always let sexist slurs slide by.

Again, it boils down to a matter of judgment. The seriousness of chauvinist expressions varies, and so do the ways you handle it. So much of sexism is assumption and habit rather than intent that it's just not worth getting defensive over. Other more serious matters should be dealt with head-on.

Women are as guilty of sexist assumptions as men. I recently called an airline to reserve a roundtrip flight from Los Angeles to New York, also requesting that the airline make a hotel reservation for me. After some of the details were covered, the clerk asked me for my boss's name. I asked her why she wanted to know that. "For the name on the reservations," she replied. I told her the reservations weren't for my boss. "Then what's your husband's name?" she retorted, never considering the tickets were for me. That's sexism out of habit.

A director of research for a large chemicals company told me about a problem she had. "I applied for a telephone credit card. I had one issued by the company, but I also wanted a personal one. A friend of mine who is a professor at a local college had just gotten one. When I called to request one, a woman at the phone company told me that it was impossible. I told her she had issued one to a friend of mine, a college professor. She told me they would for important people like that, but not for me. I asked her why she thought I wasn't important. I was indignant."

Often women are as much to blame for male chauvinism as are men. They allow it to happen, and, in some cases, even encourage it. But most often, they allow it to propagate. A division of a large corporation had a position called assistant marketing manager. Most of these assistants were men, and it was discovered they were doing mostly clerical duties. These men were reassigned to other duties, and replaced by women, at less pay. Not one of the women protested.

As long as secretaries continue to get coffee for their bosses, it will be expected of them. As long as women in business allow themselves to be used, men will continue to take advantage of us. I can't say I really blame them.

Positioning yourself as an executive is crucial. You must act like an executive if you expect to escape stereotyping, like the assumption that you are a secretary.

Being taken for a secretary is a commonplace annoyance among executive women. The more often it happens, the more irritating it becomes. Its frequency is indicative of how the male chauvinist mind thinks. He'll assume that you're a secretary, no matter where you may be sitting or what you're doing. I had a sales rep walk across an untended lobby into my office one day. He saw me working behind my desk, and asked if my boss was out for the day. He assumed I was the receptionist sitting at my boss's desk. I had to explain that I was the boss. This type of annoying occurrence happened to me often.

A friend of mine, a finance executive, told me she had a salesman walk up to her at an open house and start the conversation with "I just adore secretaries." As it turned out, she was the boss of the man who bought from him.

Everybody shares these experiences. They are common misassumptions. But you can fight against them by making a conscious effort not to do certain things that would put you on the same level as a secretary. You should make a conscious effort to position yourself as an executive in others' minds. You can fight to alter the stereotypical secretarial syndrome by following these rules:

1. Be careful taking notes at a meeting.

If you take notes, make sure there are others in the meeting doing likewise. Don't be the only person taking notes. If notes should be taken, call a secretary in. Behave like an executive.

2. Never admit that you know stenography.

If you take notes in a meeting, use a yellow ruled letter tablet, preferably enclosed in a leather holder. Never use a steno pad. Never use shorthand for taking notes in front of others. Always take notes in longhand. A San Francisco advertising executive agrees with that advice: "I used to be good at shorthand, but now the only time I use it is when nobody's looking. At a client meeting, I write everything down in longhand, even though it will take longer. I don't want people to know that I can take it."

3. Never type your own letters.

The fact that you can type is acceptable, but never type your own letters. Only type interoffice memos if others on your level do. Your method of correspondence indicates your status within the organization.

Keeping a typewriter next to my desk was a problem for me, as I needed it for writing advertising copy. So I compromised and intentionally bought a portable model that was obviously different from the sleek machines that secretaries used. I had a friend that went so far as to use a manual machine to avoid appearing to be a secretary.

4. Rarely get the coffee.

I say rarely because sometimes you should get it out of common courtesy, like it's your turn, that kind of thing. If you notice coffee is absent from a meeting, the best thing to do is ask one of the secretaries to bring it in. (It's degrading for a secretary to bring your coffee when you are alone in your office, but it's acceptable for her to bring coffee in to a group, especially if there are outside visitors.) Getting the coffee can be a touchy area, and one that you should avoid as this West Coast paper executive found out.

> I used to have big problems feeling equal to men, even if I were above them. I always felt that I had to look good. I would subordinate myself purposely, hoping that I could maintain my femininity. When I was in a meeting with men, I would always offer to get the coffee so they could watch my legs, and I could remind them that I was a woman. But when I'd return to the meeting, and try to participate as an equal, it wouldn't work. You just can't switch roles like that. I stopped doing that. The last few times I've been sitting in a meeting and someone asks me to get the coffee, I flatly refuse. Now no one asks me just because I am a woman. I don't allow that to happen.

5. Never clean up after everybody's left.

Even if you have an overwhelming compunction to do so, don't. The only exception is if very special circumstances dictate otherwise, or everyone else is helping. Even if you're itching to get your hands on those dirty coffee cups, keep your hands in your pockets.

I have a peculiar obsession about emptying ashtrays. Men will let them pile up with ashes and debris until they're absolutely disgusting, and then use them as a centerpiece on a conference table. I resist the urge to empty them everytime I see one.

6. Never pose as a model.

If someone wants to take your picture because you're you, such as for the company newspaper or annual report, then go ahead. But refuse to pose in any pictures as a model demonstrating a product, no matter how flattering the offer is to your ego. The use of you as a sex object is demeaning to you as an executive.

The closest I ever came to modeling for a photo was agreeing to do the make-up of a political candidate before we taped a commercial of him. But when it came down to actually doing it, I was sorry that I had agreed. All of a sudden it seemed like a sexist thing to do. Besides, I felt awkward touching his face and hair.

You'll encounter many insignificant sexist slurs during the course of a business day. Sometimes you may have to let them pass due to the delicacy of the situation. But most of the time you should point them out, as gently as possible. The best way to deal with them is with humor, or at least good-naturedly, with a smile. Try not to antagonize the offender, but make your point. Here's an example of what I mean.

Male Chauvinist: (seeing an elevator full of women) "Is it safe to get on here with all you ladies?"

Rejoinder: "I don't know. Do you think you can handle yourself?"

Male Chauvinist: "I'd like you meet Acme's finest lady executive."

Rejoinder: "Well, thank you, Ralph, for that introduction. You're one of the best *male* executives that I know."

Male Chauvinist: "Hey, honey, how about doing me a favor?"

Rejoinder: "How about doing me a favor. My name is Sarah."

Male Chauvinist: "You girls are sure doing a great job."

Rejoinder: "We girls try as hard as you boys."

Male Chauvinist: "You're the best-looking production manager I've ever seen."

Rejoinder: "I didn't know what I looked like had anything to do with my job."

Confronted with the situation, you may prefer to let some sexist slurs ride. But as long as he calls you "girl," for example, he's thinking of you as one. You owe it to yourself to correct that impression.

The best time to correct a sexist slur is in a one-on-one situation. If you point them out when they occur in front of a group, you run the risk of embarrassing the offender.

A San Francisco sales representative had this story to tell about attending her firm's annual sales meeting in New York.

> Last year I was at a sales meeting with the vice-president of publications. We got into a conversation about the movie *Shampoo*. I was the only other one at the table who had seen it. He said to me, "Aren't women stupid! All they think about is their hair. If they get up in the morning and their hair doesn't look right, they run off to a beauty parlor to get it fixed."
>
> I finally said to him, "You're wrong, Gordon. You're all wet about that movie. It had nothing to do with hair." He looked at me as if to say, "How could you contradict me?" He never liked that. I know he's the type of person that will never forget that. You just don't put him down in front of ten people and have him forget about it.

Speaking up in a group does raise consciousness, and you should do it if you feel secure enough. Here's what one gutsy executive did:

> I attended a conference on motivation. The conference leader was explaining motivation. The example he used was his secretary. He had to prepare a report once a week and submit it to the vice-president of the division. His secretary, he told us, was so motivated that all he had to do was gather the information. She analyzed it and wrote the report, and then typed it. That, he said, was motivation.
>
> I said, "No! That's not motivation." I do try not to embarrass people publicly most of the time. But in this case, I said, "That's not fair. You have a low-paid clerical woman doing your job, doing all the work, and she hands you the finished product. You submit it, and take all the credit for it. You call that motivation. It's not helping her one bit, and it ought to be stopped."

The same fiery lady took a position that got her boss upset with her. You always run that risk.

I had a friend in my company who applied for another position in the company, at a much higher grade. She saw a memo about the job, and someone had written in the margin, "We can't have a girl handling this job." She protested that, for months talking at every opportunity. As it turned out, the job had already been filled by a "buddy" who was living in Boston and wanted to return to Minneapolis. They created this job for him; obviously she was very upset. I wrote to the chairman of the board outlining what had happened. That upset my boss very much. Going over heads like that upsets people. But she got the job. The buddy in Boston came here and got another job.

You can afford to be forgiving about everyday sexist assumptions, but hold your ground where overt discrimination is involved. Write the chairman of the board about obvious injustices, and be prepared to shake up a few others along the way. But first feel certain you are on firm footing, or you could fall on your face.

Taking legal action should always be the final recourse. You endanger your career by doing so, so make sure the cause justifies the fuss. I spoke to many women who felt their own careers had been hampered by others taking legal suits against their companies, that somehow management was taking punitive action against them in anger over a distasteful law suit.

But there are times when legal action is necessary. The laws exist to be enforced, and you should take advantage of them. Be prepared to lose the suit, as happened to one New York executive who sued a professional organization that barred her from attendance. She is a writer for a large business publication. The organization sent her employer an invitation to attend an important meeting. Her boss asked her to go, so she called to confirm the invitation. She was told women were barred from the meetings. She called the manager and protested, and finally he reluctantly agreed to let her enter. But he told her they were concerned "that if we let women in, we will have little

Smith girls showing up for dinner, looking for a chance to spend an evening with two thousand men in black ties."

She went to the dinner and chanced upon some associates she knew from a stock brokerage firm. They invited her to sit at their table, which she did, or at least until someone came over and told her she was not allowed to sit at a regular table, that she must sit at the table marked "press." She relented and sat with the press.

But later, she protested officially, which did her no good. So she filed suit against them and lost. A private club, even though they hold their meetings in a public place, has the right to exclude women. Since then, the club has opened up to women, but it did so in stages. First, they allowed women only for the program, but they weren't allowed to eat. Then women were permitted to eat dinner, but at a special table. Just this year women are allowed to eat at the same tables as men.

It's interesting to note that this same woman who had pressed suit against that organization stated that legal action taken by another female against her company had hurt her career. I asked her if she would ever consider suing her company over an injustice and she replied, "No. I would never sue my company. The possible repercussions could ruin my career."

The executives that I interviewed differed in their attitudes about male chauvinism and prejudices against women. Some felt that it wasn't much of a factor in their career while others had many bitter experiences with it. One black executive, who had been with the phone company for twenty-five years, had this to say about it.

> I deal with discrimination head-on. But I've learned to do that over the years. Now I just go to the person and tell him I feel he is prejudiced against me, and I deal directly with the issue. But in twenty-five years, my attitude has changed. The realization that comes after a while is that there's very little you can really do in terms of changing people's attitudes. Unless people decide for themselves that they want to open their minds and take a different look at prejudice then there's very little anybody can do. Of course, I can't discern if their prejudice is against my sex or my color.

In contrast to this woman's experience were other women who felt they hadn't faced discrimination at all. One woman stated that she felt the men around her were more sensitive to chauvinism than she. She refused to acknowledge its existence. Another woman said, "I don't see male chauvinism as a problem to me. Sometimes I wonder what some women are talking about. They must walk into places with chips on their shoulders in order to get the reactions they claim they get. Maybe it's because I've only been an executive for a few years, and things have changed that much. But I can't say I've experienced much in the way of male chauvinism."

If you are one of the lucky ones who feel male chauvinism isn't a problem, then you won't need the advice I give in the next chapter on stroking the male business ego. But if you find that your femininity is a disadvantage, then you must learn to turn it into an advantage. That's what the next chapter is all about.

❧ 3 ❧

The Power of Femininity

Two young women, Jane and Peggy, were hired by a large corporation to participate in its management training program. The two were the first women in the program, and, as you might expect, a dubious management was watching them carefully. Both women were hired because of an outstanding academic record.

Jane came on like gangbusters. She wore mannish clothes and smoked a pipe. She swore like a shipping clerk. She displayed no emotions, and only related to her co-workers on a business basis.

Peggy, on the other hand, was a femme fatale. She flirted with the men, cooing and giggling coyly. She fronted a huge bust, and wore clothes that accented it. She applied her make-up with a paint roller, and you could hear her drugstore jewelry clinking three offices away.

Neither woman lasted a year. About Jane they said, "How come she can't act more like a woman?" With Peggy, they said she acted too much like a woman, the kind that make fetching secretaries, but not serious executives.

Both Peggy and Jane illustrate different personality types that grate against the collective nerves of corporations. Both are doomed for failure, or at least will find career growth a sputtering struggle. The rungs on the ladder will always be greased and slippery for these kinds of women.

Corporations are unlocking their doors for a certain type of woman. She is intelligent, articulate, assertive, but not overly aggressive. She has a pronounced way with men. These traits were common among all the women with whom I talked. And although they possessed a multitude of personality types, they were in unison on another factor. Despite their business toughness, which is vital for survival, they all had clung to one very feminine aspect of their personality, and waved it with honor during their relationships with men.

The exact kind of feminine manifestations varied vastly among the women. Some were tastefully feminine in their clothes, hairstyles, and make-up. Others tended to dress down but used other devices to display a sign of femininity. One woman who always wore pants had lovely long hair and beautifully manicured nails. Another woman, a brilliant journalist, kept a freshly baked batch of cookies on her desk. She said that as a younger woman the cookies helped bridge the gap between her and the older men who worked for her.

I asked the executives I interviewed if they ever used their femininity in business. One woman responded, "It's important to look like you're not trying to be a man. I have subconsciously picked up some mannerisms from men, like putting my feet up on the desk drawer, and I have to be careful not to be too casual. Men want you to act like a woman."

Another woman said, "I use my femininity constantly. There are certain ways a woman can act that a man can not. To balance the disadvantage of being a woman, there are distinct advantages, and femininity is one of them. You can deal with a man on a certain level that has nothing to do with sexuality."

That's an important comment. Femininity has nothing to do with sexuality, at least as far as our discussion here is concerned. Acting feminine and acting sexy are two completely separate behaviors. One you do in the boardroom, and the other in the bedroom. There's a big difference between them.

Using your femininity softens the competiveness and aggressiveness you must have to win in business. It makes you more palatable to the male hierarchy. You give the conservative businessman hope that his world is not changing too much, that you can compete in business and still be a "woman."

But more important than what the businessman thinks of you is how you feel about yourself. You will be a more integrated person by clinging to some feminine domain. Cultural changes are being made for future generations, but we were raised in a sexist society, just as the men were. Just as men need to feel masculine for ego gratification, we need ot feel a wee bit feminine some time or other. The business experience tends to be slightly desexing, and huge doses of self-confidence are necessary. Consequently, a successful integration of your personality to the environment is vital for your survival.

A study done by Dr. Margaret Hennig at Harvard discovered that successful businesswomen have resolved their identity crisis by acting feminine. "One of the major reasons for their success at the top was their ability to accept themselves as women and act like women. This combination of early technical skills with human skills made them unique."

Apparently, those findings were significant, but I am not surprised by them. Women with a certain blending of masculine business traits and feminine personal traits are succeeding all across America.

One executive, who had described herself as "often too aggressive and abrupt," had this to say about herself. "I use femininity with men in business to get what I want all the time. I believe very strongly that there are two sexes, and they are different. I once took a test that measured personality. The psychologist told me he never had anybody measure so high on the femininity scale. He asked me if I felt I was 'compensating,' but being feminine means something positive to me. My femininity is also my individuality."

That executive expressed the key to successful integration of the feminine aspects of your personality: let being feminine be something positive for yourself and others, and it will be. Being feminine does not have to mean being submissive and indecisive. You can be feminine and assertive simultaneously, the two are not mutually exclusive. You can give femininity a positive connotation.

Rather than discard or attack the concept of femininity, give it a new meaning.

"Femininity is a masquerade," says Letty Cottin Pogrebin, a feminist author. Rather than getting into a semantics game, I suggest we accept femininity as something beautiful and positive. You should never feel ashamed of your femininity. You can be an executive and still be feminine.

Betty Friedan felt that holding on to our femininity would prevent us from knowing our real selves. But I know myself, and I know that there's a part of me that wants to be feminine. So sometimes I express it. And I am not alone. "Feminine" women executives understand all the options of behavior available to them, and they have chosen to hold on to some manifestation of their femininity.

Femininity, then, takes on an entirely new meaning. By acting feminine, many women feel they are signaling inferiority. But if acting feminine makes a woman feel inferior, then the deficiency lies within her own self-image and her image of other women, and not with women in general. There is nothing degrading about being feminine.

Some feminists would try to make us feel guilty about using our femininity to our own advantage. Yet where is there a better example of how men use their masculinity to succeed than in business?

Furthermore, as a strategy for corporate success, the power of femininity works. It worked for me, and for most of the women I interviewed. And it will continue to work in the future. Perhaps it's too bad that women must consciously resort to any ploy to win at business, but until the structure changes from within, which will be sometime to come, we are forced to use all the tools we have. And our femininity is one of them.

My advice on using femininity is directed at younger women. Once you get older and higher up the ladder, you can use the inherent power of your position to gain power over people. A younger woman doesn't have the strength of title to depend upon, nor can she easily intimidate others. Using femininity takes the disadvantage of being a young woman (and therefore presumably being someone not to be taken seriously) and turns it into an advantage.

One woman admitted that she had used femininity early

in her career, but now she didn't think it was fighting fair. But she also said that she didn't have the same problems of being taken seriously now that she was older. *As long as you're not devious or insincere, using femininity is fighting fair.* Men likewise use their masculinity. In fact, men admire those who use their wits to get ahead.

Using femininity is not a step backwards as some feminists would have you believe. It is a necessary interim device that compensates for the continuing existence of male chauvinism. Learning to use your femininity is essentially maximizing your leadership skills. Most female executives know how to use it.

Barbara Walters in her book *How to Talk with Practically Anybody About Practically Anything* (New York: Doubleday, 1970) has a chapter on the art of talking with lady executives. She makes an interesting observation about them which supports my arguments:

> The image of the lady tycoon is too often a merciless one. There's a myth that she succeeds by means of jungle tactics, that she's a ruthless, predatory, castrating monster.
>
> In fact, most of the time, curiously enough, the lady tycoon is much more feminine and fragile-seeming than her housewife counterpart. It may be that the really threatening women, the kind who match the misconception of lady bosses, are passed over for promotion and leadership. Whatever the reason, I find that the lady tycoon who achieves the most gives the appearance of being absolutely guileless.

The point is that looking or acting feminine, in ways that are acceptable to men, gets you much farther in the male chauvinistic business environment than does acting either masculine or sexy. The feminine model of the new executive woman falls somewhere in the middle, and she is the one who is getting the promotions, the big offices, the plush expense accounts. Business is allowing competent, feminine women to enter their chambers.

Femininity is power for the intelligent woman. Consider your femaleness as an advantage, and it will be. You, of course, can also use it to your advantage, especially if you have a negative concept of femininity, and react accordingly.

If women are to succeed in business, and they will, they must exploit their own possibilities of action to the maximum. Women are winning by using their wits and playing up the obvious. Men can tell you're a woman, so go ahead and act like one, in a positive, thoughtful way.

About half the women I interviewed actually felt that being a woman was an advantage to them. Whether or not it actually is an advantage is meaningless. What counts is the fact that these successful women regarded their sex as an advantage. They possessed a positive self-image. They accepted their femininity as a positive aspect of their personality.

The power of femininity works because men need to feel masculine. They satisfy this need in many ways. They talk about sports and tell dirty jokes, they smoke cigars and drive big cars, all in the quest for masculine reinforcement. Another way they get their masculinity reinforced is by being around a "feminine" woman who, by her very presence, reinforces their security about their masculinity. Help a man feel good about himself, and you have a friend and supporter. Make a group of men feel good about themselves, and you get the same reaction, only enlarged.

Every man craves positive assurance that he is masculine. It's basic to his ego requirements. Like all of us, his ego is near and dear to his heart. A man will do all sorts of weird things to reconfirm his sense of masculinity, from jumping over canyons in a motorcycle to ruining a political career over a striptease artist. Male egos need to be stroked.

That's why getting what we want from men is so simple; we've been learning the part since the day we were born. It's virtually instinctive. In fact, we may not even be aware of our powers of persuasion, slightly seasoned with sexuality, when we employ them on grocery clerks or gas station attendants, husbands or fathers. But we all use them at some time in our lives.

If we're smart, we'll maximize their possibilities to the fullest. The same time-honored techniques that Eve used on Adam will help you taste the heady sweetness of business success.

Your basic strategy is to achieve your own goal, but not rob him of his power or prestige, nor diminish his sense of masculinity. As a matter of fact, you'll help nourish it.

The Art of Stroking the Male Business Ego

Stroking the male business ego is an art perfected by most executive women early in their careers. It is a subtle art that requires skill and sensitivity, and although many are reticent to admit it, most women executives have used it. (Successful men do it too.) As long as the people who give you promotions and raises, and decide your career path, are men, then it is clearly more pragmatic to humor them than to offend them. No woman gets anywhere in a man's world without catering to men's needs. This will be true as long as men hold the power, which will be for quite a while. The business system will only change from within, and the changes are occurring slowly.

The need to stroke the male ego lessens as you get higher within the power structure and obtain more visibility. You can relate to top management with the strength of your accomplishments. But when you are beginning your career, your achievements are few, and the competition is keen in the crowded pool of entry management. The goal of young executives is to get noticed by the higher-ups and somehow stand out from the rest.

Using feminine charms receives the best results when they are from a younger woman to an older man. So use it while you've got it. As you get older and gain status, you will need it less, and it will become less effective for you. Exploit your possibilities during the first ten years of your career. As a younger woman, you can't possibly "win by intimidation" or any of those other male-oriented techniques for gaining personal power. A twenty-eight-year old woman simply is just not going to intimidate a man old enough to be her father without creating an unfavorable impression on him. A woman must play by a different set of rules. She wins by using her wits and her wiles, dealing the cards from her own deck.

Replenish the male ego, don't threaten it. Because you are a special person, a woman executive, your attention to his ego is even more meaningful. Just as women are drawn to successful men, so men are drawn to creative and productive women, provided they do not deliberately or unconsciously belittle them. You will find yourself a very popular person, a politically wise thing to be.

Just like popular actors and politicians, your charisma is partially based on sexuality. Underlying all relationships is a level of sexuality, and these undercurrents exist in business relationships, too. So in a very subtle way, you are using sexuality, ever so slightly. Don't flash it, but use it gently as the situation dictates. You will find it a very effective tool. Because of your sexuality, you do have certain advantages over men, and you should maximize them accordingly. But if you place too much emphasis on these ego-stroking techniques, you would have been better off without them at all. Treat them lightly.

My tips for stroking the male business ego are common techniques offered by many authors and lecturers on the art of developing a winning personality. Charm is a leadership trait. Most of these techniques work for anybody, on anybody. But they work much better between a man and a woman because of the inherent magnetism of the underlying sexuality in the relationship. Learn to use the art to your advantage, and what an advantage that will be.

1. Learn to make friends with a wide variety of people.

Until we reach adulthood, most of our friendships have been with people our own age who share our interests and attitudes. The people that we socialize with are very similar to us. But once you enter into a business environment, you are thrust among a wide variety of people.

If you are going to pursue a career as a business executive, you must learn to relate to people different from yourself. At some point you will be dealing with the top executives, who tend to be older, and you'll have to relate to them on an equal basis if you are going to be considered a candidate for promotion. Your job may take you out to the factory where you may have to deal with the foreman or the shipping clerk. They may chew tobacco and have eagles tattooed on their arms, but your job requires that you develop a relationship with them. You will find it a very enriching and eye-opening experience to develop relationships with people other than those formerly within your circle of friends.

If you are younger, you may find it difficult relating to the establishment businessman. He represents the generation that you were demonstrating against a few years before, and now you want to become one of them. You will find yourself liking and trusting people over thirty. And you must bridge the generation gap yourself. This is a difficult transition, yet one you need to perfect.

You need to be able to develop close working relationships with people whom you may not like, at least on a social basis. Your views on abortion or prison reform may differ drastically. In fact, you may find some business associates intolerable outside the business environment. But your abilities as an executive will transcend individual philosophies and preferences. You need to be able to make friends with anybody and establish open channels of communication with them. You need to become a politician.

2. Create a comfort level between you.

The seasoned executive prides himself on his poise and self-confidence. He feels he can handle any situation. At least he thought so, until you came along. A new breed of woman, you are a misfit given his accepted stereotype of women. You are not someone else's wife, a person to be taken lightly, or a sharper-than-average secretary. But neither do you fit the inaccurate stereotype of the cold, calculating female executive, ready to claw out his eyes to get to the top. You are a woman, who accepts herself as that, yet you are also a competent executive. You confuse him and make him feel uncomfortable.

Assume the responsibility for putting him at ease. You can do this by finding a mutual interest and using it as a basis upon which to establish a comfort level between you. Look for something in common with him.

One executive with a houseful of children divulged how she used this technique: "There was this one executive vice-president," she recalled, "who was very family oriented. When I was with him, I always talked about my kids. I could tell he was uncomfortable with a female executive, so I had to push the relationship on another plane. I had to remove myself from my role as an executive for a while, and place myself on the same level as his wife. That way he could relate to me."

The key to discovering the common ground is to get

him to talk about himself. After some conversation, you may discover that you both live in the same neighborhood, or love opera or country music. Or you may discover that he has an interest that is boring to you, but you should still learn to talk in terms of his interests, with the object of establishing a comfortable relationship.

A transportation executive said on this topic, "Let's say I find out he likes golf, and I know nothing about it, nor do I care to. But I'll put up with a few conversations about it because it's his interest."

After the relationship has progressed, you may find him eager to talk about how he feels about women in business. Opening a discussion about some of the difficulties he may be encountering in relating to you is an effective way to break down the barriers between you. Wait and do this only after you've established some other lines of communication, or you may make him feel self-conscious.

Most men are ignorant as to what male chauvinism is all about. As the feminists would say, their consciousnesses have not been raised. I frequently broach the subject with my clients after I have known them for a while and am continually amazed at their ignorance and interest in learning about it. Often they meekly ask, "Do you think I'm a male chauvinist?" I answer as truthfully and as tactfully as I can. Once the subject has been aired, men seem to feel more comfortable around you.

3. Learn to compliment him.

I was having a disagreement with a client one day, and we both had been at it for some time. I could sense he was getting a little annoyed with me for not backing down, and we were polarized in our positions. Rather than arguing back after a point he had made, I said, "George, I love that tie you are wearing. Where did you buy it?"

He stopped for a moment, slightly startled at the comment, and then broke out into a huge smile. "Why, Marci," he said, "do you really like it? I picked it out myself, but my wife hates it." His mood changed from argumentative to agreeable immediately, and I won the argument. A casual compliment had done the trick.

I had successfully employed an old trick as familiar as Dale Carnegie, the sincere compliment. My timing was unusual, but the ploy is not. No doubt you've used it yourself before. You know flattery works wonders. But you may meet a businessman who is seemingly tough and feel like such a remark would be inappropriate or too mundane for him. Just the opposite is true. The businessman dresses impeccably, and he values being well-dressed. He appreciates a sincere compliment just like anyone else. Be unafraid to compliment him, but do it discreetly. Most men long to be taller, younger, leaner, or all three. So if he's wearing a suit that makes him took taller or thinner, tell him so. He'll appreciate the compliment more than a simple "I like your suit," and you'll have made his whole day.

Sometimes a compliment is embarrassing to the receiver. For example, Ted from engineering had a prematurely balding head, and rather than get a Kojak haircut, he chose to rearrange his meager locks around his shiny head. Never compliment him about his hair, as even the topic is painful to him.

Complimenting a man on his aftershave is slightly sexual in overtone, and therefore extremely flattering. Yet it's not too sexual to use on businessmen. If they choose to wear it, they hope to smell attractive and sensual. Commenting to him on the pleasant way he smells is approving of his sexuality.

Never make a personal compliment to a businessman when others are around. It's in poor taste. Even the most poised and powerful tycoon can be self-conscious, and you could embarrass him. Save the compliments for private.

Besides personal areas, you can also compliment a man on his business achievements, and you can do that in front of a group. Sometimes, the more people, the better. In the game of corporate politics, one wants a large scoreboard. Getting noticed is part of the game. Compliment the male chauvinist in earshot of the bigwigs, and he'll become putty in your hands. Plus you stroke his threatened ego.

4. Ask his advice.

When you ask someone his opinion, you acknowledge that person's worth and you make him feel important. Asking for advice is a form of flattery that should be broached when the two of you are alone. The key to advice-asking is to avoid overkill. You can overdo a good thing and look like a witless nincompoop crying help every time a problem arises. But once you learn a few ground rules for stroking the male ego by asking advice, you will find it a useful tool.

The types of advice to ask for fall into three categories: very personal, personal/business, and business. There is a different philosophy for each, and you should choose your counsels wisely for each.

For personal advice, such as romantic problems, you should only confide in very special friends, those whom you trust explicitly. You never want your personal problems discussed over coffee break. As a tool, you can ask for personal advice to deepen an existing relationship, one that you wish to strengthen beyond a normal business association. A special chemistry should already exist between the two of you before you air your private life. Selectivity is paramount. If you feel uncomfortable talking about your personal life with him, then don't. That's probably a sign that you should stay on a more formal basis with him.

Feel free to ask for personal/business advice from employees, colleagues, higher-ups, anybody. The key is to make sure he knows about the subject you're asking, and you'll flatter him greatly.

If one of the men who works for you has a special interest in cars, ask his advice about your muffler or motor when you need it. Thereafter, you'll be able to relax him by bringing up the subject every time you see him. One of your colleagues may be a whiz at the stock market, and perhaps you could pick up some hot tips from him. Your business knowledge should include some knowledge of the market and how it works (if anybody really knows), and it's a favorite topic among some businessmen. Or you may be considering investing in some real estate, and you know it's in the same neighborhood the vice-president down the hall lives in. At a convenient time, stick your head in his door and ask him about the area. Thereafter, you'll have more than just a cursory relationship with him.

Asking for business advice is another matter. Never feel ashamed to ask advice if the problem warrants it. Avoid crying wolf. Business itself continually asks for advice from a bevy of consultants. The profile of a good executive is one who has the sense to ask for advice when she needs it. Always ask for business advice from higher-ups. It's bad management to discuss problems with employees and may be bad politics to discuss them with colleagues. But you gain exposure to higher-ups by asking intelligent, thoughtful questions. You can actually improve their impression of you by asking astute questions.

Many women have developed mentor relationships starting from asking for this kind of advice. If an older executive is willing to be your mentor, jump at the opportunity, for he can help smooth your career climb. Discern between asking for help and appearing helpless. Maintain an executive posture.

Of course, you don't have to take the advice that's offered, but you run the risk of offending someone if you choose to ignore his well-chosen words. One way to avoid this is to use the advice as a point of discussion and never arrive at a clear-cut conclusion. But from there on in, by asking advice, you pave the way to a productive relationship. To discourage someone from making arbitrary recommendations, you could ask him the pros and cons of a particular situation.

5. Develop timing empathy.

None of the previous advice is worthwhile unless you develop timing empathy. Knowing *when* to approach others is almost as important as knowing how to approach them. For this you can use your female intuition.

If you're sensitive to others and have the opportunity to observe them on a daily basis, you can spot moods in others as well as in yourself. Most of us are so absorbed in our own feelings that we fail to spot signals from others that can tell us much about their moods. The fascinating new science of biorhythms teaches that we all operate on a different daily time cycle as predictable as the moon. Each day, during certain times, we all experience feelings of lethargy or energy, the blues or elation, the highs and the lows. You can increase your skills in dealing with people by observing these patterns of behavior with them and watching for signals of receptiveness. Learn to read the people who are critical to your career growth. These can either be subordinates or superiors.

Some people feel refreshed in the morning, so that is the best time to approach them. Others start feeling like themselves in the late afternoon, and you should arrange your meetings accordingly. Anybody who has dieted knows there are times when they are particularly vulnerable.

In short, being sensitive to others' moods and biorhythms tells you when you should ask for a raise and when you should steer clear of your boss altogether. It could be the best time is after work. Observe his patterns, and plot your strategy based on his moods. Most business executives set aside a certain time every day for paperwork. Don't interrupt executives during that time, as you are apt to annoy them. Instead, observe when the best time would be, and then approach him.

One executive woman had this to say about timing empathy: "You must read the person you're talking to, and he may change from hour to hour, or day to day. Like my boss, for example. I learned to ask for things from him on Mondays, after he's fresh from the weekend. On Fridays, everything was no. One of the managers who worked for me was just the opposite. He was always in a good mood on Fridays, and that's when I approached him."

I had one client I avoided on Tuesdays because he was normally uptight about a weekly report he made on Wednesday morning at a staff meeting. I found that if I waited until after that meeting was out of the way, he was much more agreeable.

Being in the right place at the right time is more than luck. Make things happen for you by developing timing empathy.

6. Master the techniques of body language.

One of the ways you can become sensitive to others' moods is by interpreting body language. It's amazingly simple to read others' body language, and unless you are dealing with an actor, you can read them perfectly. If you haven't done so, I recommend you read Julius Fast's book *Body Language* (New York: M. Evans, 1970). It's full of valuable insights on how to tell what other people are feeling by the position of their bodies, arms, legs, etc. This knowledge adds to your timing empathy.

Besides reading others' body language, you should be sensitive to the signals you emit yourself. In his book, Fast refers to a pertinent study done by Dr. Albert Scheflen, Professor of Psychiatry at Albert Einstein College of Medicine in New York City. Scheflen observed male and female executives doing business and found that they both used sexually based body language while they were conducting business together.

Dr. Scheflen reported that "a certain business routine takes place, but it's spiced by a strong flavor of half-teasing sexuality. The participants, without any expectation of sexual gratification, are still exploiting the fact that there are sexual differences between them." The reason the two participants are not reading sexual overtones into the encounter has to do with their verbal communications. Because they are discussing business, the encounter is maintained at that level. It's hard to be too sexy when you're talking about the shipping department or industrial maintenance.

According to Scheflen, sexually based encounters are typical behavior of a successful businesswoman wanting to gain the attention of a businessman, for the sole purpose of doing business. He says, "She acts as a sexually aggressive woman does, but to a lesser degree. [The male and female executive] are using body language that in other circumstances would invite sexual advances, and yet quite obviously these two have their minds entirely on the business matter at hand."

Turn this bit of knowledge into an advantage and use it to your benefit. If you want to gain attention from a male in a business situation, it is acceptable to use sexually based signals, *as long as you are talking business.* Fast says these signals include "flirting glances, holding his eyes, putting your head to one side, rolling your hip, crossing your legs to reveal part of the thigh, putting your hand on your hip, or exposing your wrist or palm." (Exposing your wrist or palm? That's what he says!)

The reason you can get away with this subtle art form is that one or more of the signals expected in a sexual encounter is missing. The missing element may be eye linkage, a low and private voice, or any number of other intimacies.

Another way women let men know the encounter is not sexually based is to interject a disclaimer in the conversation by referring to your husband or lover. This lets the partner know the signals are not for real. I found this to be effective. If I sensed a man was coming on to me, I would mention my husband in the conversation, and immediately he would back off.

Never come on like a femme fatale or you will be regarded as such. In fact, I can't think of a less professional thing to do. But a bit of subtle body language sensibly applied can help you gain the interest of a man and make him feel masculine. Because his ego has been reinforced, he'll feel good about you and be in a more receptive mood for whatever you have to say. You're more apt to make your point and create a favorable impression. It's a wonderful way to stroke the male ego.

None of these tips for stroking the male business ego are earth-shattering revelations, nor are they devious. Developing charm is essentially developing a leadership trait. These tips are simply ways to help you overcome the inherent disadvantage that you have as a woman, and turn it into an advantage.

But no matter how gracious and charming you are, you're bound to face resentment from others. You'll encounter resentment from those whose jobs you threaten, from those employees who feel uncomfortable working for a woman, from the man whose job you took, from secretaries who are jealous, and from those who think it's easier for you because you are a woman. Some of it simply cannot be avoided.

You can often avoid or work around resentment by dealing with it head-on and acting in a manner that will not antagonize others. For example, you and three men on your same level are being considered for a promotion to manager of your department. You get the job, and you know the others resent you for it. It's human nature. Since now they report to you, it is vital that you elicit their support. How should you behave?

First, you should not be arrogant about your success, although neither should you be humble. Accept it matter-of-factly. After the initial sting of your success has subsided, call each man into your office to talk with you individually. Your conversation should open something like this: "George, I know you wanted this job very badly. We all did. But only one person can have it, and they've chosen me. But don't worry about your future. Management has their eye on you, or you wouldn't have been considered for this job. Just keep doing the same kind of job that you are doing, and you'll get your reward. In the meantime, I need your support and cooperation. How do you see your future here with the company?" You can do much to minimize the antagonism toward you by simply being cognizant of others' feelings.

Some people will automatically resent you because you represent a symbol of authority. Others may dislike you merely because you are something new. In these situations, time is your ally, and once they become familiar with you, you are more apt to be accepted. And as to those die-hards who will never accept you, you just must work around, over, or behind them. Unfortunately, there will always be a few.

You need friends within the corporate hierarchy if you hope to succeed. Here's what one research executive said about the need for business friends. "Business dynamics are such that most things are people-related, so if people want to help you, or want something to happen for you, it will. It has really nothing to do with your credentials, or how well you've thought out the problem, or how good your solution is. All those things help. But if people really want to help you, they'll bend over backwards to do so. And they'll take risks for you. You can be the brightest person in the world coming down the pike, but if people don't *want* you to succeed, you eventually won't."

You need to establish close relationships with men in business if you are going to succeed. As I've pointed out, you'll gain more success by supporting male egos than by threatening them. You'll need to make friends with that "locker room fraternity."

❦ 4 ❧

The Locker Room Fraternity and You

As long as it's predominantly men who inhabit executive chambers, the business world remains their territory. They make the majority of decisions, including the ones about your career future. Your fate is in their hands. As I said in the last chapter, you should emphasize your feminine individuality, to make yourself more acceptable to men. Use your wit and wiles, and play by your own rules.

But you must understand men and their rules if you plan to survive. You need to be cognizant of male achievement models and how they affect the way men think. You need to grasp why men appreciate certain qualities in business people, and how you can apply this knowledge to your own career growth.

The male achievement model that has had the biggest influence on the business world is sports. Since the businessman has little opportunity to demonstrate his physical prowess, an ancient symbol of virility, he releases this need by watching athletic competitions that depend on strength and courage. Sports, then, have taken on an important meaning to the males in our society, and nowhere are the effects more felt than in the business community.

Unfortunately, many men think less of women because many of us don't understand sports, not because we have never played them. Many men have never played them either. But women were not born disliking sports. We learned not to like them, and our attitude has nothing to do with intelligence or aptitude. What is important is that men understand them and talk about them, and by doing so, exclude us from their society.

Sports in a Sexist Society

When I was in sixth grade, I was on the classroom softball team that was comprised of both boys and girls. I played first base because the position required only short throws of the ball. Our team won the elementary school championship, and being a part of that team was one of the greatest thrills of my young life.

The next year I was in junior high and suddenly we ceased playing sports with the boys. They had their gym classes, and we had ours. That was also the year we began to shower after class, ridding ourselves of any unpleasant odor that nobody noticed the year before. Rather than playing in our "school clothes," we wore institutional shorts that made even the most shapely of our pubescent legs seem gangly, and we closed our blouses with snaps instead of buttons.

The boys held their physical education class in the same gymnasium as ours. Despite a thick canvas curtain separating us, we could hear each other over the general din in the room. But all we saw of them was an occasional jock strap flung over the curtain by some brave soul flaunting his virility. When one of the strange contraptions arrived in our midst, we'd shriek and giggle, and dare one another to pick it up. We were even unsure of why the boys wore them, until one enlightened coed filled us in.

But there was more than thick curtains and jock straps that separated us from the boys. We had a completely different curriculum than they. While we learned gymnastics and calisthenics, they learned about team sports, such as basketball and football. Boys learned to compete in team sports while girls learned to be cheerleaders. And that trend continued through the remainder of our formal education.

Not only were we not encouraged to participate in team sports, we were never taught to understand them either, specifically football. We did learn a diluted form of basketball, but football was never mentioned. It's little wonder many women don't appreciate or understand the details of the game.

I personally think it's a shame that most women are ignorant of games like football and basketball, for they can truly be exciting spectator sports. For me, football makes the coming of winter bearable, but for a lot of women, it is poison. I am a recent convert to football. My husband watched it constantly, and rather than fight it, I decided to join him. Gradually, I increased my knowledge of the sport, and found that I enjoyed watching it as much as he did. In fact, my passing interest turned into avid fanship that has helped me to augment my income by writing freelance stories on the Los Angeles Rams. This had been a totally new learning experience for me, as I had to start from ground zero. But by doing so I've gained wonderful insight into the strategies behind the games, and I have gained invaluable insight into the corporate mind.

I'm not advocating that you suddenly develop an unnatural interest in football, for the thought may leave you yawning. Business certainly doesn't require that you know it. There is an advantage, however, to following local teams, and it is one that I exploit constantly. The ability to discuss the game is a terrific icebreaker for me. An incredible number of businessmen are armchair quarterbacks and will enthusiastically discuss football at the drop of the helmet. It's a constant topic of smalltalk during the season. Indeed, two people need only share a love of a particular team, and a close friendship can develop from nothing more than that.

Love of football is a common bond I share with men. But, despite its advantages, learning about football, or any other sport, for that matter, is really not essential to corporate success. What is necessary, though, is that you perceive why businessmen like football, and why it is such a prevalent male achievement model. By doing so, you gain valuable insight into the corporate mind.

Business and Football: A Love Affair

Professional football would not be on television, at least to the saturation point, were it not for the love affair between business and football. Advertisers sponsor the extravaganza in order to reach an elusive but lucrative prospect for their wares: the business community. Running an ad on pro football is one of the best ways to reach the affluent businessman with money to spend, because the majority of them follow football.

There are many reasons why the businessman loves football. His like for the game is indicative of the type of person he is and how he regards his world. I recently attended a marketing meeting for a major airline, and the main speaker, an executive vice-president, spent ten minutes comparing his organization to a winning football team. This comparison is drawn so frequently, it's almost a cliché.

The businessman is also intrigued with the business of football, and big business it is. Most corporate transactions are confidential, but the business dealings of pro football teams are blasted across the sports page. Sports sections serve as gossip columns for men. The businessman is fascinated with how sports business runs, because he can relate it to his own experiences.

This scene is repeated across America every morning. The husband grabs the paper, pulls out the sports section, and hands his wife the rest of the paper. He browses through the sports and on into business, which is usually in the same section. He folds the paper back up, grabs his briefcase, and rushes out the door. He has caught up on both the sports and business news of the day, which are both lively topics of conversation around the water cooler. This is a ritual that executives go through every morning. If they read a paper at the office, it's usually *The Wall Street Journal*. But you can bet they've already read the sports section to catch up on the latest sports gossip.

In addition to their interest in football as a business, men thrive on the exhilaration of competition. The desire to win, whether it be at war or politics, business or sports, is the motivating force behind the American way of life. This is the energy behind capitalism, and part of a value structure that is common to both football and business. One of pro football's most lauded heroes, coach Vince Lombardi, is often quoted ("Winning isn't everything, it's the *only* thing") at sales meetings and other places where management wishes to motivate personnel. Management wants sales people to regard the sale as winning, and winning is the most important thing. Victory over competition is the name of the game in corporate life.

Businessmen would like to believe their jobs involve virility and that competing in business is a very masculine pastime. Fortunately for us, this is simply not true. The ability to compete in business has nothing to do with brawn. Nevertheless, some male chauvinists would like to believe that masculinity has something to do with corporate success. That's why some will indeed resent the intrusion of women who are successful, as they feel feminine success threatens their masculinity.

During a game, the businessman fantasizes himself an athlete, competing with physical prowess, being strong and courageous before cheering throngs. Sociologists claim this is a throwback to Cro-Magnon days when a person's survival depended on physical aptitude. Businessmen have this challenge taken from their lives as they sit in overstuffed high-back chairs and plush automobiles, and they face this challenge vicariously as they watch the game.

A businessman likes to relate to athletes, and to believe they are just like him. Banks and other sophisticated businesses have capitalized on this and often hire football players in the off-season as public relations officers for them. They will make calls to customers or just have lunch with a big client frequently, and it provides enough influence to make the sale go the company's way. Doing business with an athlete makes the businessman feel like he's just like the athlete, and having the athlete compete in his arena is proof positive. The businessman would like to think he can compete with strength if he really had to.

I attended an advertising convention hospitality suite that had hired two members of the championship Pittsburgh Steelers to stand around so businessmen could talk football with these two superstars. I went like all the rest and stood in awkward silence, not sure of what to say and secretly embarrassed for being there to begin with. Most people asked for autographs but used the feeble excuse that it was for a youngster back home. When I left, there was a lineup down the hall awaiting entrance to the suite, as the athletes were such big draws. To many, meeting them was the highlight of the convention. They stood in line all aflutter with excitement like kids waiting to see Santa Claus and repeated their exact conversations with the athletes over and over. These are the same men who are fearsome in a boardroom.

Businessmen also like the concept of keeping score. Doing so is the only way to measure competition. The executive's scoreboard is salary. It symbolizes value. Executives seek more money, often not for the added luxuries it can bring, but because of the sheer ego gratification of a large salary. Being highly paid means you're highly regarded and winning against the competition.

The corporate team has its scoreboard, too. It's the annual report, which is an annual financial statement required by law for any publicly held corporation. Anyone can get hold of these reports, and businessmen love to check and see how their company's profits and sales compare to the competition's. Thumb through one of these reports, and it's easy to tell if the company has been winning or losing. The annual report becomes a report card on how well the corporation is being operated.

As you might expect, the annual report is scanned and analyzed by management. Producing one is a very painful experience for everyone concerned, and much masculine ego is involved. I was involved in the production of these reports as part of my advertising duties, and learned to dread annual report time. One fussy president brought two suits, three ties, and his wife with him to take his official photo. After all that, he still returned for two more sittings. The amount of ego involved is incredible. Nevertheless, the corporation that is winning is eager to have its successes published. Success means virility to most men.

Men like to compete as a group. Most of their masculine experiences are group-oriented: military, fraternity, team sports, Boy Scouts, summer camp, etc. Some of their best experiences were in group situations. Men were taught as boys to value group activity, whereas women were taught to value individual efforts. (This puts women at a slight disadvantage, but it is an area in which we can certainly compensate.) Businessmen are stimulated by the concept of team play. They love to arrange their executives into management teams, and some even call their business plan a game plan. The language of sports echoes throughout the corporate halls of America.

The importance of teaming was impressed on one industrial executive. She was discussing how a particular manager in her company had been hired. "The man who hired him told me that before the interview had gone very far, the candidate mentioned that he played ice hockey. He said that was all he needed to know. If the candidate was an athlete, he must be a team-player, so he hired him on that basis alone."

Male Un-Bonding

Male bonding is a term used by sociologists to describe men's inclination to gather together and form exclusively male groups. As we have seen, as youngsters, men experienced some of their most pleasant times in all-male groups, and they tend to recreate these experiences in later life. Lionel Tiger in his book *Men in Groups* (New York: Random House, 1970) suggests male bonding is a throwback to primitive societies. He claims men instinctively gather together in all-male groups.

But I challenge the continuing validity of male bonding. Fraternal feelings can be shared among any group with a common denominator. These feelings could be described as group bonding. For example, I participated in band and orchestra throughout my school days. Girls and boys competed for "chair" assignments determined on the basis of quality of performance. We earned our respective positions because of ability, and neither sex dominated the competition. Like athletic groups, the band travelled together frequently, and eventually a feeling of warmth and closeness enveloped all the groups I was in. I have never experienced a greater feeling of group affection than in those music groups. I experienced group bonding.

In their youth, males were grouped together for most of their recreational experiences, and these experiences are very fond memories. These exclusively male groups have been perpetuated in fraternities, clubs, corporations, and the military. But as children, if girls were included in these groups, as they are now starting to be, the phenomenon of male bonding would be nonexistent. Instead, only group bonding would exist. I believe that adult males can also learn to share group bonding with women. It's a learned experience for both of us. I've felt a bond with business groups that were predominantly male, and some of these friendships have remained throughout the years.

I suspect some men fear group experience with women merely because they have never had any. Fear of the unknown is a prevailing reaction to many situations in life. Given a little time, these men's attitudes will change. As increasingly more women compete in business, some of the barriers of male bonding will melt.

The best way to un-bond a male group is to find a common denominator between you and them. Business provides the single largest bond, but often that is not enough. You may need to find a commonality on another level. I use sports, specifically football. But there are other ways you can establish a bond. Bonds exist between people who attended the same school, are close in age, share the same religious or political beliefs, love rock music or Chinese food, live in the same neighborhood, or have a variety of other shared values and experiences.

Group members benefit from a sense of shared identity, and, as individuals, they enhance one another's sense of self-esteem. However, if men have bonded in a group to reinforce their sense of masculinity, then you are in trouble—you may never be let in. You will have a much better chance of succeeding if the men around you are secure.

Some men will welcome you into a group because they may feel you enhance its status. Other men may find you a curiosity factor and include you because of it. Whatever the reason, in some work situations, you will have the opportunity to become "one of the boys."

Many of the women I interviewed felt they were accepted as "one of the boys." One very feminine chemicals executive said, "I have a comradery with the men who are on the same level with me. I have been able to fit into a group of men and share male values. I can fit into their group beautifully when we talk business, and this is enough. Seldom do I fit in when they talk sports or politics."

You may be included in a group of men and discover that it's really not what you wanted, anyway. This happened to this transportation executive: "For the first couple years I was in training, I desired to become part of the group of boys. But one time I went out with them, and I was bored to death. I thought they were very immature. I realized what being 'one of the boys' meant, and I knew I didn't want it."

Several women felt they had become "one of the boys" when men would tell dirty jokes in front of them. One said, "I know I've been accepted. They used to stand up at sales meetings and say they would tell a joke if I were not there. It bugged me, but I would make a joke about it. Now they've learned they can say anything around me and I'm not shocked." Another one said, "I guess I'm really one of the guys. They'll tell a dirty joke in front of me."

One of the ways men will test you is with off-color humor. And if they say they won't make a joke in your presence, they are being patronizing. Put a stop to that immediately, either by a witty remark or by just telling them you don't expect them to act any differently around you. You want the male chauvinist to get over his feelings of uneasiness and relax around you. Then you will become accepted.

Another manifestation of the locker room fraternity is swearing. Some men have the annoying habit of swearing and then apologizing to the "little lady." Put a stop to that immediately, too. One woman claims, "I've used profanity to relax the men I'm with. At least, it's had that effect." You don't have to go that far, but she has the right idea. Don't allow male chauvinists to think they must behave differently around you.

To Putt or Not to Putt

Traditionally business in certain circles is frequently conducted on the golf course, and more recently, on tennis courts. This is an awkward situation for the new executive woman.

The business/golf relationship is an area where the men can continue to exclude women. The ability to play golf could even be a hidden criterion for hiring an executive. Legend claims that Henry Luce, founder of Time-Life, Inc., demanded that all his executives shoot a skilled round of golf. He so believed in the benefits of doing business on the golf course that he made playing part of job requirements. This attitude puts most women at a disadvantage.

The matter of golf presents an interesting question. Should you play with a group of men? I pondered over this for quite a while. I talked to only one female executive, an out-doors type, who had ever played golf or tennis with business associates. But even she seldom played with them. (Incidentally, she also played on a woman's softball team, and said that she felt men gave her credit for participating in that sport.)

But for most women, I think golf is out, unless you are very good at it. If you're just a beginner, practice with someone other than those you do business with. Golfers tell me that it is very frustrating to play with or behind someone who is a novice player. It slows down everybody's game. The purpose of playing golf with associates is to create a relaxed, friendly atmosphere where you are doing business as "friends." If you come along and clog up the flow of the game, you'll annoy them. It's better to leave well enough alone. The same applies to tennis. Play only if you're good enough to compete. If you can win, then do it. Deliberately losing to bolster a male ego went out with garter belts.

There's another reason to avoid the golf and tennis court routines. Most often these rituals take place in country clubs where the businessman has a membership, often paid for by his company as an entertainment expense. Some of these country clubs exclude women. As long as they are private clubs, they can do so legally.

One of my clients invited me to lunch one day at his country club. During the drive over there, he was telling me how eager he was to take me to a particular room there, as it was his favorite place to eat lunch. When we got there, the maître d' stopped us at the door. "You can't go in there, Mr. Carlson," he told my client. "Ladies are barred from this room."

The client and I were both extremely embarrassed. We ended up eating in the Ladies Tea Room, where he was the only man. During an awkward lunch, he confessed that women were allowed on the golf course only on Thursday afternoons. This discrimination is more prevalent in California than on the East Coast. A New York executive told me about her country club on Long Island. "If you can establish that you work so many hours per week, women can use the tennis courts during the same times as men, but not if you are unemployed. But as far as golf goes, they are not interested in the least at letting people play."

The moral is: if you are invited to play in a golf or tennis match at a club, ascertain beforehand that you are allowed on the course, or you may have to sit in the car as your group of four becomes a lopsided threesome. Also make sure you are good enough to compete.

In all practicality, I don't see how most women can fit into athletic outings. We're better off passing rather than exposing ourselves to a vulnerable area. Men do not expect us to be like them. None of the women who said they felt like one of the group resorted to playing sports with the men around them. The fact they didn't play apparently did not endanger their career. You can develop satisfactory relationships without resorting to sports participation.

What is important, though, is to develop a feeling of empathy between you and a group of men. In corporate politics, when a group becomes your ally, the members will help block discrimination against you, as well as include you in a power cluster. Perhaps for the first time you will develop a closeness with men other than in a romantic relationship. The relationships that you develop could be very rewarding, as well as vital. Becoming part of a predominantly male group can help your career climb. *In business, personal success requires group effort.* You must join a tribal society if you are going to survive in the corporate jungle.

⋖§ 5 §⋗

Fighting It Out in the Corporate Jungle

As I said in the last chapter, men like to think of corporate life as surviving in a dangerous jungle because it makes them feel masculine. Indeed, corporate life can sometimes seem to be a teeming jungle full of predatory monsters ready to devour your job or authority or snuff you out of the competition.

Actually, many sociologists feel that corporate behavior does stem from primitive man. Hence the rash of "jungle" books likening corporate life to the most primitive of civilizations. One of the most popular of these books is Antony Jay's *The Corporation Man* (New York: Random House, 1971). In it he says, "Managers are driven by primal urges that constitute the heritage of their apelike ancestors of millions of years ago."

Advocates of this science of extrapolating primal behavior to explain human conduct draw analogies between business behavior and the rituals of mock combat, aggression, territorial imperative, male bonding, and so on. The theory of male bonding (men's tendency to form exclusively male groups) pops up again. If this theory is true, then women have been culturally excluded from learning the laws of survival. While men learned to play Tarzan, we were cast as Jane.

The example most commonly used to illustrate jungle behavior is office politics, those messy, irrational melodramas that unfold across corporate America daily. Fortunately, not all companies are highly political. Corporations, like people, tend to have distinct personalities. One of the ways that companies differ is in the amount and type of politics that are played in them.

As a rule of thumb, office politics increase in seriousness the higher you go up the ladder. They are stickiest and most intense at the top. But junior executives are in training for office politics, as much pettiness is found in the lower ranks.

Political acumen may not be a factor in the job you currently hold, but you can bet that you will become involved in office politics at some stage in your career. As you climb higher, you will undoubtedly encounter other executives who are politically victimizing you in order to eliminate you from the competition. In order to survive, you must develop an awareness of office politics and learn how to combat them.

You are apt to find more politics in companies that don't focus their competitive energy on the competitor's products, and instead the employees compete with one another. I had one client who always kept competitive charts and graphs on the company bulletin board, had frequent meetings to inform employees how the company was faring against the competition, and singled out his salesmen for outstanding achievement. There was very little evidence of office politics in that company. Another client was just the opposite. Nowhere in his building was any indication on how they were doing and everything was very hush hush. That company was a political rat's nest, with managers competing against one another rather than against the competitor's products. The need to compete was misdirected and only caused a loss of efficiency. Most businessmen need to compete, and have chosen a business career as one way of fulfilling this need. Smart organizations know how to handle this drive. Others flounder around, becoming a victim of their own internal affairs.

It would be great to avoid office politics altogether if that were possible. But capitalism encourages our competitive instincts, and business gives us an arena in which to manifest them. As long as there is business, there will be office politics. Although you should never take office politics too seriously, it is wise to understand their dynamics.

Briefly, they reflect the human desire for power. Most executives have a thirst for power combined with a desire for money, and the drive for power seems to increase the more money an executive earns.

Public politics exemplify this quest for power. Wealthy people thirst for power and are willing to finance their own campaigns in order to get it. A Rockefeller never considers earning a living yet may seek public office. The late Mayor Daley of Chicago couldn't have cared less about how much money he had. His greatest objective was the supreme power that he held in that city.

Once they obtain power, some executives are reluctant to use it. I had lunch one day with a public relations executive who was complaining about what a tyrant his secretary was. He claimed she bossed him around the office, yelled at him when he was late for appointments, and was often rude to his clients. After hearing this for a while, I asked him why he didn't fire her. "Simple," he said. "I'm afraid to." He had power but was afraid to use it.

Your problem will seldom be executives who don't use their power but will be the others who are willing to stretch their authority to the fullest in order to gain more. The power-seeker is the individual you must watch out for. He's the guy who will snuff you out on a moment's notice if you threaten him. He'll eliminate you from the competition by trying to make you look bad. But he's clever at it, so you never catch him or confront him with his deeds. The masterful politician always covers his tracks.

The following describes some of the more common political games found in offices. As an executive woman, you are more vulnerable to politics because of the types of slights that can be used against you. Here are some examples of what I mean.

Types of Political Games

Men have long propagated a myth that gossiping is purely a female pastime, that women are the only ones that can be accused of talking about others behind their backs. Nothing could be further from the truth. Many men are worse gossips than women. A political game of the business gossiper is to spread untrue rumors about you in order to discredit you. Both men and women can be accused of this, but don't let your guard down because you believe the myth that men don't gossip.

Grace was a sales representative for a major foods company. Her duties included calling on wholesalers, explaining special pricing deals, and boosting the volume of sales for her territory. Jack was also a sales rep for the company, and his territory was equivalent to Grace's. Although he had been with the company longer than Grace, already she was outproducing him, and Jack was worried. Before she came along, he felt that he had the sales manager's job wrapped up, but now he was concerned that they would select Grace over him for the promotion. Since Jack was a male chauvinist, he felt even worse about the turn of events because he was being shown up by a woman. How could he ever face his friends in the bowling league!

Grace came down with the flu, and was bedridden for a couple of weeks. So management asked Jack to cover for Grace in her absence. He was resentful of the additional work load, but he had no choice. After Grace returned to work, she noticed a different attitude toward her from management. The sales manager, who had always been so helpful was suddenly not available. She sensed that people were whispering behind her back, but about what she didn't know. And nothing had changed with her accounts. She was bewildered by the situation and finally confronted the sales manager, asking him if anything was wrong. "No Grace," he said. "Why do you ask?"

But later that week she discovered the problem. A friendly secretary told her. It seems there was a rumor circulating around the company that she was sleeping with her accounts. That, of course, explained her increase in sales volume, while at the same time shed dim light on her credibility. The sales manager had been too embarrassed to ask her about it after Jack had come to him with the inference.

Jack had employed a common male chauvinist tactic against women in business. Men love to gossip about sex and will jump on the slightest innuendo and snicker over it after work at the local bar. Grace was the unwitting victim of a malicious and untrue rumor. She finally left the company, for she knew that the people there wanted to believe that she was sleeping around rather than that she wasn't. Once a rumor like that gets started, there is little you can do about it except confront it and hope that it goes away. At best, it will die down slowly.

If Grace had decided to stay with the company, she could have acted in another manner. She could have immediately gone to the sales manager and told him that she was aware of the rumor, that it was entirely unfounded, and that she would like to have a meeting with Jack to discuss it. By confronting it, she might have been able to squelch it. Most companies are run by decent people, and a person like Jack could have been fired for his unethical and despicable behavior. If she had confronted the issue, she might have had the satisfaction of seeing justice done by his being fired.

If she wanted to take further measures, Grace could have asked that a complete report be placed in her personnel file. This is an extreme measure, but if the job is worth keeping, you should be willing to take full action to preserve both it and your reputation. Your survival may depend on such decisive action.

In the game of politics, subordinates as well as superiors threaten you. You can be undermined by your own employees. A Minneapolis engineer told me about such an incident. She was friendly with one of the engineers who worked for her, a young, bright man. Many nights they would both work at the lab, and since neither was married, they would have dinner together and continue discussing work. She was much older than he. Another man in her department was jealous of this relationship and started a rumor that she and the young man were having an affair. Because she had access to lines of communication inside the company, she was able to learn where the rumor had started, and she fired the man who had started it. Only in some cases will you have that much power to fight back. The sad part about these sex-related rumors is that the double standard lives on. Men often benefit in the eyes of their peers by a reputation for sexual promiscuity, whereas women are only hurt by it. Indeed, this type of thinking is changing, but corporate America will be the last to let go of it. It will be the last holdout for male chauvinism and related attitudes. Many men can still only think of women as sex objects or figures of authority. If she is younger the chauvinist will think of her merely as a sex object.

Besides sexual slander, you may be the victim of assaults on your work behind your back. Here is what one San Francisco advertising account executive told me about her experiences with office politics:

> I was working as an assistant on our vice-president's accounts because he was overloaded. Apparently I was doing too good a job because seemingly non-purposeful things were happening around the office, little undercuttings that were a bad reflection on me. This vice-president was supposed to be my friend, so I never suspected that he was behind the strange occurrences.
>
> One day the president of the agency called me in to talk about my progress on the accounts. He told me reports were coming in that I was doing a bad job and that my copywriting was particularly poor. Well, this was news to me. All the copy that I had written had been approved by the clients, and I wasn't aware of a single problem. I asked him where he heard that from, but he refused to tell me. He said he had promised not to tell where he had heard it. I told him that was childish. Finally he said if I promised not to tell, he'd tell me. He told me it was my supposed friend, the vice-president.
>
> I marched right into that vice-president's office and confronted him. I demanded that he tell the president that what he had said was untrue, but he refused to do it. I left the agency within four months because I had lost all the trust and confidence that I had in the vice-president. I guess you could say that the vice-president won the political battle. Thank goodness the company I'm with now is apolitical.

The withholding of information is another common tactic employed in office politics, and you can be victimized by anybody in the company. Employees or colleagues can "forget" to give you some vital information you need to make a crucial decision, or "forget" to tell you that you will be required to make a special presentation at a meeting until the night before. If someone is out to make you look bad, this is often the simplest way to do it. No one can be held responsible for occasional lapses in memory because we all have them. So the resentful employee delays informing you that production will be late until you can do nothing about it. Or a colleague lets a circulating memo sit on his desk until you've already missed the meeting you were supposed to attend.

Once this happens to you, there is very little you can do to rectify it. You might as well pack your briefcase and look for another job. Then thank your lucky stars you got out of the company before it sucked you up in its political quagmire.

A highly political company is a disastrous place for a female executive to be, for you are at a disadvantage when it comes to politics. Many women have told me about situations where employees or others in the company go over their heads to get a decision to go a certain way and use their femaleness against them. These people will go to your boss with a problem or request, saying they have difficulty working with a woman. If your boss is on your side, he will tell the guilty party that he must get used to working with a woman, because that is now part of his job. But unfortunately, many of them will sympathize with the male chauvinist rather than helping you. If you have a boss who is unwilling to support you, your best bet again is to look for another job. If he has any sympathy for the male chauvinist, he will never give you the additional support you may require. If you are going to succeed, you must have the support of management.

Ways to Combat Office Politics

We have been discussing some of the more common types of political undermining found in business. The best method to combat them, or to rise above them, is to gain power for yourself, and gain it quickly. Power comes with seniority and promotions. Unfortunately very few women are promoted as fast as men, and most of us still don't possess individual power.

You can, however, gain some political power by becoming part of a group. If you are in a political company, this becomes mandatory for survival. You will need to develop an alliance with the locker room fraternity to survive politics. That's why it is so important to know how to stroke their egos.

In most companies, you will find several clusters of managers who flock together because of similarities of age, experience, job responsibility, religion, race, or a dozen other common denominators. Depending on the size of the company, you will find a variety of groups. Some are in the softball league, others may belong to the same country club. Still others may bond together just because they work in the same department or are in the same job level. Because of our sexist society, the common bonds between you and these men are limited, but that does not mean that you can never become part of a power cluster. But before you make any moves, determine where the real power in the company lies. There are winners and losers in business social dynamics, and if you must become part of a group, pick the right one. There will be one group where the power lies, and that is the group you should attempt to enter. You want to be around the people who are making things happen, because they can help make things happen for you.

In order to determine the groups with power, you must first be clearly aware of what's going on around you. Learn the organization chart so you know the formal lines of communication, but then throw it away. Observe where the real power lies. Often, people with lower titles are privy to helpful information, and they may be worth cultivating. Rarely are companies actually run as they are theoretically structured to operate.

As in all groups, power clusters in business have leaders. All that is necessary, then, is to develop an alliance with the leader or leaders. Once the leader of a group accepts you, the rest will follow suit, but they'll first look to him for guidance. Approach the leader individually. Never broach the group as a whole. If a power cluster frequently lunches together, never ask to go along with all of them initially. Instead, ask the leader to have lunch with you, and by doing so, he will feel obligated to ask you along the next time. Let him think it was his idea.

A New York executive explained her strategy for breaking into a group. "You have to force yourself," she says. "Keep inviting them out to lunch until they feel guilty and start inviting you. After a while, they will accept you and really enjoy your company. Never attempt more than two men at a time until you know them."

She carried her quest one step further. "Sometimes, a group would go out after work for cocktails. A lot of decisions and plans were being made, and I was being left out. Finally, I swallowed my pride, and invited two of the men to after-work cocktails. They in return invited me to come along with the group, and now I've been accepted and am part of the flow of information. Without that, I don't think I would have survived in my job this long," she admits.

Another woman said she would exchange tidbits of information with certain men in order to gain an alliance with them. She was very careful about what and whom she told, but she claims it worked for her. I feel this is a dangerous way to make business friends. The male chauvinist thinks of women as gossips, and by sharing pieces of information, you may reinforce his opinion. Nevertheless, you may be forced to use this technique if your survival depends on it. But never divulge confidential information—it is unethical, unprofessional, and could get you fired.

As you see from the examples, the amount of aggressiveness you demonstrate often determines how successful you will be at becoming part of a power cluster. But you should be gently aggressive. That's what using your femininity does for you. It softens the sting of this kind of thing. It allows you to be aggressive and assertive without threatening or irritating the men around you, while simultaneously achieving your business goal.

You can survive without being part of a power cluster, but if your company is politically oriented, you will find it difficult. This is one of the biggest obstacles you will face. You need to become part of a peer group, but the majority of your peers are male. They naturally exclude you. You need them far more than they need you. You are forced to make the overtures and bridge the gap between the group and you. The dynamics of business politics demand it.

No matter how charming and capable you are, there are just some power clusters that will never allow you to enter.

The fraternal bonds of brotherhood are too great. Male bonding reigns and you will be kept an outsider. You can still survive under these circumstances, but it will be necessary to develop lines of communication external to the power groups. Sometimes you can find sympathetic secretaries who are traditionally excluded from power groups, and they can become your allies and feed you information. If you ever become part of the group, however, count out the secretaries being your friends. If they are jealous of you, they are more apt to become your foes. But once you become part of a group, you won't need them anyway.

As for combating office gossip, you are best off if you hold a strong enough position that you don't need to worry about it as much. Like the engineer in Minneapolis, who can fire the purveyor of untrue rumors, or at least get high enough to remain untouched by them. Because you have the confidence of those around you, your position is firm. But like the advertising account executive who confronted her superiors, the only way to combat gossip or untruths about you is to isolate the source of the problem and deal with it head-on. With enough persistence and some luck, you should be able to identify your enemies. As painful as a confrontation may be, it is the only way you can crush a rumor before it does too much damage. And even then, you may not succeed.

An insidious method for fighting corporate politics is to discredit the competition. I personally would prefer to move on to another company if I had to resort to bad-mouthing others to survive in office politics. Never try to build a career with that kind of behavior. Those who belittle others in order to glorify themselves eventually end up losers. You want to win on the basis of your own merits, not because of someone else's shortcomings. Putting the opposition down is a trait of the insecure competitor. Public politicians use this technique frequently. It's tacky and I don't recommend using it. Nevertheless, if you ever need to resort to such a tactic, you should be aware of its usefulness in combating a corporate foe.

If you are going to discount your competition, you should be subtle and do it in such a way that cleverly disguises your intention. Let's say you are talking to your boss about an important meeting both you and your arch competition Ronald are invited to attend. You say to your boss, "I hope Ronald will be able to go to the meeting with us tomorrow. He's several days behind on his department forecast, and I know he's worried about completing it in time." You've told the boss Ronald is behind in his work while on the surface voicing good intentions.

Here's another example. Your department has a weekly scheduling meeting at which both you and Ronald are required to provide information. You know that Ronald always procrastinates until the hour before the regular afternoon meeting. So that morning, you ask your boss if you could possibly hold the meeting before lunch, as you have an important reason to be gone in the afternoon. You know your boss will agree, and you also know that Ronald won't have his report done in time. Again, you're making him look bad, while creating a favorable impression of yourself. This is a devious, but often effective, political ploy.

I've watched enough men who are masters at politics to believe that they come more naturally to them. Women, as a whole, have yet to learn how to play the game. The competitive instinct has been nurtured in men, while it has been stifled in us, or at least channeled toward getting a man or having the shiniest floors. We learned to not compete with men, only with each other. The women who have made it thus far in business are the ones who are instinctively competitive and know how to play politics with men, or are perceptive enough to learn the rules of competition quickly. If you find yourself in a political situation, you must set your competitive wheels in motion if you are going to survive.

Besides our lack of competitive aggression with men, other cultural traits are shared by most women. We are eager to please. We put others' feelings before our own. Men represent authority figures to us, and we are therefor easily intimidated by them. We are often the unwitting victim of power by intimidation because we are so easy to intimidate, partially because we are apt to react emotionally to stress (but see "6. You're too emotional" under "Eleven Common Male Chauvinist Misconceptions about Businesswomen" in Chapter 2). Stress is one thing business is full of. How you cope with intimidation and stress, pressure and frustration, will in part dictate your executive success. Emotions are a fact of business life, and a vulnerable area you must learn to deal with.

◆§ 6 §◆

Whatever You Do, Don't Cry

During the Senate Watergate hearings, I was fascinated by the attorney for H.R. Haldeman and John Mitchell, two men who could afford the best. The attorney, John Wilson, was a crusty old coot and defended his clients with all the dignity of a merchant marine. During the course of the hearings, he would rant and rave at the senate investigating committee and its chief counsel, Samuel Dash, reveling in every opportunity to be abrasive toward them. This was his method of operation. *Time* magazine reported an incident in which Wilson called one of the committee members, Senator Inouye from Hawaii, a "little Jap." When the Oriental senator demanded an apology, Wilson asked, "Why should I apologize? I wouldn't care if he called me a 'little American.'" Wilson was attempting to win for his clients through intimidation, a popular device used by power-seekers in business and politics. Several bestsellers have been written on the subject, and the techniques are common knowledge among the ruling classes of government and business.

As I said earlier, women, especially young women, can seldom intimidate others without compromising their positions. Intimidation is a tool that works best for men. In fact, women are often easy victims of intimidation. As Michael Korda points out in his book *Power: How to Get It, How to Use It* (New York: Random House,

1975), women are often not aware of the power games men play and unwittingly become part of them. Or more frequently, they are easy victims for them. It is easier for men to gain power over us than vice versa. A sharp man knows this and will try to use it against you if you let him. Tennis star Bobby Riggs knew about women's vulnerability to verbal intimidation when he played Margaret Court. He used it successfully and beat her because of it. When Billie Jean King came along, it was another story. She understood the glib hustler's ploy, and was able to guard against it.

Some men will exploit your emotional vulnerability. They will attempt to control you through intimidation and victimize you through your emotions. Like Billie Jean King, though, you must not let anybody intimidate you. You must learn to guard against any susceptibility you may have to buckle emotionally when pressured.

But most men, rather than exploiting you, will just discount you. They fear that a tendency toward emotionalism will keep you from being a competent executive, that because of your emotional makeup, you are unfit for executive responsibility. They fear you can't make difficult decisions because you will collapse under pressure.

Are women more emotional than men? Yes, according to Dr. Ashley Montagu in *The Natural Superiority of Women* (rev. ed. New York: Macmillan, 1968). He says women are more apt to show their emotions. Conversely, because of this penchant, he claims that women are more mentally stable than men, illustrated by the fact there are more men than women in mental institutions. Women are quicker to respond to both physical and mental stimuli, he says. But because quickness is equated with excitability, it causes the myth of greater feminine emotional weakness. We can draw from his conclusions that women are indeed more emotional than men, that women are healthier because of it, and that emotionality is not necessarily a weakness.

We may be more emotional than men, but we are less quick to show anger. Montagu discusses some scientific studies done at Oregon State College and Columbia University that compared male and female emotional responses. Under the same given periods of time and under the same conditions, it was found that the average man lost his temper twice and the average woman once.

What that study really illustrates is that American men are more apt to show anger than American women, a conclusion that any casual observer of our culture could certainly draw. What the study failed to mention was the number of times those women had manifested their emotions in another way—by crying. American men have been taught that the only acceptable emotion for them to express is anger. Crying is considered unmanly. Look at the chiding Senator Edward Muskie took from the press after he cried after losing the New Hampshire primary. American men, or northern Europeans in general, differ from Latin or Mediterranean types who are permitted to cry or let their emotions show in other ways.

There is nothing inherently wrong with crying, and in fact it can be quite healthy for you. But in our culture men consider it unacceptable to cry, and this same attitude prevails in business.

On the other hand women, in our culture at least, have been trained to cry. And when we do cry, we often find that it is a nifty way to get what we want. Some men will do almost anything to get a woman to stop crying. But crying has no place in business; it is one manifestation of our femaleness that is not tolerated by the business society. Crying may receive immediate sympathy, but in the long run will endanger your career. Learn to control your tears. Mary Tyler Moore may be able to get away with it, but you can't. Whatever you do, don't cry.

I asked each of the women I interviewed if she had ever cried in a business situation, and I received many interesting comments. Most of these executives cried either once or not at all in their careers, and all remarked that they had learned to control their tears. One said, "I've had to close my door and compose myself a few times, but I'd never allow myself to cry in front of anyone." Another said, "I cried once because a mistake I had made was pointed out during a board of directors meeting. I was so embarrassed I cried. The whole time I sat in that boardroom with tears in my eyes and said to myself, 'This is why women don't get ahead in business. We haven't learned not to cry!'" One woman had an interesting comment. She said, "I only cried once, and that was in front of a woman. She didn't know how to handle it either." A San Francisco sales rep told me about the time she cried in front of her boss: "I was there with ice cubes on my eyes, so my eyes wouldn't swell, and talked to him. I looked terrible, and once I started crying, I couldn't stop. It was a horrible experience." You might be interested in this bit of advice she offered. "Somebody told me tea bags are good for crying. You just dip them in water and lay them over your eyes, and the swelling and redness are reduced."

A high-powered female executive gave some good advice on how to handle a situation where you feel like crying:

> One time I was severely criticized in public by a manager whom I respected. He was several levels above me. I was so humiliated because I wanted to impress him. As I reflect on it now, it was probably a mild chiding. But I cared so much about my career, and, being so supersensitive, I got so hurt and upset I felt like I was going to cry.
>
> I ran out of the meeting and held the tears in until I reached my office. I closed my door and cried, and then got hold of myself and marched into his office. I told him how unfair I thought he had been, and how much he had hurt me.
>
> He said to me, "I saw you welling up to cry. And I decided that if you came in here and started to cry I was going to fire you on the spot, because I cannot handle that emotion. The fact that you went out and took care of it, and then came back in here with very logical, objective facts, and more importantly, the fact that you could articulate the problem you're having makes me want to deal with it and help you. Just don't ever come in here and cry."

The attitude expressed by her boss is common to most businessmen. They would rather see you get angry than cry. So it's important that you learn to show anger. Most executive women have learned how to channel their feelings toward anger rather than tears, assuming it is necessary to show any emotions at all. The best, but impossible, alternative is never to get upset at all, but none of us can be that fortunate.

Women who have used crying to get what they want in their personal life will try the ploy unsuccessfully at the office, where it is a completely inappropriate tactic. Here's what one woman had to say about this:

> A lot of younger women who can't cut it are using crying to gain sympathy. But business doesn't have a place for that. That is not to say there aren't occasions when you shouldn't cry, or that crying is bad. Even in a business situation, when someone is brutal or says things to humiliate you, you have the right to use all the defenses you have. More importantly, you have the right to express your emotions whether it be in a business atmosphere or not. But you must recognize the consequences, and the fact you'll have to bear them. As a woman, if you resort to crying in those situations, then you'll be considered emotional and unstable, just as a man who can't control his temper is.

So if you feel an emotional outburst coming on, recognize your vulnerability to crying, and channel your feelings into anger.

Aside from cultural reasons, there is another reason why women are susceptible to crying (and men are susceptible to anger). We all have emotional cycles, highs and lows, on a regular basis. Women are more fortunate than men, however, because we are very aware of our cycles, since we have a monthly reminder of them. Jokes and mock concern over women's inability to hold positions of power because of our menstrual periods are annoying. Men are just as susceptible to emotional outbursts and depressions during regular intervals in their lives too. They are just not as aware of them.

Smart female executives turn their knowledge into an advantage and learn to schedule accordingly. They know *not* to schedule an important presentation or meeting during certain days of the month when they are more susceptible to pressure. Of course, the schedule may be out of control, but most big, potentially volatile showdowns are usually scheduled in advance. If necessary, you should try to influence the meeting date; at least you should be aware of your increased sensitivity and a hormonally caused tendency to overreact to stress situations.

Of course, the worst can happen, as one West Coast manager discovered:

> I had one terrible situation with my period. It was particularly heavy, but I had cocktails after work with some of the people from the office. We'd been sitting there for an hour, and suddenly I felt the need to go to the ladies' room and change. Well, I was about halfway across the restaurant when the whole world dropped out and was running down my legs. But I just continued to walk across the room to the ladies' room where I gave myself a bath. I removed my nylons, put on my raincoat, and came back to the table and excused myself. They thought it was really serious, like I was hemorrhaging, and I was so embarrassed. The next day I saw them, I pretended nothing had happened.

Fortunately, nightmares like this rarely happen. Dealing with one's period during business life is really not a problem most of the time. Once you become sensitive to the potential problems, you can compensate for them. This was something that I too learned the hard way.

David was marketing manager for a foreign manufacturer, and his company was one of the early clients in my advertising agency. Our first assignment was to come up with a new ad campaign, which we did. I made a presentation a couple of weeks later, and everyone was wild about the new campaign. David asked if he could keep the preliminary art and copy we had prepared so he could show it to someone else. This wasn't an unusual request, so I agreed readily. But a few days later I began to call, asking for approval to start final production, but he wouldn't take my calls. I could never get past his secretary. Finally, after we had missed the deadline, he called, full of charm and apologies, saying that they loved the ad, but they would like to postpone its final production for a month or two. They had an unexpected slowdown on the production of the product line. We amicably discussed the change of events and agreed I would bill him for the work-to-date. Any apprehension I felt about the security of our relationship was dispelled about that conversation. He promised to call me the minute they were ready to proceed.

One morning a couple of weeks later I was browsing through a copy of the publication we had chosen for the client's ad, casually sipping a cup of coffee, and enjoying the rare luxury of a few uninterrupted moments. I turned the page to find a very familiar-looking ad on it. I stared at it in disbelief. It was the same ad I had proposed to the client, the one they had wanted to postpone. Of course, David had never paid the bill, and I could see he was not intending to. He had taken the concept and copy to an art service which is less expensive than an advertising agency, and had the ads produced there. I first called the publication to determine who had shipped them the materials and then called my attorney to begin legal action. I was seething with anger.

After he received a letter from my attorney, David called me, again full of charm, and suggested that we discuss our disagreement over lunch. We agreed to meet the next day. The meeting started rocky, as I was still trembling with anger over the creep's underhanded business dealings. He was cordial and controlled, as he made some ridiculously low offers to settle the bill. We argued, my voice cracking from emotion. The more we debated, the more agitated I became, until I finally started crying. Tears welled up in my eyes, and I was hiccuping and sobbing out of pure frustration.

He took advantage of the situation and used it to intimidate me. He began making fun of me for crying. He began attacking me as a woman. He told me that I had no place in the business world, that the only place for me to work was on my back. Never in my life has anybody been more hurtful toward me, and all I could do was cry all the more. The frustrating part was that I had the upper hand because I had legal grounds, but he knew how to win through intimidation.

Finally, I gained my composure enough to know I should remove myself from the situation. As I got up to leave, he delivered the final blow. He said, "Marci, I hope the next time we meet, it won't be during the wrong time of the month. Maybe you can keep from crying," he said, the personification of the male chauvinist pig.

The incident upset me so much I drove home and called my secretary to cancel my appointments for the rest of the day. I was totally drained. I was in no condition to finish the day. My personal feelings of anger and frustration had overtaken me, and I had allowed myself to blow the encounter entirely out of proportion.

The irony of that incident, and what made me feel worse, was that the creep was right in his assessment of my volatile emotional condition. I was due to start my period any minute, and I am more prone to emotional outbursts during that time of month. I decided that in the future I would be more cognizant of my periods and that I would avoid planning potentially explosive confrontations such as the one I had just experienced during that time.

Dealing with your period during your business life shouldn't present any problems for you once you learn to be sensitive to your own emotions and compensate for them. The best method I have found to keep my spirits high is to wear my jazziest outfits on the days I feel worse. It's simple psychology. If you feel you look your best, you will feel good about yourself. If you feel good about yourself, you can better keep your emotional stability on an even keel.

Don't Take It Personally

Women are apt to become emotionally involved with everything they do. Whether it be the education of our children or civil rights issues, we are an impassioned sex and are just beginning to experience our potential. Often women become too emotionally involved with their work, to the point of losing objectivity. This is often a fault of female managers.

Successful women executives have a clear picture of themselves, and they understand their propensity toward hyper-involvement in everything they attack. Because we throw ourselves, body and soul, into our endeavors, we regard them as ever so important. I asked one businesswoman what her biggest problem was, and this is what she said: "I've been so attacked over the years that I felt like I had to prove myself over and over again. Now I'm always on the defensive. I also tend to back down too easily, and I overreact."

When we allow ourselves to overreact because we have put too much importance on the details at hand, we fail to see the big picture. As the saying goes, we can't see the forest for the trees. This is an undesirable trait for a manager, and one that you should guard against. It's not that solving the problem at hand is not important. What counts is the amount of importance you put on the problem. If you are too involved with it, you may not be able to view the situation objectively and see things for what they really are. Your decision-making ability will suffer because of it.

There's seemingly a dichotomy here. A successful executive must immerse herself in her corporate responsibilities, living and breathing the corporation. She makes important decisions involving millions of dollars, and frequently her career is on the line. There are always more problems to solve than one has time to adequately consider; there are always more things that require doing than time to do them. And business executives are achievers who demand a high quantity of output from themselves and those around them.

But because business is such an encompassing lifestyle, you must not get overly involved with it, or it can devour your energy and spew you out an emotional wreck, unable to realize any other portions of your personality. If you spend yourself at the office, you will lose your soul to work. You will have nothing left to give to your family or friends, or more important, yourself. So it's important for several reasons not to get too emotionally involved with your career objectives. Somehow, you must maintain a distance from them. Your overzealousness could mean defeat on the really important jobs. You must demonstrate that you can remain clear-headed under pressure.

Both male and female executives are guilty of becoming too emotionally involved with their jobs, and they pay for it as their careers progress. Most executives are fired at least once along their careers. There's an old reverse snobbery in business that says you're nobody until you've been fired at least once. But consider what happens to you personally if you get fired when your job becomes too important to you. If the company becomes your entire life, what happens when you lose it? You can become shattered and despondent and lose your sense of worth, or even your self-confidence to try again. Pity all those stockbrokers who jumped to their death after the market crashed in 1929. Business was the only thing in life that mattered to them. You want your life better balanced than that.

If you let your job control you, any minor irritation during the day flares up to crisis levels in your mind. You live on antacids because your stomach is a wreck, and you can never relax enough to enjoy the work. I know this is a strong tendency of mine, and one that I must continually guard against. Moreover, if you take your job, and yourself, too seriously, you will be obnoxious to be around. A perfect example of this is Lily Tomlin's brilliant portrayal of Ernestine, who works for the phone company. She's too caught up in self-importance and in following the rules. My favorite hyper-zealot is Hot Lips Hooligan of M*A*S*H fame, who, with her prissy boyfriend, loses touch with the humanness of our endeavors. Taking your job too seriously can actually be a hindrance rather than a help. Bogging yourself down with inconsequential problems and becoming overly upset at the wrong things are signs that a person cannot set priorities. A person overly concerned with details often fails to see the big picture and will be a less effective manager because of it. A manager with vision and scope will progress much faster than the one who wears blinders and can only view her tiny world.

You will also be judged on the way you handle criticism. If you graciously accept it as good advice and don't become defensive over it, you'll go much further. You are then considered "teachable." No one ever expects you to be perfect, and, as a decision maker you are bound to make mistakes. When they are pointed out to you, don't take it as personal criticism, but only as a chance to learn how to do a better job. Learning to graciously accept criticism is part of your executive training.

It's no wonder, however, that women in business tend to be on the defensive. Men have put us there by constantly making us feel like we must prove ourselves. Staying on the defensive, then, becomes almost an automatic reaction unless you learn to guard against it. Don't view criticism from your boss as an attack on you as a person, but only on the way you are conducting a certain function. Management is more concerned about profits than it is about your feelings, so you must develop a thick skin. And remember, making errors is part of the growing process. If you didn't make mistakes, you wouldn't be learning from your experiences, a valuable thing to do.

Women tend to be overly sensitive about criticism because they are not programmed to accept rejection. For example, in the dating relationship, the male was assertive and the female passive. The boys did the asking, and the girls did the rejecting. The male traditionally dominated the marriage and protected his wife from unpleasantries. Before marriage, our parents acted as our protectors, stunting our ability to cope with life while keeping us delicate and fragile. Toughness was not considered a desirable feminine trait, but it is certainly a required business trait if you want to compete with men. A certain kind of toughness is necessary just to get through the day. And you'll have so much to do, you won't be able to worry about your feelings anyway.

Just as women are overly sensitive to criticism, they also tend to seek approval from others just for the sake of pleasing them. Men rarely seek approval for its own sake the way women do. There's fault in being too eager to please, for it indicates insecurity. Men value the ability to be concerned most about doing a job and less about always pleasing those around them. You should, too. Being too eager to please means not knowing when to say no. Marilyn never knew when to say no. Every time someone came to her with a request, she would agree to do it. She worked fourteen hours a day and was always dashing around in a frenzy because she didn't have enough hours in the day. Her performance in some of the areas of her job was slipping. One day her boss called her in to discuss why she couldn't keep up with her work. She told him that she was constantly interrupted during the day by people with urgent needs to fill, and she was continually detained. Her boss told her that she wasn't doing her job properly. "Why, isn't filling people's requests part of my job?" asked Marilyn. "Of course," said her boss. "But another important part of your job is establishing priorities, and we expect you, as a manager, to do that for yourself. You must learn to evaluate which requests are important and which ones get pushed aside. You can't please everyone all the time. Sometimes you must say no."

"But what if people get angry with me?" Marilyn queried. "That's okay," her boss told her. "You are not here to win a popularity contest, you are here to do a job. By doing so, you might step on a few toes, but that is all part of what we expect you to do."

Marilyn had to learn how *not* to always please others, and this ran against her inclination to do so. Women often put others' feelings before their own. Watch out for this tendency in yourself.

Handling Pressure

Picture the stereotype of a business tycoon. He sits behind a large rosewood desk frantically answering a dozen telephones and popping Rolaids because his nervous stomach is acting up again. He meets an associate for lunch and gulps three scotch and milks before the meal. His afternoon schedule is hectic, and he is especially concerned about a presentation he is giving to the board of directors that afternoon. He hopes his stomach won't act up again, as he is afraid to stand in front of the board chewing antacids while trying to deliver his presentation.

He returns from lunch to find his secretary in a state of panic. He had accidentally taken with him to lunch the presentation she was supposed to type, and now it will not be ready for the meeting. He sees a pile of phone messages on his desk, and he methodically sorts them with one hand while he pops Rolaids with the other. He sees a call from his biggest customer and immediately returns it. The customer is fuming and cancels his order because the merchandise is late again and he can't go into production without it. The businessman vows to visit the doctor and do something about his stomach. For sure, he must have an ulcer now, but he has been afraid to go to the doctor and find out. He knows the doctor will order him off of booze, and he doesn't know how he can stand the pressure without a few drinks.

This could be you. Women are not exempted from the stereotypical stomach problems, ulcers, excessive drinking, high blood pressure, and the other health problems that are common to executives. You are just as susceptible as men to these corporate woes. You are just as apt to feel the pressures. How you react to them is up to you.

One of the ways to counteract pressure is to build up a tolerance for the minor annoyances that plague you during the course of a day. You may start out in the morning fresh for a day's work, and by noon you have so many problems you are starting to get in a bad mood. By the time you go home at night, you feel your whole day is in shambles, and you are emotionally exhausted. But if you let minor irritations bounce off your back like Ping Pong balls, you can leave your problems at the office and relax when you leave at night. A Los Angeles banking executive has the right idea. She says, "I just don't get upset, no matter what happens. I never show anger, or lose my temper. But that's because when I leave the office, I leave the problems there, and that helps me to unwind. If I think about work all the time, I find I am less effective with dealing with the pressures."

She has been an executive for many years and has learned to cope with stress. It wasn't always that way for her. She told me about one of her first jobs, at the Los Angeles office of the J. Walter Thompson advertising agency, where she worked for Bob Haldeman:

That was the most stressful situation I've ever been in. I felt that if I could survive and work under the conditions he required, I could work for anybody.

Ron Ziegler was a junior account executive at the agency, working on the NBC account. It was my job to create the traffic schedules for production. Ron would come back from NBC and tell us they wanted to run an ad the next day in the *Los Angeles Times*. This was impossible. There just wasn't enough time. I never knew if he didn't realize how much time it took, or did not understand the logistics, or was just plain stupid. I also worked with Dwight Chapin, who was assistant to Haldeman. When Watergate surfaced, I thought it was so stupid when they were making surreptitious phone calls and charging them to their expense accounts. I decided I wasn't so wrong after all in my evaluation of their intelligence.

You will probably never work for Haldeman, but corporate America is full of equally tough task masters, and you'll need to hold up under the stress of tough bosses, sticky problems with no clear-cut answers, and all the other causes of executive pressure. It's possible that at home you react one way and at work you react differently. You develop an alter ego, in a sense, that allows you to do this. You cannot afford to react the same way at the office that you do at home.

When someone is angry at me for a mistake I have made or if I feel irritated at something, I find that if I tell myself "it's only business—it's not so important to warrant getting upset over," it helps me get a clear perspective on what is happening. Then I can maintain an unemotional involvement and make decisions based on fact. It also keeps me from feeling too bad if things are going wrong.

Another businesswoman gave her advice for handling pressure: "I used to get uptight, but not anymore. If I worried about every problem that came up in my job, I'd be a wreck. But if it seems like I have too much to do, I stop everything for a minute and realize that I can only do one thing at a time, that I am capable of thinking problems through to logical conclusions, and that this problem is not different. Instead of running in fifty different directions, which I could easily do, I work at taking a calm approach."

Another woman is still working on the problem. "When I'm really busy, I go bananas. I also tend to worry too much. I blow so much energy on worrying. But I'm really aware of the problem, and I'm trying to do something about it. I've taken up list making. Every morning I write up a list of five must-dos and establish my priorities that way. When I've completed one task, I cross it off the list, and that alone is very rewarding. If I have any time left, I then approach the lower priority work."

The main thing you must have is control—control of yourself and of your time. As an adult, you must accept full responsibility for your actions. As a manager, control is mandatory. Here's what one executive said about control: "Psychologists will tell you control is a bad way to deal with your emotions. But when you have a job to do, you have to decide that controlling your emotions is going to be your objective. And you may have to sacrifice to get to that point—you may have to sacrifice your personal feelings. But if your goal is paramount, then you'll be able to control yourself."

If you feel uptight at the end of the day, physical exercise is the best way to rid your body of tension and do yourself a favor at the same time. Physical exercise seems to have the side effect of making you feel more in control of yourself, and this alone will help you.

Don't give in to being too emotional just because everyone else expects you to be. Your overemotionalism will keep you from the big promotions and the large staffs. If you can't control yourself, how can you be expected to manage other people, one of the most difficult tasks you will have? Before you can manage others, you first must be able to control yourself.

❧ 7 ❧

Managing Other People

Part of your responsibility as an executive is to manage other people. Managing others is a difficult art because you have your own emotions with which to contend and also the emotions of your subordinates. Because each person on your staff is different from the others, management becomes a highly personalized endeavor. The seasoned manager must also be a psychologist, reading each employee's individual needs and knowing how to respond to them.

For a woman, the difficulties are compounded. You must be particularly conscious of the way you handle people. Men get away with shoddy management, especially if they are one of the good old boys. Women, on the other hand, must be masters of management before they will be given control. Management must back you completely before they will relinquish to you the same responsibilities that a man would automatically receive. You must prove your worth as a manager.

If you are to gain equality in business, you must demand that you manage the same size staff that a man would in your position. Don't let your management discriminate against you by holding back the number of people that you supervise. Managers who are responsible for larger groups usually earn a higher salary. Consequently, you must master the perplexing art of managing so there will be no excuse for your not being given the same power a man would receive.

The way you approach managing other people is all a matter of style. Volumes have been written on management style. You can never know too much about the elusive science of managing others, and most writers in this area each have their own particular approach.

One of the most popular of these is Douglas McGregor's classic X and Y theory of management, which he describes in his book *The Professional Manager* (New York: McGraw-Hill, 1967). He upholds that a manager's style of supervision reflects her assumptions about people. In brief, managers who believe in theory X assume people need authority and coercion to motivate them and that satisfactory performance will only come by ordering them around. A theory X manager rules through fear and unbending authority.

The theory Y manager is more benevolent. The executive who subscribes to this theory assumes that people are capable of disciplining themselves. She feels people respond better to challenge than to authority and that high expectations of employees result in higher achievements. Theory X emphasizes the worst in people, and theory Y the best.

Rather than ordering people what to do, a theory Y manager works with her employees to help them set meaningful, reachable goals and then removes the obstacles to the employees' achieving them. She assumes people can motivate themselves. The supposition here is that employees will be happier working toward goals rather than just showing up for work every day and performing a dull routine, with each day being identical to the rest.

In short, theory Y managers are more humanistic in their approach, more caring about providing a stimulating environment for their employees, and more sensitive to meeting each employee's individual needs. And the theory Y style of management will work best for you, the new executive woman.

The theory Y manager is not as altruistic as she might seem. Caring about her employees' needs is self-serving. This West Coast finance manager had the right idea: "I see my role as manager as a supportive position to my subordinates. As a manager, your reason for being there is to support all these people, and to do whatever is necessary to develop them. That of course becomes your own personal gain."

A theory Y manager sees her role as balancing the needs of the company with that of her people. She tries to make work fun and personally rewarding to her employees. A successful blending of these two elements benefits everyone concerned. These should be your objectives when you manage people.

Personnel handbooks list nine subconscious desires shared by all people, and you should know these desires in order to effectively handle and motivate others. You motivate your employees by satisfying their subconscious desires. If the employee does well, respond by recognizing him and praising him, and he will continue to achieve if only to gratify his ego. The nine subconscious desires are emotional security, recognition of efforts, creative outlets, sense of personal power, sense of roots and belonging, immortality, ego gratification, love, and new experiences. You can seldom offer emotional security and love, and certainly not immortality to your employees, but you can appeal to the rest of their desires. For example, you can offer them recognition of efforts, creative outlets, and a sense of belonging by merely being a sensitive manager. And their job may be the only arena they have in which to become fulfilled. Thus they are dependent on you, as their manager, for a sense of fulfillment.

Because the role you play in meeting the needs of others, you may find your maternal instincts coming to the fore. An older executive told me she often had maternal instincts toward the men who worked for her, and she felt these feelings set her apart from her male counterparts.

> I realized I had maternal feelings one day when I was sitting in a management meeting. One of the men who worked for me was giving the presentation. He did an excellent job, and I was very proud of him. I experienced the same feelings when my children did well in school. Yet I discovered that my male colleagues were threatened by him. They felt he was a bright, young star out to take their jobs. I had such an entirely different reaction than the men. I decided that it was because I am a mother and a woman. I

may naturally feel maternal toward younger people rather than being threatened by them.

If you sense that you are relating to your employees with maternal instinct, do nothing to stop it. It can only make you a more sensitive and caring manager, and today that is the kind of manager to be.

We Have Met the Enemy . . .

Practically nobody wants to work for a woman, which is one of your biggest problems. And women want to work for women even less than do men. *The Los Angeles Times* (April 22, 1976) published a Gallup Poll that asked the question: would you rather work for a man or a woman? A larger percentage of men said it made no difference whom they worked for. Men are more readily accepting women on the management scene than we women are ourselves. This same poll also showed that more men than women favored the passage of the Equal Rights Amendment. As the feminists say, "We have met the enemy and they are us."

Women who work for women usually fall into two categories: they will either adore you or abhor you. Very seldom is there any in-between. Experts feel that the reason women often resent working for other women is that girls more resented being disciplined by their mothers than boys did. The intricate dynamics of a mother-daughter relationship are often replayed when one woman works for another.

If you are not overtly supportive of the women who work for you, they are apt to harbor resentment and jealousy toward you. And women who don't like working for you will be harder to manage than men. With men, you can simply reinforce their masculine ego. With women a different tactic is required. To gain their support, you must demonstrate that you will use your power to help them. Those women whom you support will love you dearly. Often a woman may initially resent you, but she will alter her attitude as the relationship progresses. One woman who worked for me told me, "I always said I would never work for another woman, and when you offered me this job, I was very hesitant to take it. But now I've changed my mind. Since you were also a secretary once, you are an easy boss to work for. You understand my problems. I've changed my mind about working for other women."

A Minneapolis executive told me this about her relationship with female employees. "The women that work for me like me because they feel I've been helpful to them. I fight to get them good salaries and encourage them to apply for other job openings. If they run into snags, I always go to bat for them. There is one thing that annoys me, though. Sometimes I've offered a woman a new position, and she says she must go home and consult her husband before giving me a decision! I'd expect that only if we were talking about moving her out of state."

If you support the women below you, they are apt to become loyal and productive employees. Their inherent prejudices will melt away, but you must give this process some time.

Are there differences between supervising men and women? One banking executive thinks so. She says, "Women are insecure about their decision-making ability. As a supervisor, you must develop it. With a man, you bolster his masculine ego. With a woman, you develop her intelligence. Managing people is such a personalized endeavor, however, that I doubt that either men or women as a group are easier to handle." I tend to agree with the woman who told me, "There is no difference supervising men and women. I had a younger brother and sister whom I supervised, and I learned very early to treat everyone as equals."

Management Without Emasculation

Many of the women executives I interviewed felt they had an easier time supervising men than women. One said, "From my own experiences, it's been easier with men. They're great to deal with. The only times I've had to go to my boss and say 'Will you please order someone to do something,' it's always been a woman." She was a beautiful lady with flowing blond hair, and I suspect that her female employees were jealous of her and tried to usurp her power by refusing to acknowledge her as boss. There's no question about it. If you are attractive, you will have an easier time getting along with men. "With men, I've tried the teamwork approach," said another manager. "My attitude is 'work with me, rather than for me.' Then I don't have to worry about feelings of emasculation. But that doesn't always work because some people need firm leadership."

Herein lies an enigmatic problem when dealing with the male employee. You need to provide strong leadership, yet you must do it without emasculating him. If your authority over him is flaunted in a way that is belittling to him, you will have a problem to deal with. To handle authority correctly, you must be a master politician for it is a sensitive area. An experienced executive who manages over forty men told me, "Sometimes when men are performing ineffectively, I find it's because of our sex differences or his macho attitude. I'm sensitive to this attitude, and when I'm aware of men with a problem like this, I deal with them quickly and talk it out of them. I never approve of their attitudes, but I'm willing to discuss it with them." She also told me that the more men she managed, the easier it was for them to accept her. Since there was such a large group under her and so many men were in the same predicament, they accepted her more readily.

The easy solution to the management without emasculation dilemma is to hire only enlightened men who have strong egos. Hopefully, you will have some of these types of men working for you, and you will have a wonderful relationship with them. But since there are so many male chauvinists in the business world, odds are you will manage your share. The problem with the male chauvinist is this. He sees your supervision of him as a reflection of his own inadequacy. He asks himself, "What kind of man works for a woman?" and he deplores the mental image of a pussy-whipped Casper Milquetoast that he conjures. Because he himself would think less of a man who works for a woman, he projects his feelings on others. He may even take some ribbing about it from the boys at the lodge. His wife may also be a chauvinist, and your status belittles him in her eyes.

How the male chauvinist regards you as a supervisor depends on his attitude toward women in general, and toward his mother and wife in particular. To command his respect, you must be able to overcome prejudices that have been reinforced all of his life—or until he met you. You must alter the male chauvinist's concept of women.

Be somewhat sympathetic about the difficulty a male chauvinist may be having in dealing with the fact that he works for a woman, but don't let your sympathies hamper your ability to evaluate his performance objectively. Give him time to readjust his thinking. But never verbalize your sympathies with him or he will think that you approve of and accept his behavior. You may detest the necessity of ever giving the male chauvinist special consideration, but you must realize that his attitude could hamper his performance, and in turn become a negative reflection on you. And you will be evaluated on his performance.

There are certain considerations that you can pay male employees that will help soothe the sting of your supervisory capacity. For example, when I was at an industry function with one of the men who worked for me, I was always careful to introduce myself as working with the employee. I never made it a point to even mention my status unless it was necessary for some business purpose, and I think those men appreciated that. But most of the special courtesies that you can extend to your employees to help earn their respect can be applied to both men and women. Being cognizant of others' feelings is specially important for you, because as a woman you must try harder and use more skill than your male counterpart.

The Care and Handling of Employees

One fact of management is that you and your employees are mutually dependent. You fulfill some of their needs, and they become dependent on you. You, in turn are dependent upon their good performance. A rule of human behavior is that dependence engenders hostility. As children, we learn to resent the authority of certain individuals, such as parents or teachers. Much resentment is directed toward law enforcement figures, and many of us hang onto these feelings throughout our lives. We all, at some point, consciously or subconsciously resent authority. Your employees may resent you because you are an authority figure.

Since you are dependent on your employees, you may also feel resentment toward them, but it is much easier to deal with your own feelings than it is to deal with the feelings of others. For example, say your employee agrees to furnish you some information next Tuesday for a report you need to make on Wednesday. On Tuesday morning, he tells you he won't have it in time. Consequently, you are late with your presentation, and since you must accept the responsibility of the actions of your staff, it is your fault you were late. Because your success partially depends on your employees, it is easy to become resentful of them if you are not careful. You must make allowances for their shortcomings whereas seldom will they understand yours.

Some employees will also feel hostility toward you because you must criticize them. It's frequently a hard thing to learn that you're not in business to be liked but to do a job. You may be forced to take corrective action that will increase the resentment an employee feels toward you, yet you must do it, because you are responsible for that employee's actions.

If you are the least bit sensitive, criticizing others can be excruciatingly painful. When you first start out, you may find it an exceedingly difficult task to perform. I talked with one woman who said she felt uncomfortable criticizing the men who worked for her: "In my first management job, I supervised women who were professionals and they were a snap. The first time I really had problems was when I began supervising men. They tended to be either prima donnas, or they didn't want to work very hard. At first, I dreaded having confrontations with them, but I knew that they were necessary. It took a while before I could handle them and maintain a firm grip over them. But my stomach was churning for a while every time I was forced to do it. Finally I got over it."

There are certain constructive ways you can criticize with the least detriment to your relationship with the employee. If you approach criticism humanely, your employees will appreciate you for it. There are courtesies that you can extend to the people who work for you that show you respect them as human beings even though you are criticizing them. A few words of praise before you criticize soothes the sting of harsh words. A little extra time in caring about your people's feelings will help you gain their support. As a woman, you should be particularly sensitive to this.

If Ted, who is an engineer in your department, works on a project for three months and comes up with an unacceptable design, you might approach him like this: "Ted, I'd like to talk to you about the engineering design you submitted. I can tell you've worked hard and long on it, and some of the designs are absolutely brilliant. There are a couple areas, however, that need cleaning up, and I think you may have to start over on some of them. I'd appreciate your thoughts on the matter." Then you can proceed with the criticism without attacking Ted's ego.

Another manager, a male, might take that engineering drawing and fling it in Ted's face, ordering him to create a new design in two weeks or he will be fired, and that tactic might work for him. Ted may feel resentment toward the man, but he may also feel envy about the forceful way his boss handled himself. Ted may wish he were as forceful and adopt his boss as a role model. You will never become his role model, nor will he admire you for your forcefulness. He is more apt to resent you. You must become a master of diplomacy to gain the support of your employees.

One more word about criticism. Although you should be cognizant of others' feelings when you criticize them, you should never be reluctant to offer constructive criticism. Even though such sessions are dreaded by managers, most learn to accept them as an unpleasant but necessary evil of management. You will be judged on the firmness with which you handle difficult employees. When there are problems in your department, and there always seems to be something awry, your management will observe how quickly you isolate the problem area, and how you go about solving it. If firing an employee is necessary, you must show that you are capable of doing it. How well you replace the person who has left is also part of your responsibility, and you will be judged accordingly.

Although it's important always to have control of the situation, you can control with a gentle hand. That's the management style that works best for the executive woman. It calls for applying your femininity, which in this case means being especially sensitive to the feelings of your staff.

Some supervisors manage by embarrassment. They wait until a group has gathered before they criticize poor performance, and by doing so, they hope to spur employees on to greater achievement. They operate on the premise that people will work harder to escape the fear of being embarrassed in front of their peers. And sometimes this works, however cruel it may seem. I had a boss who successfully used this tactic on me. Every time we had a staff meeting, I would live in fear that he was going to embarrass me again. I was always well prepared.

Embarrassment is an offshoot of intimidation, and therefore it's a less effective tool for women to use because of the inherent resentment that others have toward businesswomen. Although you should never be reluctant about criticizing an employee's performance, you should try to be gentle about it and avoid doing it in front of a group. No use increasing the intensity of their resentment toward you.

If you sense a great deal of animosity from an employee when you criticize him, then discuss his feelings with him immediately. After you have attempted to change his attitudes and he is still unteachable, then use your power to the fullest and fire him. You cannot afford to have people working for you whom you can't control, or with whom you can't communicate. You must have channels of communication to keep a contented staff. You must learn what's bothering them so you can remove the obstacles, or at least smooth the wrinkles. And you can benefit from the input, too. If you hear what criticisms your employees have of you as a boss, you can improve your methods.

If you suddenly have a big, unexplained turnover in your department, investigate it thoroughly. An extraordinary loss of personnel is a reflection of mismanagement, poor employee selection, or both. Here is what one utilities executive discovered about employee management.

I know a lot of managers who are slave drivers. They just tell their people what to do, and never ask if they are happy. I make it a point to call my employees individually into my office about once every three months and discuss their gripes with them. This sounds very sensitive, but it is really self-serving. I know that if I train someone and they leave, then I have to go through the training process again. The company has an investment in that person, and, as a manager, I should do everything to keep the competent ones happy. And I find that my department is much more efficient. As a result, I have been given more and more people to handle. I know that's not the only reason, but it sure has helped me run a happy group.

This same woman also mentioned another important courtesy. It is vital that you respect your employee's confidence. Never talk about them negatively with other employees. Never partake in office gossip about your employees, and never discuss salaries with anybody but the personnel department and the employee himself.

It is a good practice never to divulge salaries to anyone, for the lower-paid employees will resent those who make more money than they and cause dissension in your department. If no one ever knows, then you don't have that problem. Of course, they can confide in each other, but it is amazing what a sensitive subject salary is. I've heard some managers boast about the money they pay their employees, like they are trying to appear more important because they have access to privileged information. You should be secure enough not to resort to that kind of tacky behavior. You have a responsibility to uphold your employees' rights of privacy, and you should respect that right.

As a manager, it is your job to make your employees' tasks easier and to help remove the obstacles that are keeping them from performing their jobs. There are times when you need to offer criticism and times when you need to support them. You should make it a rule always to stand behind them if you feel they are competent individuals. Be loyal to them, and you'll receive loyalty in return.

Hiring

Hiring employees is often a bigger gamble than putting all your money on one number in Las Vegas. At least

THE NEW EXECUTIVE WOMAN 97

there, you know what you are betting on. When you hire an employee, all you know is what you think you're betting on, but in reality, you won't know the outcome for a few weeks or months. It will take that long to adequately evaluate an employee's performance. Usually, the higher the status of your employees, the longer it takes to evaluate their worth. The more managing they do, the more intangible the process becomes. You will know after a few days if a secretary will work out, but for a manager, this may take months.

Your company probably has a personnel department that will assist you in finding qualified applicants, testing them if necessary, and conducting preliminary interviews. Once the applicant moves past personnel, he'll spend time interviewing with you. Usually, the ultimate decision is left to the prospective supervisor, but the personnel department can do much of the leg work for you.

You need a high percentage of good hires if you expect to run an efficient group. You must have a clear image of the function the employee is to perform and knowledge of the type of personality and job skill required. This is invaluable information for the personnel department. Job skills are simple to determine. Evaluating the intangibles like the person's dependability, integrity, and true personality behind the facade of his best foot forward is difficult.

Interviews either bring out the best or worst in people. A glib talker may impress you the first time out, whereas a shyer person might crumble under the strain of interviewing. The shy applicant may become more relaxed with you the second or third time you see him, and the shininess of the extrovert may tarnish a bit after a while. Sometimes there is a temptation to hire the first qualified person who comes along, but each decision should be important enough for you to give it proper time. It is much easier to use care in hiring than it is to suffer through the ordeal of firing someone. Give some thought to employee selection.

One executive considered hiring to be her biggest problem in business, and her job required her to hire predominantly male applicants. She claims she was very successful at this. "Hiring is a gamble," she said. "But as a woman, I have more of an intuitive feeling that helps me. I think women are more sensitive to feelings and to signals that people emit in a conversation."

Is there such a thing as women's intuition? If there is, it sure comes in handy when you hire. Intuition becomes your biggest asset, and I truly believe that most women possess it. That's not to say that men can't have it too, nor that they don't. But women have been trained to be more sensitive to nuances and to others' feelings, and to rely on vibrations rather than logic. Since we have nurtured these aspects of our personality, then we ought to be better equipped to make hiring decisions, where the ultimate decision is usually one of intuition. Of course, you'll never sell yourself on a job because you possess women's intuition, but if you learn to use your intuition, you will have a good record of hires and will receive rewards because of it.

One thing you should always do when interviewing prospective employees is to ask them how they feel about working for a woman. By bringing the subject up yourself, you can test the applicant for signs of antagonism. If you sense that he would find it difficult to work for you, then don't hire him. You must feel you have control of your staff.

One research manager said she got right to the point in her interviews. "When I interview men for jobs, and I decide I want this particular person, I say to him, 'This job involves traveling with me. Is this going to be a problem for your wife?' This usually leads into a conversation with them about their previous experiences. So far nobody's ever indicated that it was a problem." She handled that situation perfectly. She conceded that there was a potential problem, but she maintained the upper hand while discussing it. Complications like this should be ironed out before you hire someone. If he quits over something like that, it will only serve to make you look bad. Be outwardly firm, but inwardly sympathetic, to the problem. You have a responsibility to alter male chauvinist misconceptions, but you can't expect to change a society overnight.

The Queen Bee and You

In January 1974, *Psychology Today* published an article by Graham Staines, Carol Tavris, and Toby Epstein Jayaratne called "The Queen Bee Syndrome." Their findings created quite a furor among feminists and other interested readers. The epithet "Queen Bee" became the latest buzzword for women who had succeeded within the present business system, and, used accusingly by the feminists, stereotyped these successful women as antifeminist.

To conduct their research, the authors sent out a questionnaire to the magazine's readers asking them questions about their life-style, and their attitudes toward the women's movement, and about life in general. From their responses, the writers drew some preliminary, empirical conclusions about the woman who had succeeded in business, and they created a profile of her. They tagged her a "Queen Bee," and her beliefs, in brief, were as follows: Other women could succeed in business if they worked as hard as she did. The only way to succeed at executive levels was through individual effort. The Queen Bee had worked hard to attain her position, and she felt "Why should it be easier for others?" She had a high-status job with good pay, and she had achieved social success. She was also eager to succeed in the traditional feminine role of wife and mother.

Most important for our discussion here, the article indicated that the Queen Bee selfishly refused to help other women because she enjoyed her unique status, and because she was fearful of the competition.

I believe there is some fact and some fiction in the *Psychology Today* profile of the successful businesswoman. Some of the Queen Bee beliefs are obviously true. Individual endeavors *are* the only way to succeed in business at executive levels. That's how business chooses its leaders and rewards its stars. Women who have succeeded understand that, they have learned to play by existing rules, and they are winning—as individuals. Business only rewards those who play by its rules. That's the way the executive system operates. Indeed, most successful businesswomen have been individualists, as the article points out. Success in business and individualism are interrelated.

But today's successful businesswoman doesn't possess all the attitudes attributed to her in "The Queen Bee Syndrome." For example, I found in my interviews with executive women that most were very concerned about helping other women, contrary to the Queen Bee belief that they weren't. Most had made a conscious effort to help when they could. And you should too. By doing so, you are helping yourself. In the long run, it will benefit you if women are accepted on a wider scale. We need a women's job network that can compete and counterbalance the old boy's network that has assisted men so much.

But herein lies a sticky problem for women executives—the hiring of other women. It's imperative that you help other women, and one of the ways you can do this is to hire them. But it's unwise to help other women to the point of endangering your position. If you hire a predominantly female staff, most managments would take you by the earring and toss you out the door. Compromise is the only practical solution. Attempt to hire a balanced group.

If there is a woman applying for an opening with the proper qualifications and you feel she has potential, then hire her, and give her special attention to augment her progress. Even during these days when reverse discrimination is in vogue, *you* cannot afford to hire a woman just because she is female. Determine first if she has the proper qualifications, or you are helping no one, least of all yourself. Some companies keep records on your percentage of bad hires to assist in evaluating your worth as manager. Judge both male and female employees with the same criteria, and you should have no problem. If a woman survives your careful scrutiny, then by all means offer her the job first. And consider yourself lucky if a qualified woman does apply, as she can be an asset to have around.

But remember. You are extremely vulnerable every time you hire a woman. If you hire a man, and he fails to work out, not much would be thought about it. But if a woman doesn't work out—and, in truth, many times she won't—everyone says, "I told you so."

As an East Coast executive told me, "My first experience in trying to help other women was a couple of years ago. I promoted my secretary to technical writer, then to head of the department. Two months later, she came and told me she was pregnant and was leaving her job to stay home and raise a family. I was so disappointed and embarrassed because I had personally championed her cause to management."

Quite frankly, there will be times when it's prudent not to hire a woman, and you should be realistic about this. I had the privilege of talking with a woman who had just been appointed city manager for a suburb of Chicago. She was the first woman manager in the state and knew she would be closely scrutinized. She was previously assistant to the manager, and now she had to hire a new assistant for herself. I asked her if she would hire a man or a woman. "I will hire a male assistant," she told me, "but for the wrong reasons. I don't want the board to think I'm going to build a female dynasty. I feel almost forced into hiring a man." Rather than bowing to feminist idealism, she understood the realities of her position.

My best advice to you is to help other women fairly and assertively as much as you can, but don't jeopardize your position—and theirs—in the process.

Firing

Firing, for most executives, is the most distasteful part of management. Everyone hates to do it. Telling employees they are failing is never an easy chore, and it is probably harder for women because we tend to be more sensitive and sympathetic and we dislike hurting others. But your ability to fire is as important as your ability to hire. You must learn to make those kind of arbitrary decisions.

Most managers procrastinate too long before making a decision to fire someone. Yet you will be judged on your ability to make expedient firing decisions. If you determine that a particular employee is the source of a problem, if you can't turn him around speedily, the quicker you get rid of him, the better off you will be. You should also fire any employee whose resentment about working for a woman gets in the way of doing his or her job. You will probably detect a few undercurrents of resentment toward you in most situations, but most of the time the situations are operable. There will be situations, however, that will lead to insubordination of an employee, and if this happens, fire him. You cannot control male chauvinists in the executive chambers, or even in the next department, but you can sure do something about them with your own staff. Do not tolerate any outward sign of antagonism.

Your job is tough enough without having to put up with that.

A brilliant research manager who supervises a staff of chemists had learned to accept firing as part of her job. "It never bothers me to fire people anymore," she confessed. "I don't allow it to become an emotional decision. I think about it intellectually and have never done it precipitously. If it's necessary, then I do it quickly, and in such a way that it doesn't destroy the person. I help them realize what their opportunities are, and that it's better for them to have a chance to go somewhere else where they would better fit into the organization. I never give them any recourse, and that works out better.

"The rotten apple syndrome is really true," she said. "If you have people who are contributing less than they can be expected to do, you're going to spoil it for the other persons in the department. I feel an obligation to the other people to keep the environment clean for them."

This is the professional attitude you should assume about firing people. Charity begins and ends at home. If someone is not carrying his weight, then you have an obligation to let him go. The process of firing brings out volatile emotions in everyone, so you should strive to keep it on an unemotional level.

Women tend to be extremely conscientious, almost to a fault, and you are apt to feel badly because you made a wrong decision about someone. This same research manager confessed that she feels like she has failed every time she fires someone. "I have a strong sense of pride," she said. "If someone who works for me fails, and it's my responsibility, I'll tend to feel low over that. I find myself magnifying my failures at the expense of the successes. It's hard to see the successes sometimes. I tend to blow my failures out of proportion, and get depressed over them."

Remember what I said earlier about taking your job too seriously, so much so that it affects your emotions outside of work. There is no use getting upset over a failure, as you are only human, and no one expects you not to make any mistakes. You certainly are not expected to be perfect at the uncertain task of hiring personnel. Learn from your errors, and you will grow because of them.

I'm sure most managers remember the first time they fired someone. I know I do. He was the first art director I hired for my advertising agency. He was a middle-aged man around 45, and I was just 23. From the first, I had problems controlling him. Dave would listen to my instructions about what the client wanted and then proceed to layout an ad the way he wanted. After giving him careful instructions, I would ask if he understood what I needed. He would shake his head yes, and then proceed to do whatever he pleased. I'm sure his justification was that he knew more about the advertising business than I did, and he was probably right. I signed his paycheck, yet I felt out of control of the situation.

His insubordination continued until I reached my limit. At first I tried to understand why he was insubordinate. It was probably due to the huge disparity in our ages. I finally decided firing was the only solution, but I procrastinated in doing it. By the time I finally got the nerve to call him into my office and lay it on the line, I was a nervous wreck. I was so worried about doing it that I could barely sleep the night before. All I could think about was his family. Images of his children kept popping into my head, and I wondered how he was going to feed all those little mouths. Somehow, I felt responsible for them.

With trembling hands, dry mouth, and a knot in my stomach the size of a watermelon, I called him into my office. He walked in with a cup of coffee, sat down in the chair across from my desk, put his feet up on the chair next to him, and clasped his hands behind his head. "What's up?" he asked.

"Dave, I've decided to fire you," I blurted. "I don't like your work, or anything about you, for that matter."

"What?" he said. "You're going to fire me? Marci, that's ridiculous."

"What do you mean, that's ridiculous?" I demanded. "You work for me, and I have the right to fire you any time I want."

"Yes," he said, "but you will never survive around here without me. You need all my experience."

"Don't kid yourself, Dave. I can hire guys like you for a dime a dozen," I said, my voice quivering.

"Why you snot-nosed kid," he retorted. "How dare you have the audacity to fire me!" By this time we were shouting."

"Just pack your stuff and get out of here," I told him,

while trying to control the tears that were welling up. "Just get out. I never want to see you again." I grabbed my purse, and ran out of the office. I jumped in my car and drove around for a while, trying to compose myself. I knew I had made the right decision, but firing Dave was more of a trauma on me than it was on him.

Later than afternoon, after he was gone, I called a friend and told her what happened. "Why, Marci," she said, "you handled that all wrong. You don't just blurt out that you are going to fire someone. Soften the blow by telling him how much you think of him, but the situation you're in hasn't worked out. Tell him that you know that if he leaves, he can find a situation more suited to his talents. Just don't take someone by surprise. And the way you approached it offended his male ego."

I soon replaced him with another art director who worked for me for years. Although, he, too, was quite a bit older than I, he didn't give me the same kind of problems. But we discussed his feelings about working for me at great length before I hired him. I didn't want to make the same mistake twice.

The next time I decided to fire someone, I decided to be gentle. Karen was a secretary close to my age, and we had developed a social friendship outside of work. She began taking advantage of our relationship, asking for time off to plan a party, or leaving work early when she felt I would be tied up at a client's for the day. I found it difficult to say anything to her because we were friends. Finally I decided that work was more important than our friendship, and I would have to fire her.

"Be gentle with her," I told myself. "Don't let happen again the trauma you had in firing Dave." So I called her into my office and gave her a long dissertation on how much I liked her and thought of her as a person. As tactfully as possible, I told her I was letting her go. She seemed to take it well, and I went home relieved that the unpleasantness was over with.

The next morning I came in to find Karen sitting at her desk working, like nothing had happened. I was speechless. There she was, all bright and shiny, ready for a day's work. I thought I had fired her! I called her into my office again.

"Karen," I said, "didn't you understand that I fired you yesterday?"

"You did?" she replied. "Is that what you were getting at yesterday? I couldn't figure out what you were talking about."

With Karen, I was so tactful that she didn't even comprehend the communication. I think the idea that I would fire her was so foreign to her, she didn't realize what had happened. And I had to go through the process again. Since then, I've learned to be gentle, but make my position clear. Firing someone once is bad enough, but having to do it twice is torture.

Socializing with Employees

The difficulty in firing Karen was compounded by our friendship. Our relationship outside of work interfered with my ability to adequately supervise her. Once this happens, the difficulty is reestablishing a business relationship in the office. As a supervisor, you can criticize an employee without antagonizing him. As a friend, you will strain the relationship and create bad feelings around you. So my advice based on my experience is to avoid personal friendship with subordinates. That doesn't mean you shouldn't be friendly toward them, and be friends to them when they need it, but it's a good practice to avoid social friendships with your underlings.

From a career building standpoint, there is a reason why you want to avoid socializing with them. It's a matter of positioning, and this is important especially when you are younger. You should select friends who are on the same level, or higher, in the company. Be status conscious on the job. There's an old saying that you are known by the friends you keep. You will be more easily accepted as an executive if your peers are executives. Business is very status conscious and will observe with whom you socialize. If you want to be seen as an executive, you must act like an executive. And executives almost always socialize with other executives.

Since you are apt to be in the minority, you may get lonely for female companionship. I know I did, and struck up kind of a work friendship with a couple secretaries who were near my age. But I was very careful whom I selected as friends, and I avoided seeing them too much outside the office. This is a good practice. Many people use their work as their social outlet, but too many problems can arise from that. You should always have friends outside of work, if for no other reason than to help you keep a good perspective on the world. You are apt to become so engrossed in business that you become one-sided. That's easy to do, and keeping friends in other professions helps broaden your insight.

I worked for a company that was ultra-social. All the executives would dine together, with their spouses or whatever, at least twice a week. Everything was fine until the president's wife began messing around with the neighbor of one of the chief engineers (they met at a party which we all attended). Complications set in, and it was sticky from there on in. I think everybody in that company learned a good lesson.

Incidentally, not all executives agree with me about this. A high ranking West Coast lady told me, "To me a secretary is not a secretary, she's a person doing a job. I either like her or I don't. If I wanted to develop a personal relationship with her or go have drinks with her after work, the fact that she was a secretary wouldn't matter. She could work in the mail room or be a president of the company. The personal relationship matters."

She does say, however, that secretaries are hesitant to invite her to lunch. "They get over that, though," she says. "Eventually they feel like they can invite me to lunch. I don't mean to sound like it works easily. It doesn't. There are very few people I relate to in the company. I've changed jobs five times now, and the nice thing about that is that I've made friends who have lasted with every job."

Since she believed in being so friendly with her people, I asked her if she would ever confide in them. "No," she said. "I would never confide personal problems because that would display weakness. But I may confide a personal problem if it relates to work."

That is a good rule to follow. You will need to confide in someone about work-related topics. Everybody finds somebody in a company in whom they confide. But be careful whom you choose. Remember, loose lips sink ships, and the ship could be your career.

Special Care and Handling of Secretaries

Your secretary serves as a personal extension of you. She becomes such a vital part of your work efforts that she deserves special attention.

The ultimate status symbol is a curvaceous blond sitting outside your office, waiting for your beckoning call so she can serve you. This, of course, is the male chauvinist idea of what a secretary should be like. Oddly enough, many women like to play the role of office wife, waiting on their man at the office just like they would at home. So when you interview prospective secretaries (and we'll assume they are women), ascertain that your choice is not one of those women who get off on playing office wife. You can sometimes almost tell by looking at her and her reactions to you whether or not she's the one for you.

Within certain elements of the business community, the trend has reversed itself. Executives wishing to create a serious image often go for a plainer type, and the plainer the better. I also suspect that their wives are the jealous type, and they also feel more comfortable with a plain secretary. Fortunately, you needn't worry about what your secretary looks like. You are not trying to impress the locker room fraternity. What you do care about is that your secretary is competent and likes working for a woman. Some women actually prefer working for other women. This is the type of person you want.

Since your secretary is normally required to answer your phone, her telephone voice is very important. Never hire a secretary without first listening to her on the phone. If you are thinking about hiring her, call her and see how she answers the phone. Determine whether she has a cheery, friendly voice or sounds like a cold fish, and notice how she comes across. Someone who sounds acceptable in person may sound rotten on the phone, and you should check this out before you hire her.

You may, of course, hire a male secretary, although that tends to be a little too cute. But I talked to one executive in San Francisco who had a male secretary, and she claims he was the best secretary she ever had. One man called up in response to a classified ad I had placed, saying he was a qualified secretary—and a transvestite. He said he wanted to interview for the job, but only if I would let him wear women's clothes to work. Although I was slightly intrigued by the idea, I doubted if some of my more conservative clients would appreciate it, so I turned him down. "I thought for sure *you* would understand," he countered before slamming down the receiver.

Here's a special word about the handling of secretaries. Be cognizant of how you treat her. Don't expect her to be your office servant. You should get your own coffee and place your own phone calls. The only exception is when you have a guest in your office.

Starting at a New Company

You may find yourself hired to manage an existing group of employees who may have worked together for some time and have developed a closeness with each other. This is a tough situation to walk into. Here are some hints on how to handle it.

When you first meet your new employees, meet them at their work stations so you can identify their jobs with their names and faces. Get them to tell you what their responsibilities are, and by encouraging them to talk about themselves, you'll get clues as to their personalities. Never approach them as a group, but meet them individually. You need to maintain the upper hand from the outset, and this is easier to establish on a one-to-one basis.

After you have met each employee at his work station, call each one into your office, and discuss his job with him again. Ask him if he has any suggestions for improving efficiency or communication, and listen to his gripes. He will be flattered that you care about his opinion. (Remember, a Y theory manager always cares about her employees' needs.)

After you have gotten to know them individually, observe them as a group, at lunch or coffee breaks. Isolate the clique and see who the leaders are. If you get them on your side, you have it made.

Sometimes if you are replacing a man, and other men in the department have been passed over for the promotion, you might find some antagonism from one or two, especially those who thought they should have gotten the job, and they lost out to a woman no less. If you sense resentment, you may have to fire one or two.

One management philosophy is the "clean broom"—when you start at a new company, fire a few, or everybody, and bring in your own people so that you have control from the beginning. If you are hired to clean up a department, you may sense hostility from the survivors and may have to terminate one or two to shake up the troops enough to establish your authority. In situations of insubordination, nothing gains an employee's attention more than firing a few of the co-workers.

If a department has gone sour, the best way to handle it is to get rid of everybody and start over again. This is a drastic measure, so do it only when necessary. You may earn the respect of those you hire, but you will experience a tremendous loss of efficiency in the process. Don't do anything until you've had a chance to properly evaluate the situation, and never start firing without letting your boss know what you're planning, or you could be in a heap of trouble.

When you start a new job, expect those whom you manage to be wary of you. A top executive in the Federal Reserve Bank in Chicago told me, "I have a number of men who directly report to me, and when I became their boss, they were skeptical. A man would probably receive the benefit of the doubt, and they would assume that he knew what he was doing. With a woman, they feel like maybe this is affirmative action, and so they approach you with some uncertainty. And that's irreparable until they get to know you. Once they do, I've never found any problems."

Some executives take their secretaries with them when they change jobs, and this can be a good idea, especially if you feel you can work with nobody else as well as you can with your secretary. However, there is a disadvantage. The existing secretary will know more about the company and its operations, and can be of great assistance to you. If you bring your secretary along, there will be two new people on the job, and the transition may be rocky because of it. A better way, if you can't live without your secretary, is to hire her after you have been there for a while and are more established yourself.

⋘ 8 ⋙

Your Office: Creating and Controlling Your Territory

Thank goodness that keys to executive washrooms are declining in popularity as executive status symbols. Women couldn't use them anyway (unless we demand our own executive washroom, too). The trend now is for private bathrooms complete with showers. This is just one way companies reward their executives. A plush and spacious office is another, and it is the most visible measurement of esteem a company can bestow on an executive. Many power-seekers prefer a larger office to confidential salary increases as recognition of their efforts. An impressive office is an unmistakable sign of authority.

Although the size of the office communicates territorial rights, and indeed indicates status, its relationship to the powerful corner offices is important. Corner offices are the most desirable, and offices diminish in importance the closer they get to the middle. One of the reasons corners are status is that they contain more windows. Windows, then, also become a symbol of authority. In most companies, having an office with a window indicates a certain degree of status. From there, their size and the number are significant.

Furnishings are also an indicator. The more an office looks like a living room, the greater distinction it has. Overstuffed sofas and easy chairs are popular. Other desirable trappings are muted lighting, preferably by table lamp; rosewood paneling; fireplaces and wet bars; custom wall coverings and drapes; and fine original art or signed lithographs. Desks should be solid wood and look like tables. The ultimate office doesn't even contain a desk. Even the quality of the carpeting has crept into the arena of executive status, thanks to a manufacturer's advertising campaign: "A name on the door rates a Bigelow on the floor." Exposed filing cabinets and typewriters are un-status symbols.

Another rule of corporate status is that the less work you have showing, the more important you must be. Over-flowing in-baskets, piles of papers, and scattered books are out for status-seekers. Instead, the discriminating executive prefers to keep just a minimum of work visible. Multiple telephones are acceptable and, in fact, are encouraged, as are leather-bound books arranged in library fashion on the wall.

These trappings may seem insignificant to you, but within the value structure of business, they are very important. One of the ways a company may discriminate against you is to withhold some of these fringe benefits that a man would receive in your position. Government can regulate salary and even tangible fringe benefits such as life insurance or stock options, but it cannot provide you with an equal office. You must demand that for yourself. Status symbols are even more important for women because we do not receive the assumption of authority that a man automatically receives. If you have an equivalent office to the others on your level, it indicates the company regards you just as highly. Don't accept any form of differential treatment, and offices are one of them.

You may not control the size of your office or the number of windows in it, but, company policy withstanding, you can decorate your office to reflect your individuality. (Some firms require that you obtain permission before hanging anything, others forbid it altogether, but most are willing to let you decorate to suit your taste.) The amount of individuality you put in your office usually is in direct ratio to your position in the company. It is worthwhile, then, to invest some of your own money into your decor. As subtle as it may be, it will help position you as an executive.

Besides the status of a tastefully decorated office, you

will feel more comfortable in an office that you have personalized. A touch of femininity is appropriate here. You shouldn't be frilly, but you can reflect a certain warmth and softness to make your surroundings more soothing. Provided you have ample lighting, plants are perfect. A bouquet of freshly cut flowers every week will do if you don't have the proper conditions for plants. I spoke with one executive who kept a freshly baked batch of cookies on her desk.

Professionally framed paintings or lithographs that you have personally selected are a delightful extension of your personality. Many people hang posters, but they tend to give an office the feeling of a college dorm rather than a sophisticated business atmosphere. Choose art with a discerning eye for quality, for nothing is more tacky than cheap art. You're better off with nothing.

Photographs of your family or friends should be kept at a minimum, and you should use only photographs taken by a professional. Snapshots, especially in those plastic cubes, are unsophisticated, despite their popularity among middle management. Be snobby about what you buy for your office, for it reflects your good taste, and discerning executives will appreciate you for it.

The Use of Space

Have you ever been sitting in a chair feeling vaguely uncomfortable until you realized that your uneasiness was because your back was facing the door? If you have, it's human nature, and it is something that you should remember while arranging your office. Place your desk so you sit facing the door, but not so you are backed up against the wall. Spaciousness gives a feeling of power, and you should give yourself as much room as possible. So arrange your desk so you have ample space behind you, otherwise, even if you have a big office, you are apt to feel cramped and less in control. If anybody needs to feel squeezed, it should be your visitor and not you. The more space you dominate, the greater chance you have to achieve the upper hand in the relationship. Your desk and chair should be your throne, giving you authority over whomever comes in. Use the space in your office to help you gain power over others.

If you are fortunate enough to have a window, sit with the light beaming over your shoulder. Never sit where you have to squint, for squinting causes premature crow's-feet, and we all get them soon enough. Make your visitors look into the light. This also puts you at an advantage.

When you are negotiating, always sit across from the people with whom you're bartering, and give them as little space as possible. Keep *their* backs up against the wall. When you wish to appear on more equal footing, a round conference table is perfect. In a round table, there is no position of authority as there is with a rectangular one.

The distance between you and your visitors will depend on the nature of your discussion. According to Julius Fast, author of *Body Language*, if you wish to relate at a normal business level, seat people from two and one-half to four feet from you; seat them closer for more personal interraction. If gaining power is your goal, always position yourself higher than your visitors. Dominance through height occurs throughout the animal kingdom, including man.

If you are an average-sized woman, you will have to make some conscious adjustments here. The best thing you can do to gain power is to keep your guest sitting, and you stand. Put three men on an overstuffed couch, sit across from them in a straight-backed chair, and watch them squirm. You will hold the position of power.

Because tallness contributes to dominance, taller people have an easier time gaining power. Now this presents some problems for women, but you can compensate. For example, I arrange my office so that there are two easy chairs across from my desk that are significantly lower than my desk chair. When someone comes in my office whom I want to dominate, I always ask him to sit in one of those chairs. I also have a round conference table. If I wish to deal with people on a more equal footing, I ask them to sit with me at the table.

I also use a five-foot-long desk rather than the standard six-foot version. I feel dwarfed behind the larger desk. I use a low-backed chair rather than those black leather thrones so many business executives use so I don't look quite so small. If you have the luxury of selecting your own furniture, order it scaled to your size.

A buyer in Los Angeles has a notorious reputation

among salesmen because of the way she uses the space in her tiny office. She keeps a bar stood next to her desk, and when a sales rep comes to see her, she sits on the stool and towers above him. She further intimidates him by asking how much time he'll need (sales reps frequently fudge, saying ten minutes when they plan to take thirty), and she keeps him to his word by setting an oven timer for the amount of time he says. When the time is up, the bell rings, and she sends him out the door. She is unpopular with the sales reps, but they respect her. She knows how to keep them in control.

Get in the habit of asking people to sit down when they come into your office to talk with you. Don't stay seated and let them tower over you. Either direct them to sit, or stand up yourself. Staying seated can put you at a psychological disadvantage.

People who hold meetings in their offices have authority. If you wish to control a group of people in a meeting, either hold the meeting in your office or in a neutral conference room. But don't hold it in another's office, as he will automatically play the role of host and therefore leader.

According to Michael Korda in *Power: How to Get It, How to Use It,* you can also gain dominance over another by entering his office, and, in a sense, invading his territory. But this technique of gaining power is only useful if you step beyond the accepted bounds of behavior, and infringe on the other territory. Korda suggests such ploys as using items for ashtrays that were meant for something else, giving orders to his secretary, spilling coffee and other assorted examples of obnoxious behavior. But what he means is to "take over" the office, and in doing so, immediately gain dominance over the one whose territory you have invaded.

Such calculated behavior is inappropriate for many office situations, but you should be cognizant of dominance ploys. If you walk into a subordinate's office, you can gain dominance by merely remaining standing while you talk with him. Or you can sit down and pull your chair around the desk so you are sitting next to him. Ir you can pull up a chair and lean over the desk, occupying a larger space, and therefore gaining dominance through territorial rights.

You don't always have to gain power over just subordinates. You may wish to make an impact on your supervisor. Here's what one finance executive told me about confronting her boss: "There is a point you reach once or twice a year when things aren't going your way. So you take a stand, and an absolute stand is necessary. I always do these things standing up. That's part of making an impact. Sometimes my boss will even ask me to sit down, but I always remain standing, knowing that by doing so I will be more effective."

The posture you assume, the way you hold your arms and legs, and your facial expressions, can all indicate authority. Actors and politicians know how to effect gestures and stances that suggest honesty, competency, and personal power, and you can too. According to Korda, the position of maximum power, while seated, is to have both feet firmly planted on the floor and lean forward with your hands on your knees. The person who is devoid of nervous gestures and twitches is thought to be powerful. A serene, confident facial expression can mask the turmoil and uncertainty that may be churning inside.

I was curious about the teenage hysteria over television's "Happy Days" and its cocky superstar, the Fonz. When I finally switched on the program one night, I was shocked and amazed. Somehow, I expected the Fonz to be much taller than he is. He's the shortest male actor on the program. So how does he gain all that power and authority? The answer is simple: body language. The Fonz is a master at standing with the posture of authority: legs slightly spread with feet firmly on the floor, his arms either extended from his body in a typical "Fonz" pose, or hands on hips. He has a cool, confident look on his face; he speaks with authority, gestures with his hands to indicate sincerity, and he uses eye contact. He's an exception to the truism that tallness equals dominance.

The lesson to be learned here is particularly pertinent to executive women. Despite your probable height disadvantage, you can still gain dominance by using other ploys. Learn when to use them, and know when others are using them on you.

Learn to Leash Your Libido

Everyone in the company knew about Linda's affair with the president. Since they were both single, she saw nothing wrong with their relationship, and she was, in fact, proud of it. When they moved in together, she was jubilant, and she shared her joy with several people in the company. After all, who could challenge her relationship with him, since he was president and majority stockholder.

Linda's affair with the company president lasted several years, and during that time her career progressed with the company from secretary to an entry level management position in the marketing department. She was a loyal, dedicated employee and a zealous supporter of both the president and the company. After work every night, the two of them would discuss the events of the day over dinner. They both lived for the company. Linda, out of loyalty, began reporting observations she made about the marketing department to the president. When things weren't going the way she thought they should, she felt obligated to reveal her findings to the president. She justified her actions this way: "I fought what I saw as injustices. In a lot of cases, there were things that the president was just not seeing that were detrimental to the company. My problem was that I was too concerned about the company; somehow I felt it was my place to reveal what was really going on."

The president trusted Linda's judgment and through her became unusually well informed about the day-to-day activities of the marketing department. Mark, Linda's boss, was bewildered by how the president knew so much about what was going on in his department and mentioned his concern to a colleague. "Don't you know?" his colleague asked. "Linda is living with the president."

Mark detested the concept of one of his employee's cohabitating with his boss, for he could see the unnecessary problems it was creating. Linda ignored the possibility that her relationship could jeopardize her job and continued to play watch dog for the president, dutifully reporting daily the occurrences of the marketing department.

One day Mark had had enough, and fired a flabbergasted Linda. She couldn't believe he could fire her, and went running down the hall to the president's office. But he just shrugged his shoulders and said, "Sorry, Linda. I can't help you. If Mark wants to fire you, as your boss, that's his prerogative. And you know I never interfere with my managers' decisions because that's the only way I can demand total accountability for their departments. Go on home, and we'll talk about it later."

A confused and unhappy Linda went home and packed her bags. She felt the president could have saved her job and that he should have if he cared about her. But she could see the company would always come first, and she knew the relationship would have to end. The next day she moved out and eventually took a job in another city.

Linda is very bitter about the whole experience. I know, because she is a friend of mine, and I knew her and the president quite well. I often felt she abused her relationship with the president and that one day it would catch up with her. And true to form, it did.

Most job-related affairs end in disaster, or at least leave both parties feeling they have undergone a traumatic experience. The more serious the affair, the more serious the ensuing trauma. In Linda's case, she lost both her job and her romance simultaneously. Losing just one of them is bad enough, but she was forced to endure both. She vowed that she would never get into that kind of relationship again.

Having romantic relationships with the men you work with—and this includes your clients as well as your colleagues—could be dangerous to your career health, although many people continue to get involved. For a female executive, office affairs can be particularly explosive, and you should be aware of the pr⃝⃝ems that you may encounter. Since the majority of rel⃝⃝nships end, you must first examine the repercussions of a⃝ office affair to determine if it is worth the involvement. Things can be going great as long as the relationship continues, but once it ends, you may find that person very awkward to be around. You may continue doing business with him, he may still be your boss, employee, or colleague, but you will likely feel vaguely uneasy in his presence, and this could affect the way you handle yourself. It's difficult to face someone on a daily basis if you've had a disastrous affair with him, and you should consider this seriously before you get involved.

Another problem for female executives is that you are fulfilling a stereotype by having an office affair. You spend years trying to alter the male concept of woman as sex object, and then you turn around and act like one. This is not to say you should deny yourself romantic involvements, but you should be wary of job-related ones. At work, you do not want to be thought of in sexual terms. If you are attractive, it is almost impossible to engage in an affair without reinforcing the image of being a sex object.

Men find it difficult to simultaneously treat women as colleagues and as lovers. Be aware of this before you enter into an affair. Once a man sees you as a sex object, making the differentiation in his mind between your professional side and your sexuality creates a conflict in his mind. From there on in, he will continue to see you as a sex object even after the affair has ended, and there is little you can do to stop it.

No matter how discreet you are, other people will find out. Perceptive people can pick up on your vibes alone, and eventually someone will see you together. Assume that your affair will not be a secret. What would be the recriminations if your boss knew? Would he care, or think less of you because of it? You have a right to a personal life that is none of his business, but if you fish in the company pond, be prepared to catch more than you bargained for.

A woman told me about two people in her company who were having an affair. "They are from different areas of the company, and they think no one knows about it. In reality, the whole company knows. She's single and he's married, and executive management looks upon them as dishonest. They've both taken off work at the same time. They are in such different areas that if you didn't know, you might not put it together. But everyone knows, and it's going to catch up with them. It always does. It's sad because it is such a loss of brain power. I think they're getting themselves in a position of frenzy. You can just see it affecting their work." A rule to remember: office gossip makes it virtually impossible to keep an affair a secret.

The double standard is alive and well in corporate America. Others can know about the affair and increase their regard for the man, while thinking less of you. Although they would be quick to deny that they felt that way, I've heard many men make jokes and innuendoes about women with whom they were supposedly having affairs. The locker room fraternity loves to believe they have mystical sexual prowess. Some men will even dishonestly imply that they are having a relationship with a woman in order to appear masculine and virile. It's devastating enough to be talked about when you *are* having an affair, but to be accused of it when you are not is one of the ways male chauvinists attempt to put you down.

One time a friendly advertising salesman told me there was a rumor around town that I was sleeping with all my clients, and that was why I was keeping their business. I was initially shocked, and then irate that I could be accused so wrongfully. I asked him to track down the source of the rumor, if possible, so that I could deal with it head-on. He was able, fortunately, to trace it back to one of my competitors in another advertising agency. I called the man and gave him a piece of my mind, but that rumor continued to haunt me for a couple of years. Now and then someone would tell me they heard it, and there was literally nothing I could do about it except hope that it would go away. Eventually, I think it did, but I carefully did nothing to reinforce it.

Despite our supposed liberated society, men still think less of women who sleep around. The generation that believes in free love has not yet reached the managemnt level, and the people with whom you will be dealing still live by the old rules. Even though you see nothing wrong with expressing your sexuality, others may think less of you. It's better, then, to keep your social life away from work.

Some companies have a policy against employees dating each other, although this is the exception more than the rule. Most large companies have restrictions on married employees working for one another, but this is usually as far as it goes. Smaller companies are more likely to prohibit it, because of the problems that can develop when you both work in close proximity. But if your company does have a policy against it, and you get involved anyway, you are more apt to be fired than the man is. This is another area where the double standard manifests itself. I don't know why the women are always the ones that are fired, but that is usually the way it works out.

A publishing representative told me about attending his company's annual sales meeting, where the national sales representatives would come in from the field and meet with the publishers and the liaison staff in New York. A regular attendant at the meetings was a young woman who was director of circulation. This particular year she wasn't at the meeting, and the publisher stood up and made an announcement. "I know you are all wondering what happened to Rosemary, our circulation manager," he said. "I was forced to fire her. It seems she was having an affair with one of you salesmen." After that comment, several people's faces turned red, and they all were embarrassed.

After the meeting, one of the salesmen went into the publisher's office to confess his involvement with Rosemary, and to tell his boss he would never get involved with a woman at the company again. "Why, Harry," said the boss, "I didn't know you were having an affair, too. I fired her because of her relationship with Sam." Harry fled from the office. His own guilt had gotten him into more trouble than was necessary.

The point of the story is that Rosemary was fired for having an affair, but the men involved weren't. I have never heard of a situation that was reversed. So if you get caught breaking company policy (and if you do, you will), you'll be the one who will be reprimanded, not the man. As I said, the double standard is alive and well in corporate America.

Most business communities are very small and inbred,

and word about this kind of thing does get around. Not only could you lose your job over it, you may have trouble finding another one. A San Francisco executive said, "I know one woman who has the reputation of sleeping around, and if she lost her present job, she would have a hard time finding another one."

Here's the predicament one couple got themselves into, as described by an executive woman in New York. "A married man who was a head of a division on the East Coast was having an affair with the woman who was head of the group on the West Coast. They would meet from time to time, and it was quite a cozy relationship. Then an edict came down from corporate headquarters to kill the division on the West Coast and lay off all the employees. He couldn't do that to his girl friend, so he deviated from company policy and didn't kill it. Not only did he lose his job over it, but he also got divorced." That's just another story of an office affair causing havoc in the lives of the participants.

One night stands can be difficult to deal with, too. Here's what happened to a West Coast advertising executive: "I attended a publisher's cocktail party one night and met another agency's client. We hit it off, one thing led to another, and the next thing I knew I was in bed with him. The next day I thought, 'That was sure a stupid thing to do,' and every time I saw him after that, I was embarrassed. I never heard from him again, and besides that, it wasn't even enjoyable. When I faced him again, he was visibly embarrassed. I pretended like it never happened."

As you no doubt realize, I strongly recommend not having romantic relationships with the men you work with. However, human nature being what it is, you probably will anyway. And I can't say having relationships with colleagues is all bad. I met my husband because he called on me to sell me printing, invited me out to lunch, and we began dating almost immediately. He was one step removed from my work situation, even though he was a supplier, and I felt my management (I was an ad manager at the time) wouldn't object. I eventually stopped doing business with him because it interfered with our romantic relationship. If he were late on a delivery, and printers always are, I would be angry with him. It was hard to keep our business and personal relationships separate, so we gave up the business aspects, and our romantic relationship worked much better.

Several executives with whom I talked strongly disagreed with me on the subject of dating colleagues. One told me about her fiancé, with whom she shared the management of a department.

"Jim and I were co-workers for years," she said, "and my ex-husband and I would see him and his wife socially. We both attended a seminar out of town, and on this trip I told Jim that I was breaking up with my husband. He confessed that he and his wife were unhappy also, and contemplating a divorce. We started falling in love, and after a period of time we decided to live together."

I asked her how she handled the situation at work. "We decided to go to our boss and simply announce that we were living together. Much to our surprise, our boss thought it was hilarious. He's very straight, and he thought we were very daring. In fact, we thought he secretly liked having these people working for him who were so 'daring' because it made him feel like he was 'with it.' "

They were fortunate to have this kind of boss; many people aren't quite so understanding. Besides sharing the same secretary at work, their offices are next door, and they are co-managers of the same department (in a large corporate office of a major manufacturer). Amazingly, she claims they don't get tired of seeing each other. "It's also incredible to us that two people who see each other as often as we do can stand each other. But we don't talk shop at home at all."

So this is one office affair that worked. This same woman also told me about an affair she had prior to her relationship with her fiancé. It was with a co-worker in a different division of the company. "I was traveling to Brussels to supervise a photography assignment. The photographer and I traveled together for a month, and eventually it just happened. We saw each other whenever he came over to the United States. Two years ago we took our vacation together in the Caribbean. It was on that vacation that I decided I would rather be with Jim, my fiancé. But our friendship has continued. I don't know whether or not I'm unique, but I'm still close to all the men I've ever had affairs with."

I asked her if she had ever avoided entering into an affair because of the possible repercussions, and she said no. But she is the exception rather than the rule.

The most unique situation I came across was an executive who was marrying one of her former employees. When I talked with her, she had just lost her job as vice-president of a financial institution, but she felt her relationship with Hank, her employee, had no bearing on her dismissal. Instead, she felt it was a political problem. Here's what she had to say about her involvement:

> We had an employee-employer relationship during the day. At first I managed him by bolstering his ego, and we became super friends. There was no hanky panky. He had trouble with public speaking. At our first manager's meeting he had his whole speech written out. I told him that at the next meeting he couldn't use his notes at all, that he should go over his notes until he knew them and then just relax and talk like it was a conversation. I think he first developed a respect for me because as a manager I helped him get over his fear of public speaking.
>
> We worked together about five months after we had decided to get married. I told the president about our relationship, and some of the other employees knew about it. We had been to certain work-related functions together so it was not clandestine. It was interesting because I was making more money than he and was on a higher level in the company, but this never seemed to bother him.

Her relationship was most unique indeed, and even though she felt there was no connection between her getting fired and her relationship with Hank, I have to think there was. Once her management knew she was having sexual relationships with one of her employees, she was typecast as a sex object rather than as a manager. Once you are thought of that way, it is virtually impossible to shrug the stigma. Consequently, I'm sure she suffered a loss of esteem.

"Secretaries are always having affairs with their bosses," another executive said. "That's one way I distinguish myself from the other women in the company. I never date people I work with." That's another good reason why you should avoid affairs, or at least be cautious about getting into them. Develop a policy about it, and don't regard your company as a dating service. Here's what one woman said about her own dating policy:

> My policy has changed from company to company. I certainly have dated people I met through work—I'd be crazy not to, as long as there are no problems involved. Like if he is a customer of mine or if he's selling to me, then dating him is a business decision. As long as we can conduct business and keep our dating relationship separate from the business relationship, that's great. But if we start crossing wires, it's one or the other. Life is too short to have that kind of mess. You make one mistake, and your integrity is questioned, and you're put down for it. Sometimes it's not worth the risk.
>
> You have to decide what's more important. If the personal relationship is more important, then I'd get out of the company. Generally, I don't think it's a very good rule to socialize with the people that you do business with. But I've certainly dated people I met through business.

A managing editor of a newspaper had this to say about office dating:

> Generally speaking, I would recommend not messing around in the office. If the relationship doesn't work out, and very few relationships do, it can be awkward. I've dated almost every bachelor on the paper over the years, and I've made a point of remaining friends with all of them, but it hasn't been easy. Sometimes it can get very emotional. We had one divorce on the staff, and then the parties involved had to come to work every day. It was a triangle arrangement, because the wife was running around with another reporter. There's some very good reasons for not messing around in the office.
>
> Because of my present position, I don't date anyone in the company. I don't want to date anybody that I could become the boss of, because that becomes extremely awkward, and all the bosses above

me are married, so that doesn't really leave anyone else.

She has learned to pay the price of executive status and derive her social needs from outside her work environment.

Most executives have learned to be cautious about whom they date. One said, "You must decide how the entanglement would affect the business relationship. I have a potential entanglement with the salesman representing our single biggest supplier. All the ingredients are there, but I'm in a company where that sort of thing in my position would be fatal. I'm not willing to risk even a very discreet kind of situation like that."

Only you can set your individual policy on handling business-related social relationships, because every encounter has unique characteristics. Don't get caught up in passion, as did the San Francisco woman who was the victim of the one night stand, before you determine the possible ramifications of the entanglement. In business, it is better never to have loved at all than to have loved and lost.

Can You Climb the Corporate Ladder on Your Back?

There is a misconception whispered through the halls of corporate America that many successful women have used sex to get ahead, that they have scaled the corporate ladder on their backs. Once you achieve success, there will always be the slight suspicion that you might have sold out for any gains you have achieved.

Of all the women with whom I spoke, only one had ever used sex to get ahead. She reluctantly admitted that she had slept with a certain vice-president in her company to gain some information and that, quite frankly, it worked. During the post-coital pillow talk, he revealed to her what she wanted to know, and she used the information to her advantage.

But she was exceptional. Assuming that today's female executive can go from the bedroom to the boardroom is a myth. As a career strategy, it just doesn't work. It could possibly help in isolated, exceptional situations, but it is worthless as an overall career strategy. It didn't work for Scarlett O'Hara, and it won't work for you.

Several of the women I talked with admitted they had seen other women try to use sex to get ahead. One said, "One girl I worked with absolutely flaunted herself. She was a girl Friday type. Her clothing was extremely suggestive—low-cut, short dresses, long after mini skirts had gone out. She slept with our boss to get ahead, except it never really helped her. She couldn't see that he was making a fool out of her."

Another executive told me about a woman she had befriended in the process of helping her fight discrimination. The woman I interviewed had gone to bat for her to help her land a management job in another department. "This woman I helped eventually used sex to get ahead," she told me. "She developed a relationship with a vice-president, who was married, and so was she. The affair was pretty obvious. Every time she wanted something, she would go to him. And it bothered me that someone who had gone through all those fights against discrimination would then decide to fight with sex, especially because I had helped her get that management position."

I asked another woman if she had seen anybody climb the corporate ladder on her back:

> The few women I do know that are really high on the ladder got there by hard work. I've heard stories and met a few people who made some progress that way, but the same thing always happens. In nine out of ten cases, either they are found out, or the guy who's high in management and has the girl on the side no longer has any confidence in her. He wonders what she's doing with the customers or even the competition. Her credibility is right out the window, and she never progresses very far. In the meantime, she earns the resentment of everyone else in the company, and without her lover, she won't last ten minutes.

And she's right. A former lover, especially if he's married, will seldom protect you. If the affair is over, he'd just as soon you were out of his sight, because you're no use to him anymore. Others knowing about the affair endangers your career more than his. Once this happens, your only recourse is to get out of the company. And new jobs are harder to find than new lovers.

In executive chambers, seldom, if ever, will you encounter the casting couch routine—"you can have the job if you go to bed with me." Fortunately, most businessmen would never consider resorting to those tactics. Unlike Elizabeth Ray, femme fatale of the Senator Wayne Hays scandal, as long as you are competent at your job, you never will have to worry. Contribute to profits, and you will be rewarded accordingly. Those are the standards by which you will be judged.

Handling Passes

Although you may never be confronted with an ultimatum, you are bound to be the recipient of an occasional casual pass. Most female executives, especially single ones, have become masters at fending them off without hurting the other party's feelings. And the passes should never be taken too seriously.

In his book *Male Chauvinism: How It Works* (New York: Random House, 1972) author Michael Korda says this about male chauvinists. "At the back of their minds is the fear that a woman may think less of a man if he doesn't at least put up a formalized show of public interest, a kind of gesture to the gallery. Most men do not expect response."

Korda, speaking on behalf of male chauvinists, tells us that most men do not expect a response to their passes, that they are merely idle gestures of masculinity that should not be taken seriously. Think how embarrassed you would be if you responded affirmatively to an unserious pass. That reason alone may be enough to keep you from dating men at work.

Fend passes off as gracefully as possible, and with humor if you can think of anything clever to say. One woman said her boss casually dropped in on her at her office one afternoon and said "How about an affair." She answered, "No thanks, I'm already having one." One married woman said she was often the recipient of gentle flirtations:

One manager I worked with made a pass at me, but it was only by innuendo. He told me he lived at the marina, and he'd leave the back door open if I'd like to come in. I told him not to catch a draft.

Most of the time I ignore passes or deal with them with humor. Like I say "I can't find a babysitter" or "how big is your car, because you're going to need lots of room for my five children"—that sort of thing. I am very conscious of the male ego when I do it. If someone makes a pass, and you say, "Don't be ridiculous," then you're putting him down. I naturally blush when someone makes a pass, and I look very uncomfortable. Nevertheless, I would say I was very flattered, but I just can't get involved. "I'm a married woman, and I like it like that"—something to that effect.

Keep a supply of gentle refusals on your back burner, because you will need to use them occasionally. Most of the time the encounter will blow over without anybody's toes being stepped on.

When I was a young secretary, there was an engineer in my company, very obnoxious and very married, who took a liking to me. I always seem to attract the weirdos, and he was no exception. We worked in the sunny climate of San Diego, yet he wore a bright blue wool stocking cap to work every day, rain or shine. Every Friday he would come into my office and ask me to go out with him for dinner, and every week I would refuse. Finally I decided to put an end to this nonsense. The next time he came into my office with an invitation, I retorted, "Roger, you know I don't date married men, unless, of course, they have a signed permission slip from their wives." Like clockwork, the next week Roger came in, only this time he carried a piece of paper written in a feminine script giving him permission to have dinner with me. He apparently had another one of the secretaries write it out for him. But he had called my bluff. The next time I learned to say a firm but gentle "thanks, but no thanks." As in all communications of a delicate nature, make your statements tactful but clear.

If someone is really on your back, your final recourse is to go to your boss. Only do this as a last resort, as you should be able to fight your own battles. You can turn most men down in such a way so that they won't continue pestering you and without hurting their feelings. Your carriage should be professional enough so that he knows that you mean business. Men will appreciate you for turning them down tactfully, and, as an executive woman, you should develop that skill. You will find that propositions will be at a minimum if you carry yourself properly. The way you handle yourself says a lot about who you are. You are wise to keep your business relationships with men on a business level.

ᴇᷟ 10 ᷤᴏ

Business Entertaining

The higher you climb in executive life, the more your business will be conducted in a quasi-social atmosphere. Your fringe benefits include the luxury of closing a business deal over dinner in a posh restaurant and having the company pick up the check. Especially if you are a seller, part of your job may be to entertain your customers by taking them to plays and sporting events, country clubs, and even weekend resorts, all at the company's expense.

All this sounds very glamorous, and indeed it can be, but for a woman executive, business entertaining is a potential nightmare, especially if there's drinking involved, as there frequently is. Alcohol melts the inhibitions of most people, including you, and a few too many unleashes your libido, as well as that of the people with whom you are drinking. If there is ever a vulnerable area for executive women, it is during business social functions where drinking is involved.

Consequently, you should avoid having cocktails after work when only you and a man are present, unless you are totally confident that he respects the business nature of your relationship and will act accordingly. You may *think* he sees you as a business person, and very well he might, but a few drinks may blur his vision of you, and suddenly you become a sex object. After-work cocktails are potentially explosive for executive women, and you should be cautious of the danger they hold. At best, a drunken pass is awkward to handle, and is more apt to happen when the two of you are alone. If you have to conduct business after work, then do it in your office, unless it is proper to bring someone else along with you. When the purpose is merely socializing, it is permissible to invite someone else along.

Often groups of peers that have bonded together will meet for drinks after work. Most often business is discussed, as that is the common bond among the participants. Valuable information is traded, and sometimes decisions are reached. The amount of after-work socializing varies from frequent to never depending on the interpersonal dynamics of the company. The company location also contributes. Commuters in metropolitan centers are more apt to meet after work to wait until the rush hour traffic thins. If this group is a power cluster, then you should make it a point to be included. Invite yourself along if necessary, and soon they will get used to having you around. At first there may be resistance from an all-male group, and you may have to take the first step in breaking down the inherent barriers between you. But as I said earlier, your job success may depend on your becoming part of a group, and after-hours cocktails is a common ritual in some companies.

No matter who you are with, never feel you must drink alcohol to be accepted among a peer group. Drinking is a personal decision. You will not be accepted as one of the boys just because you can hold your booze like the best of them. With certain immature groups of men, this is a big deal, but don't fall into that trap. Men will respect you because of your business abilities, not because you can drink them under the table.

If you enjoy a drink or two after work (or with lunch) then go ahead. Our post-prohibition society deems it entirely acceptable. But if you are one of those people who get tipsy from the smell of gin, *never* drink in a business situation. You are better off sober and serious then giggly and girlish. If you get tipsy, you are vulnerable to exposing yourself in an unfavorable light and stripping yourself of the professional image you have built. Drinking fogs one's judgment, and drunks are notorious for telling everything they know. You could undermine your position by divulging confidential information and regret it when you're sober. So if you drink at all, do it in moderation. You'll also be doing a favor to your waistline.

Sales reps have called on me in the afternoons after they've had a few too many at lunch. No matter how good the product they sell, I am immediately turned off. One such person's speech was so badly slurred and his presentation so sloppy that I asked him to leave and return when he was sober. He called me the next morning, obviously embarrassed. But the damage was done—his competition received my business. I'm not sure how much his drunken state affected my decision, but it sure left a bad impression.

Now multiply my reaction to this intoxicated fellow by a factor of ten. That's the negative impression you'll leave on others. In our society, fraught with unjust double standards, some men consider heavy drinking manly, even though being drunk on the job is totally taboo. But for women, heavy drinking is an all-out disaster and one of the worst things you could possibly do. Being known as a boozer will destroy your professional reputation just as it will a man's, but others will be exceedingly less tolerant of your drinking than they will of a man's. Male chauvinists are just waiting to see you stumble. Everyone loves to say "I told you so" and no one more than the male chauvinist. Don't give him any fuel for his fire.

If you find yourself getting drunk, remove yourself from the situation as quickly as possible. The longer you linger, the greater the chance you will make a fool out of yourself. Getting drunk around business associates is one of the tackiest things you can do, and if it ever happens, removing yourself is the smartest. The same holds true if the situation is reversed, that is, if the person or people you are with are getting drunk. Leaving the scene may be awkward to pull off, but it is a better alternative than getting into a hassle with a drunk business associate. I speak from experience.

I invited a client to lunch one Friday after successfully selling him on a new advertising campaign that morning. Prior to the meeting I had been apprehensive about the creative approach, but Al loved it. I was jubilant over my success, and he was happy about the new campaign, so we

decided to celebrate over lunch, which was nothing unusual. We had shared similar outings before.

We drove to the restaurant in his car. Upon arriving, we
were forced to wait an hour or so for lunch, and we decided to wait in the bar. The combination of our "thank
goodness it's Friday" mood and the long wait proved to be
a disaster. During that time, Al gulped down several
drinks. When we finally reached our table, he ordered a
bottle of wine, which he managed to polish off by the time
lunch was served. By the end of lunch, he was clearly
drunk.

I had known he was getting drunk, but I felt it was not
my place to say anything to him, and the last thing I
wanted to do was offend a client. But I felt insecure about
his driving, and was reluctant to get in the car with him. I
tried to get him to let me drive, but with no success. "I am
perfectly capable of driving," he slurred. So we pulled out
of the parking lot, Al draped over the wheel, and headed
in the wrong direction from his office. I asked him where
we were going.

"Well, Marci," he replied, "we're going to the airport.
We're catching the next plane to Las Vegas. You make me
feel lucky."

"But, Al!" I shrieked. "I have no intention of taking off
with you for the weekend. What ever made you think I
would?"

"Why not?" was the answer. "You spend lunch telling
me how glad you are we bought the new ad campaign. I
know it means big revenues for your ad agency. The least
you can do is repay me with a favor. Besides, I hear you
libbers are terrific in bed, sexual equality and all that, and
I plan to find out for myself."

Angry and humiliated, I demanded that the creep return
me to my car. I told him that although I appreciated his
business, I did not find him sexually attractive, nor would
I consider developing a personal relationship with a client.
But if I had his account on those terms, then I was no
longer interested in doing business with him. On Monday
morning, I received a telegram from him firing us off the
account. I wasn't surprised after what had happened, and I
realized that I had allowed that scene to develop by know-
ingly being with him alone when he was drunk. I had
placed myself in a vulnerable position with him, and

bluntly rejecting him as a sex partner was more than his ego could bear.

After reflecting on that incident for some time, for it did cause me a large loss of revenue at a most unpropitious time, I decided that perhaps sexual undertones had existed from the beginning of the relationship, and that he had hoped all along that I would go along with him if he gave me his advertising business. But it took the lubricant of alcohol to expose his attitudes. Before this incident, never so much as a bedroom innuendo had escaped from this shy little man's lips in all the hours we spent together. I doubt that they would have surfaced had he not been drunk.

As a woman surrounded by men, you cannot escape the threat of an unpleasant scene like this one happening to you. But you can diminish the possibility by avoiding being alone with a drunk business associate no matter how harmless he seems or how well you know him. If you see the situation is getting out of hand, then leave. The immediate difficulty of gracefully leaving nowhere compares to the potential explosiveness and probable repercussions if you prolong the situation. A pass from a business associate is always awkward to handle, but a pass from a drunk one is devastating.

If you are the object of a drunken pass, don't do what I did. Don't get angry and tell him off, for by doing so you have given him the ultimate rejection. Instead, treat it as casually as possible, and don't bring it up the next day, no matter how insulted you are. Also, be forgiving for a while because men are still struggling with the role of women in society, and in one sense, you can be flattered that men find you sexually attractive. Try to get your point across without endangering his ego.

Business Lunches

Lunching with associates for the purpose of conducting business is a commonplace in executive circles. A leisurely lunch in a posh restaurant can indeed be a pleasurable way to relax during an otherwise hectic day. But for the executive woman it presents some special problems, especially if you are doing the entertaining. The most obvious problem is the one of who picks up the check. Some men enjoy the novelty of a woman paying. You may hear comments like "It's about time the tables were turned" or "Now I know what it's like to be a kept man." Accept these gentle ribbings graciously, as at least the men who say them are willing to let you pay. Unfortunately, not all men are like this. No matter how discreetly you handle it, nor how much he respects you as an executive, your picking up the tab may be more than he can handle.

I had a client who refused to have lunch with me unless I agreed in advance that I would let him pay. The first time I took him to lunch he protested and squirmed, but he let me pay. The next time the same hassle occurred, only this time I argued with him about it for several minutes, and then reluctantly gave in. He declined several lunch invitations thereafter, and I assumed he was just busy. But one day our lunching together was unavoidable, and he confessed his dilemma. He said he knew it was silly and hopelessly chauvinistic, but my paying for lunch embarrassed him. He told me that he would only lunch with me if he could pay.

Although in one sense he was blocking me from doing my job, as it is expected that advertising accounts will be entertained by their agency personnel, I decided that forcing the issue was pointless and potentially self-defeating. He appreciated my tolerance, and we shared a long and profitable relationship after that, and I'm positive I experienced no loss of status in his eyes.

If the matter of who pays for lunch is creating a conflict between you and your male companion, then let him pay, even if it is not customary in your business role. But explain to him that you have an expense account, and your company expects you to use it.

You can pick up the check in such a way that it offends no one by making arrangements in advance. If you are doing the entertaining, it's up to you to select the restaurant. Establish relationships with several restaurants beforehand, and explain to the maître d' that you plan to frequent that establishment on a regular basis for the purpose of entertaining business associates. Tell him that you want everyone in the restaurant to know that when you come in with a guest, you should receive the check. (If you don't specify this they will automatically set it in front of the man.) The best solution, if they'll cooperate, is to establish credit with them, so you merely sign the check, and they will bill you at the end of the month. In any case, make sure the personnel know you. Have your secretary remind them of your instructions when she makes the reservations, and also do it when you arrive, if you can do it surreptitiously.

Despite all this forewarning, some places will still botch it up. Your best insurance is to excuse yourself from the table directly after the meal, and remind the maître d' of your instructions. Incidentally, you don't have to give a reason for leaving the table. Just excuse yourself and leave. If you feel the need to give a reason, say you need to make a phone call. (To say you are going to the bathroom is tacky.) Or you can make arrangements for the maître d' to have your bill at his station, so it never reaches the table at all. At the end of the meal excuse yourself and go sign it. This is the best way to avoid a conflict.

If you and your companion arrive at the restaurant separately, where you wait depends on who is the host. If you are, you make the table selection. Approach the maître d' aggressively and say, "Good morning. I am Eunice Executive and I have a reservation for noon. My companion, Mr. Peppers, has not yet arrived, but I would like to be seated. Please show me to the table, and tell him I'm here when he arrives."

If you are the guest, let your host select the table. You wait in the lobby for him to arrive, and then be seated with him. You can also wait in the bar, but most women find it uncomfortable to be alone in one, so waiting in the lobby is preferable.

If you have been shown to your table first, when your guest arrives, rise and shake his hand. If someone stops by your table, you should stand and shake his hand and remain standing until the visitor asks you to please be seated. The older social etiquette dictates that a lady never stands when being introduced at a table, but in business, you would look pretty foolish if you were the only one sitting. Standing also makes you taller, and therefore gives you more authority.

Always order your own food. And if you're the host, you should order the wine, and you will be the one going through the tasting process. The only exception to this is if you know your companion is more of a wine connoisseur than you, then let him do the selection and tasting. You still do the paying.

Just a note on make-up: putting a dab of lipstick on at the table after a meal is acceptable, but anything more than that is not. Save the cosmetics for the powder room, and never comb your hair in public.

When you are leaving the restaurant, you may tip the captain or head waiter if he has given you particularly good service. Never tip him if he has kept you waiting for a reserved table. Tip your waiter 15 percent, or 20 percent if the service warrants it.

When Your Lunchtime Is Free

Even though you may not have a business lunch, you should try to get out from behind your desk at lunchtime. To perform most effectively you need a break from the stress and some time to relax. Many executives will work through lunch when they probably can accomplish as much by taking a break. Without one, your mind can grow weary, and your thinking processes will bog down.

Many women executives shop on their lunch hour, for it is the only opportunity they may have to do it. If you have an emergency, like you just tore a hole in your last pair of panty hose, then shop on your lunch hour. Other than that, it is better that you relax, and receive some nourishment. You are apt to perform more effectively because of it.

You may choose to spend lunch dining with a group of executives from your company, either in the executive dining room, company cafeteria, or outside restaurant. Everyone will pay his own way, usually by dividing the bill by the number of people present, and everyone kicks in an equal amount.

When you are having problems with a particular employee, and the situation is delicate (like you sense he resents working for a woman), and you wish to talk it out with him, lunch is a good time to do it. You see him on common ground, rather than in your office, which symbolizes your authority over him. He may respond to criticism better if you soften it by paying special attention to him. Most of all, he'll be flattered that you chose to spend your private time with him.

Lunch is also a good time to get close to your boss. You can get him away from phones and other interruptions and command his full attention. Use the time to run an idea by him, or get his advice on a problem you are having. Despite his acceptance of you, he still may feel reluctant to initiate lunchtime meetings with you. So don't be shy. If you have an important issue to discuss, then tell him you would like to discuss it over lunch. Get him used to the idea of treating you just like he would a man, and your long-term career goals will benefit from it.

Be Nice to His Wife, But She'll Probably Hate You Anyway

Besides social functions for business people exclusively, your business dealings will include gatherings where spouses or escorts are present. This could be traditional company Christmas parties, summer picnics, retirement dinners, open houses, social events of professional associations (like your local chapter of the American Management Association), or a number of other gatherings. Prudence dictates that you attend some of these functions, no matter how dreadful they are, as they are part of the ritual practiced by business executives. Being seen in the right places is important.

Attending these functions presents some unique problems for the new executive woman. For example, should you bring an escort? I asked the women I interviewed if they brought an escort, and their answers varied.

"I'd rather go alone than bring a boy friend to a company function," one single executive said. "I find it very uncomfortable for both him and me, especially if he doesn't know anybody. I will occasionally ask an escort, like the account executive from my ad agency who is apt to know some of the attendees. But I never invite anyone if I feel he would be uncomfortable with that group of people."

"I always bring an escort," another woman told me. "Those gatherings are always set up for couples, and I feel more comfortable having someone with me." Whether to bring an escort to a social function seems to be an area of personal preference, and how you handle it is up to you, especially if you are single.

If you are married, that's another story. Many women say they leave their husbands at home, because their husbands detest the role of Mr. Female Executive (this problem is discussed in detail in Chapter 14). Two women reported that their marriages had broken up partially because their husbands were uncomfortable playing this role. Indeed, it is an awkward one to handle. The ideal situation, then, for women whose husbands prefer to avoid social gatherings, is to bring along a company-related escort, but most husbands object to this. So many married women attend these functions alone.

One said, "I almost never bring my husband to an office social function. Early in our marriage I went to his functions and he came to mine. But now we are both honest in our communications, and we both are free to say no if we don't feel like going along. If I have a social commitment or responsibility, I'll go without him. This has worked out very well," she reports.

One of the advantages of having an escort is it makes you less threatening to the wives of other executives that you will meet. As an executive woman, one of your biggest problems is your co-workers' wives, who are apt to be jealous of you. To them, if you bring a man along you are less apt to be after their husbands, and they will tend to be less jealous of you.

"Wives are just terrible," said one knowing lady who supervised forty men. "They see you as a threat. The more he admires you and thinks of you, the more she sees it as a personal put down." To the insecure wife, you are everything she is not. She may resent you because her husband thinks of you as an equal, whereas he still treats her as an inferior. You annoy women who are happy staying home and playing housewife. Before consciousness raising, she would think there was something wrong with you. Now she's wondering if there isn't something wrong with her. A New York executive told me about the wife of one of her associates:

When I go to the West Coast, I always stop in Bakersfield to see a man who heads up a division there. I really enjoy his company, but we always go out to dinner with his wife, which is very difficult. I rarely run into suburban women who are strictly house-wives, and it's extremely difficult for me to carry on a conversation with that woman because she has noth-ing to say to me. She's a nice person, and always gives me a jar of homemade jam. At first she found me a great novelty, but she resented me too. Now she accepts me, probably because she sees I'm not going to take her husband away.

This will be the general attitude of most wives you en-counter. They will be resentful and jealous, but curious. That's why it's important that you make a point of devot-ing some time to the wives of your associates, and try to relate to them woman-to-woman. You may attend one of those parties where the men congregate around the bar discussing business, sports, and politics, while the wives are in the kitchen discussing pediatricians and casseroles. Your natural inclination will be to gravitate to the men, because you have more in common with them than with their wives. However, if you are the only woman talking to the men, the women will feel snubbed and will resent you be-cause of it. The wives will watch you longingly as you stand confident and secure, accepted in a group of men that excludes them, and they'll hate you all the more.

You actually make it easier for the men around you if you establish a rapport with their wives, even though this may be difficult for you to do. For political reasons, it is virtually imperative that you establish some kind of rela-tionship with the boss's wife, especially if you are attrac-tive. If she doesn't like you, she could put pressure on her husband to get rid of you. It's happened before. You, of all people, should know that you never underestimate the power of a woman, especially a jealous wife.

You can exchange social pleasantries with people with-out really liking them, and you should be poised enough to do so. Don't be like the woman who said, "If I don't feel like being good friends with the boss's wife, I won't be. And that's a big problem for me politically, but that's part of being honest with myself."

The quest for honesty in one's relationships is impor-tant, and you can conduct your social relationships accordingly. But even at a business social event, your business image comes first. Consider attending an office function as part of your job, and use other outlets for pure socializing. It's unnecessary to make friends with some-one's wife, but you can be friendly toward her. She will feel more kindly toward you and will feel less resentment.

Dress is another important concern at these functions. You may have just bought a dynamite backless cocktail dress, which you are dying to wear. Or every time you wear your red slinky dress with the slit up the side it makes you feel like Cher. Save those flashy, provocative clothes for purely social occasions. Always dress down for company events. You never want to outdress the boss's wife, especially if you are attractive.

Always conform to the establishment when you are selecting clothes for these occasions. You may be a weekend hippie, braless and barefoot, but save this image for your friends. Business is the ultimate Establishment, and to be accepted in it, you must fit in. Do so by gearing your attire down. You can still look sophisticated without wearing high fashion clothes. Barbara Walters does it every day.

Entertaining in Your Home

If you live alone, never invite a male business associate to your home when just the two of you will be there, unless, of course, you have something else besides business in mind. He might misinterpret the invitation, and the evening could turn out a disaster. For obvious reasons, you are much better off in a restaurant. If you are married and wish to entertain a business associate in your home, then it is perfectly acceptable to do so. In this case, invite him and his mate.

A sophisticated form of entertainment is the small dinner party in one's home. This is a particularly gracious way to entertain, as small dinner parties allow you time to relate to your guests on an intimate basis. In a large party, you must circulate and spend small amounts of time with each guest.

The problem at dinner parties is who does the serving. If you are attempting to position yourself as an executive, you could blow your image by playing the little woman clad in an apron, scurrying around the kitchen cooking, and then serving dinner to your guests. The purpose of your entertaining is to develop a closer relationship with your guests, and you can't do it if you are responsible for getting a seven-course meal on the table. If you are fortunate enough to have servants, then of course they do the serving and cooking. But most of us don't have them. The best alternative is to hire a catering service that will cook and serve the meal. You can write the expense off on your income tax and maybe even on your expense account. Having a small catered dinner party is classy and sophisticated, and if you really want to leave an impression on business associates, a dinner party will do the trick. And, by hiring domestic help, you can do it without compromising your position as an executive.

Cocktail parties involve more people, but you can prepare the hors d'oeuvres in advance, and then just hire a bartender, and perhaps a helper to serve trays of food, refresh drinks, keep ashtrays clean, and clear away empty glasses. You need someone to do this, and you will dilute your effect as a hostess if you are running around collecting used napkins. Get in the habit of hiring other people to help you when you entertain. If you do any entertaining, you want to do it right, and you don't have a wife to play the maid's role. So hire one.

A transportation executive felt that giving parties was important in her business life. "I have so many men working for me," she explained, "that I found if I throw a party in my home and play hostess, it breaks down the barriers between us. My problem is not that men are jealous of me, because they are used to competing. If they see me in another role, they realize I am not competing in any area but business. Then they like competing with me."

I asked her if her husband plays the role of host at these affairs. "No," she said. "Very seldom does he attend them."

"Even if they are in your home?" I asked incredulously.

"That's right," she replied. "He usually chooses not to be there, and I respect that. And rarely do I attend functions with him, as we are just both too busy."

If You Are Being Entertained

Sometimes it is more difficult to be entertained than it is to do the entertaining yourself. When you are the hostess, you are in control, but when you are a guest, you place yourself in another's domain. Expressing the right amount of gratitude at an appropriate time can be awkward. Here are some tips on how to be a gracious guest.

Being entertained at lunch is so common that a sincere spoken thank you at the end of the meal is appropriate, especially if you are frequently entertained by the person. Typed thank-you letters are always appropriate in a strictly business-to-business relationship, but would become a bit cumbersome if you wrote one to the same person every week, so use your discretion. However, if you have been entertained by a prospective employer, or anyone else upon whom you wish to leave a strong impression, handwritten thank-you notes create a favorable image. Handwritten notes are personal and convey sincerity. Never have your secretary handwrite it out for you. This is something you must do yourself.

If you have been entertained in the evening by a business person, a thank-you note is always in order. Get in the habit of sending them, for they indicate a touch of class. If you have been entertained by a man and his wife, especially if they have had you in their home, send flowers or a houseplant the next day. If you have been a guest in someone's home for more than a day, a more personal gift is advisable, for instance, something that reflects their hobbies. If they like tennis, send them a case of tennis balls, or golf balls if they like that sport. Books are always nice presents. Send them the latest novel or one of those coffee-table gift books that are so popular. Whatever gift you choose, give some thought to it.

Rules of Social Etiquette

The emergence of the new executive woman has created many questions regarding her role in today's society. The next chapter deals with questions of business etiquette, where proper behavior depends upon the business relationship of the people involved, and not on their sexes or ages.

But when the business relationship enters into a social realm, such as we have been discussing in this chapter, which rules should apply? Because of the conservative and traditional nature of the business community, if you are in a purely social situation where non-business people are present, you should adhere to the old rules of etiquette. You want to show a touch of class when you deal with others, for this is a desired trait of top executives. To accomplish this, I believe you must conform to the old rules of etiquette in purely social situations. Your proper role may seem a little confusing in these situations, and ultimately you should behave the way that is most comfortable for you.

ᥩᥩ 11 ᥩᥩ

The New Etiquette

One thing that separates business from all-out guerrilla warfare is the mask of decorum it wears. The poised and polished executive prides himself on his perfect etiquette. He is exceedingly charming and courteous, and he explicitly follows the rules of corporate behavior. In fact, good manners are a tacit prerequisite for executive status.

You too should practice the rituals of the refined as part of your executive demeanor. And you should follow the same rules that men do. This means that in business dealings, sexist rules of social behavior should be discarded, while the rules of the business community must be adopted. In business, as in all subcultures, there are rules of behavior that are indigenous to it.

I pondered the question of proper etiquette for the new executive woman for some time. I knew it would be much simpler if businesswomen followed the old rules of when to stand, shake hands, go through a door, etc. Indeed, the amenities of the older social etiquette are comfortable, and you may have a difficult time abandoning them. But I feel that it is critical that the female executive relate to others exactly as any executive would. So I took the rules of social etiquette, rewrote, and desexed them. They are the rules of behavior that I believe you should adopt in your business life.

The new rules of business etiquette depend upon the

business relationship of the people involved (e.g., buyer to seller, boss to employee, shipping clerk to vice-president) and not upon the age and sex of the participants as is the case in social etiquette. I have dechauvinized the rules of business etiquette in order to place female executives on an equal footing with their male counterparts. Chivalry is one way men patronize women, and their patronizing behavior toward you must be discouraged.

There will be considerable confusion in the minds of many men over how to relate to you. The establishment male has been taught to treat women as the weaker sex. So you must demonstrate how you wish to be treated. It is up to you to pave the way and show him you expect to be related to as a business person, as an equal. If someone offers you courtesies from the old school, accept them graciously, but, if possible, demonstrate that you wish to be treated otherwise. For example, if a man opens the door for you, and according to your business position you should be holding it for him, walk through it, but say, "Thanks, John, but that really isn't necessary." The next time you come to a door, open it for him. No use embarrassing or alienating him, because he, without thinking, is doing what he has learned is proper. On the other hand, you must not tolerate being treated differently.

Expect that the process of changing how men treat you will take a while. You are on the forefront of a changing society, and it will not happen overnight. Doors will be opened for you for a long time to come. But you can do your part by demonstrating how you wish to be treated by following these new rules of etiquette.

Introductions

The name of the person with the highest business status is said first. Therefore, unlike social etiquette, a woman may be presented to a man, depending on their relative status within the corporate hierarchy. When you are in doubt about their relative status, say the older person's name first.

Example: You are introducing Laura Logical, one of your employees, to an executive vice-president of your company, Mr. Whiz. You would say, "Mr. Whiz, I would like you to meet Laura Logical, my production assistant."

Example: If you are introducing one of your customers to Mr. Whiz, the customer's name would be said first, even though the customer may be of a lower status. You would say, "Mr. Customer, I would like you to meet Warren Whiz, executive vice-president of marketing."

Example: You are introducing an outside sales representative to Laura Logical, your employee. You would say, "Laura Logical, I would like you to meet Pamela Peddler, who is our sales representative from Acme Bolts."

After you know the person, the phrase "How's business?" has replaced "How do you do?" as the common greeting. In response to this, most people will say business is terrific, even if it isn't.

Introducing Yourself

When you are introducing yourself, also give your company affiliation, and position if it is relevant. When you enter an unfamiliar office because you have an appointment, say to the receptionist, "Good afternoon. I am Tammy Tycoon, and I have a three o'clock appointment with Mr. Bridgenose." Also give the receptionist your business card. If you do not have an appointment, tell the receptionist the purpose of your visit so the information can be relayed to the person you wish to see.

Who Goes First

Ladies before gentlemen went out with garter belts. Those with the highest status walk first. If you are hosting guests, then they always walk first, no matter who has the highest status. The remainder of the time, it makes no difference.

Holding Doors

The same rules apply as to who goes first. Hold the door open for those with higher status than you. If you are hosting guests, then hold the door for them, no matter what their status. Other than that, the first person to the door holds it open for others.

When to Rise

Always rise when you are being introduced or are greeting a visitor. Stand up when a person comes into your office, offer him a chair and remain standing until he is seated. Rise again when he starts to leave, and accompany him to the door.

Shaking Hands

Even if you have to walk across the room, always shake hands with a person to whom you've been introduced. After the initial introduction, if you see the person on a regular basis (such as another employee in your department), it is unnecessary to shake hands or rise each time you see him.

If the situation dictates hand shaking, then offer your hand first, because a gentleman will usually wait for you to make the first move. When you have been with outsiders, most business people also shake hands at the end of the meeting.

What to Say

When you are being introduced, say "How do you do, Ms. Bigwig?" or "I've heard some very nice things about you, Ms. Bigwig, and I've looked forward to meeting you." Whatever you choose to say, use the person's name while looking into his eyes. This helps you remember the name.

Your Business Name

It is proper for a married woman to keep her maiden name in business if she chooses to do so. If you marry after your career has been established, always keep the name with which you started.

Use of Ms.

Marital status has no bearing on your career, and you should adopt the use of Ms. Some women, however, are offended by it. If you are addressing a letter to an executive woman, and you do not know her preference, have your secretary check with her office.

Name on Business Card

A man never uses Mr. before his name on business cards, and neither should you. (Sorry, Amy Vanderbilt.) Use no designation, just your business name. You may still use a form of address before your name on your social cards but look for that custom to change.

Exchanging Business Cards

Although many people break this rule, it is proper etiquette to exchange business cards at the end of a meeting, not at the beginning.

Use of First Names

The use of first names varies according to geography and industry. Adopt the custom of the other executives in your industry. For example, the atmosphere around most advertising agencies is casual, and first names are used almost exclusively. In banking, however, the opposite is true, and last names are used. If you are meeting a person substantially older than yourself, always use his last name until he asks you to do otherwise.

Writing Letters

Make your written communications concise and brief. All business correspondence, except handwritten thank-you notes, should be typed on company letterhead. Many business people have adopted the use of personalized letterhead with their name on the left side. A status symbol, the letterhead is 7" x 10" instead of 8½" x 11", and is called executive-sized stationery.

Telephone Manners

The telephone has replaced the letter as the most frequent means of business communication. Most executives have their secretaries answer their phones and screen the calls, but the trend is away from that. Whoever answers your phone, there are some rules of phone etiquette that you should observe.

Answer the phone immediately and identify yourself. Even though you may be in the middle of a rush report, switch your voice to a friendly, relaxed tone. The person who originates the call is also the one who ends it, so wait for the caller to say good-by. Hang up gently.

When you are the caller, you will first go through the company's receptionist, and then the person's private secretary before you reach your party. No need to identify yourself to the company receptionist, just ask for the party. If you are calling an unfamiliar office, when you reach the secretary, identify yourself be your name, title, company affiliation, and the nature of your business.

If you are about to embark on a lengthy discussion with the person you are calling, ask him first if he has a few minutes to talk. You may have caught him at a bad time, and while you are communicating your message, he may be preoccupied. On the phone, it is harder to keep a person's attention.

If someone important has called you at an inconvenient time, take the call anyway, tell him you are exceedingly busy, and ask if you can call him later. Unless it is an emergency, never take phone calls when there are guests in your office. It is rude.

You and Your Supervisor

Wait for your boss to set the stage for the degree of formality in your relationship. Call him by his last name unless he requests otherwise. Respect his working time. Unless you have a crisis on your hands, accumulate several items you need to discuss, and cover them all at once. Keep your interruptions to a minimum.

On the other hand, keep your boss informed by sending him carbon copies of correspondence and memos. Check with him before making important decisions such as hiring, firing, large expenditures, or budget cuts. But even then, get right to the point, and tell him of your decision. Do not justify your decision unless he asks you to do so.

You have the right to disagree with your boss, but do it in a way that won't antagonize him. This is the proper time to justify your argument, and do it calmly and objectively. If you have ample justification, have thought out the solution, and have a boss who is interested in the growth of his managers, he will allow your decision to stand. Whatever the outcome of the agreement, however, his decision is the ultimate one, and you must respect that. Above all, be cooperative.

❦ 12 ❧

Traveling for Business

I was in San Francisco to attend a convention, and it never occurred to me that anyone there would think any different. But because I was a young woman traveling alone, I looked suspicious. It didn't help matters much when I asked the hotel's assistant manager, as I was registering, if a group of men from Toronto had arrived yet. They were clients whom I had arranged to meet at the convention, and we had planned to stay in the same hotel as a matter of convenience. But when I asked him about them, he took one look at me and pranced off to fetch the manager, who took me aside and interrogated me on my intentions.

I thought there had been some mix-up in the reservations my secretary had made, and my only concern was getting a room in the overflowing city. Once I explained my purpose for being there and handed him a business card, I was shown to my room immediately. Not until I reached the solitude of my hotel room did I realize the reason for all the extra attention. The hotel thought I was a hooker, soliciting the convention crowd that was milling about in the lobby below.

That incident took place several years ago, and attitudes are changing as the number of traveling businesswomen increases every year. Maybe now we even outnumber the other kind of professional ladies who frequent hotels, but don't be surprised if you are mistaken for one. The situations that you confront while traveling for business seem to emphasize the problems of being a woman. Nevertheless, once you learn how to handle yourself, you will find traveling for business a delightful fringe benefit of executive life, and one from which you can derive personal enrichment.

Air Travel

Once you reach a certain plateau in your business career, your company will fly you first class. The seats are roomier, the food and service are superb, and for a few blissful hours you can dwell with the privileged few. If your company allows you to fly first class, it is a symbol of success, and you should jump at the opportunity. You never know who you might meet, and the law of averages says that eventually you will meet potential business contacts that can in some way assist your career.

An international publishing company insists that all its sales personnel fly first class, because, as I stated above, you never know who you might meet. They claim they have sold some of their biggest advertising packages to top company officials, busy executives who would never see them during a regular business day, but are receptive during a five-hour flight. Passengers on airplanes are characteristically friendly, and visit freely with one another.

No matter where you sit on the plane, you will have an opportunity to broaden your perspective by meeting people from diverse walks of life. You can also use air time to catch up on work, but that is better left to when you reach the hotel, for there you will need to be more careful about whom you strike up a conversation with. If you have the misfortune to sit next to a boor, you can work or sleep.

Luggage

Executives are frequent air travelers, and the men have got it down to a science. Luggage manufacturers have designed a carry-aboard size bag that holds all a man needs for a two- or three-day trip. Since he carries it on the plane with him, he eliminates the possibility of the airline losing his luggage en route, and he also avoids waiting for luggage to come off the plane.

Admittedly, the carry-on luggage route is the slickest way to go, but I have never met a woman yet who could get all she needed in that small space. We just cannot travel as lightly as men, and we still face the disastrous possibility that our luggage may be lost. The solution is to compromise. Take aboard a small case containing your cosmetics, toothbrush, nightgown, and one change of clothes. Put the remainder of your belongings in another bag (especially the heavy stuff like hair dryer and shoes), and check that bag at the gate. That way, if the checked bag happens to get lost, you still have all the basic necessities with you. About the time you are desperate for the rest of your gear, the airline will have found your luggage, and you will have gotten through the mishap without enduring a horrible nightmare.

As you might expect, luggage is another executive status symbol, with honors going to Mark Cross, Gucci, or Vuillton if you can afford them. Professional travelers such as airline pilots use Halliburton luggage, which is made of a durable anodized aluminum that provides a protective armor for the contents. If your pocketbook dictates a less expensive make, don't worry about it. But do try to have your luggage at least matching. The appearance of your luggage influences how others will treat you. Don't come in looking like a character in *The Grapes of Wrath*.

If you travel frequently, create a travel kit of all the cosmetics and toiletries you need, and then only use the kit for traveling. This saves time and reduces the possibility of forgetting something. Never pack glass bottles or jars, because not only are they too heavy but they could break. Instead, use those little plastic bottles you buy in drugstores. Many cosmetics can be purchased in convenient travel size.

What to pack depends on where you are going and how long you plan to stay. If you are going to a different part of the country from your own, be cognizant of the different dress styles in various geographical regions. People in the Midwest and South dress more conservatively and are somewhat behind in fashion compared to California or New York. Especially if you are the seller in the business relationship, dress to conform to the established rules of where you are selling. Your customers will be less suspicious of you, and you will seem less the outsider.

I knew a man in Los Angeles who made sales calls to the Southeast twice a year. Before each visit, he would have his hair cut short, his sideburns trimmed, and he would don what he called his "sincere suit," an unassuming gray number, obviously worn, with small lapels and baggy trousers. He claimed that when he wore his normal business attire on these trips, he was experiencing difficulty is closing sales calls. His sales manager had offered the advice about the old suit and the haircut, and since then, his sales had tripled.

Going to these extremes may not be necessary, but there are several things you should take into consideration as you are selecting your wardrobe. Are you going to a metropolitan or a rural area? Will people in that geographical location expect conservative or not-so-conservative attire? What is the climate, both day and night? (Some warm climates have cool evenings, and you should be prepared for both.) How long will you be staying? What is the particular nature of your trip?

Some standard advice to travelers can be safely ignored. "Only pack as much as you can carry" is an example. In principle, it sounds great, but in practice, most women cannot possibly carry all that they will need, especially for a trip lasting more than a few days. Pack *more* than you think you will need, and you will never be sorry. Besides your clothes for the business day, be sure to bring along an evening dress or two. Chances are you will be going out in the evening, and you will appreciate the change from your business attire. A man can just change his shirt, and he will look presentable. For you, your business clothes are less appropriate in the evening, so bring along suitable attire.

As long as you travel to major metropolitan areas, you will probably never face the necessity of carrying your own luggage. Personnel will usually be on hand to assist you, and you should keep some change easily accessible for the purpose of tipping those who help you. From the street outside an air terminal to the baggage check-in counter, a skycap will assist you. Tip him 50¢ per bag. When you arrive at your destination, scurry down to the baggage claim area and be the first to line up a skycap to take your luggage from the claim area. Give him your claim stubs, and indicate the type of ground transportation you prefer, taxi or limousine. Then you can comfortably sit in a lounge area while he fights the crowds for you. Meet him at the taxi stand or limousine, where the driver will load your luggage. Again, tip the skycap 50¢ per bag, and more if he has given you especially attentive service.

You are not expected to tip a limousine driver, even if he helps you with your luggage. Taxi drivers, however, are a different matter. If your fare is less than $2.00, tip him 25¢ for this ride. If it is over that amount, tip him 15 percent of the total fare. If you have luggage, tip him an additional 25¢ per bag.

When you reach the hotel in your taxi or limousine, a doorman will be standing outside. His job is to help you out of the cab and supervise the transfer of your luggage. He is not tipped for these services.

A bellboy will collect your luggage while you proceed to the registration desk. He will collect your room key from the clerk and show you to your room. Once there, he will turn on the air conditioning or heater and arrange your luggage for unpacking. For these services, tip him 50¢, plus an additional 50¢ for each bag. Getting to your destination without once carrying your own luggage is as simple as that.

Getting Around Hotels

As a woman, you will have more trouble checking into a hotel than you will dealing with your luggage. You will be eyed suspiciously, as I was in San Francisco; at best you will probably be treated as a second-class citizen unless you stand up for your rights.

Here's one area where you can yell discrimination all you want, for that's about the only way you can expect equal treatment from stuffy hotel management. A soft-spoken research director, who said she would never openly accuse her company of discrimination for fear of the recriminations, employed a different tactic on hotel management:

I was checking into a hotel in Montreal with four men who worked for me. Typically, the men who work for me get better rooms than I do, even though they are my employees. Most of the time, if I am in my room and settled, I will just ignore it. But this particular time, when I checked in, the room was a mess, so much so that I couldn't stand to be in it. I went down and told the man at the desk about its condition, and he said, "Well, just wait in there, and we'll send someone up to clean it in a few minutes." I said, "I don't think you understand. I'm not going to inhabit a room like that." He refused to change it.

Finally, I said, "Would you have given that room to a man from my company?" Now, I wasn't sure if the room assignment had anything to do with being male or female. But he immediately stopped and handed me a key for another room. Whether or not that was the issue, I used it as an excuse to get what I wanted.

In situations like this where you are getting bad treatment from hotels, I see nothing wrong in applying pressure via the accusation of discrimination. Hotels shun bad publicity, and they will rush to smooth over a potential problem.

Your real clout with hotels, however, is your business status. Metropolitan hotels cater to the business traveler, a frequent guest whose pockets are lined with plush expense accounts. And as an executive, you wield possible influence over others in your organization. So inform the desk clerk of your business ties when you check in by handing your business card to him with your confirmation slip, if you have one. Make sure he knows you are a business executive, and you can count on receiving much better service, for you represent his best type of customer.

One annoyance about checking into metropolitan hotels is that they refuse to reserve a certain type room for you. They will ask your preference on size of bed, and which floor you want. When you arrive, they will put you in a requested room only if they have one available. This has happened to me several times at the Waldorf-Astoria in New York. I would request a room on or above a certain floor to cut down on the street noise, and inevitably I re-

ceived a lower room. I asked the assistant manager about
the policy, and he said that no Hilton hotel (including the
Waldorf) will guarantee a particular room in advance.
They will only guarantee that you get a room.

If you are not used to sleeping in the city, request a
room on the highest floor the hotel has, or you will have a
fretful time getting to sleep and your performance the next
day will suffer because of it. One executive recalled what
happened to her on her first trip to corporate headquarters
for an annual meeting. The first night she was restless and
barely got any sleep. The next day at the meeting, she fell
asleep during the morning session. To this day she is
teased about it, and it was an experience she would rather
forget.

Battling jet lag and time differences can quickly wear
you down, so it's vitally important you get proper rest on
a business trip. A Valium or two before bedtime assists
you in sleeping in a strange environment, or will help you
get some sleep on the plane. Putting yourself on too hectic
a schedule can also be disastrous for your effectiveness,
and there is a tendency to push oneself for efficiency's
sake on a trip. When you schedule your time, make generous allowances for getting lost, traffic jams, and rest
breaks, or you are apt to experience a frustrating and ex-
hausting trip, when you could enjoy a very pleasant experience.

Learning to indulge in the facilities hotels offer can also
make travel more enjoyable. Conducting business in a
strange environment is never as convenient as in your own
office, but hotels offer many services that makes business
traveling easier for you.

Use the switchboard as your answering service. They
will act as a message center, and even wake you up in the
morning. If you need a secretary, most hotels offer that
service also. Greet your guests in the hotel lobby, never in
your room.

The laundry and valet service in hotels is a life-saver.
The instant you check in, you can have your travel-weary
garments freshly pressed in an hour or two. I've even
packed slightly soiled garments knowing that I can get
faster service at the hotel after I arrive than I can at my
own cleaners. Most companies will reimburse you for rea-

sonable valet and cleaning charges, so feel free to take advantage of the service.

If you are in too much of a hurry, hang your wrinkled garments over the bathtub, turn on the hot water, and shut the door. The steam you generate will eliminate the normal creases from packing.

Eating Alone

Eating breakfast alone can be a pleasant transition into the day. Lunching by yourself can be a breather from an otherwise hectic day. Eating dinner alone is dreadful.

Just a few years ago, higher-class establishments refused to seat a woman eating dinner by herself. Today there is no reason why you shouldn't dine at your favorite establishments by yourself in the evening. I tell myself this every time I travel, for I feel uncomfortable eating alone in a restaurant at night. Somehow eating alone in hotel restaurants is more comfortable, for me, anyway.

What to do with your eyes is always a problem. It is perfectly acceptable for you to bring along something to read. Newspapers are an obvious choice, but somehow they never work for me. More than once I have spilled my water with my elbow while I was attempting to fold the paper to a manageable size. Once, in a candlelit atmosphere, I pulled the candle closer for a reading light, held the paper too near the flame, and suddenly had a small bonfire on my hands. The rest of that trip I chose to eat in my room.

Room service is a safe but boring alternative to eating alone in a restaurant. You still eat alone, but you will feel more comfortable in your room. If you want to kick your shoes off and lounge around in a negligee, order room service before you change, or the bellhop may misconstrue your request for service. When you're through with dinner, leave the cart outside your door, and then call for someone to pick it up.

If you are the adventurous type, you will probably prefer eating in a restaurant, for you never know whom you might meet. A New York journalist recalled a very interesting experience she had on a business trip to Tokyo:

The first night there, I was eating alone in the hotel coffee shop, and I noticed this man across the way eyeing me. This went on for quite a while. Finally, he came over and sat down at my table. He said, "You're American, aren't you?" and I replied yes. "You're the first English-speaking woman I have seen in Tokyo. Would you like to walk with me in the Ginza? I'm South African, and I just want somebody to talk to."

Well, I was dying to see the Ginza, which is a shopping area in downtown Tokyo, and he was very charming. But I was so tired from the plane trip that all I could think about was getting to sleep. I turned him down, and he was obviously embarrassed. Since then, I've wondered what would have happened if I had gone with him. I'm sorry now I didn't take advantage of the offer.

Not with My Husband, You Don't

Janet's husband is a business associate of mine, and over the years he and I developed a friendship that transcends the normal business relationship. My husband and I were eating dinner at their house recently, and we were discussing some of the problems of executive women. I mentioned the touchy problem of jealous wives, especially when a businesswoman has to travel with the husband. Janet admitted that this had been a problem for her. Roger was scheduled to go on a business trip with a female colleague. When Janet heard that her husband was to travel with a woman, she said she refused to let him go. Of course, Roger went anyway, and Janet said she was a nervous wreck the whole time he was gone. Since then she has gotten more used to the idea, but she said she still doesn't like it. "It just doesn't seem proper," she told us.

One manager noticed that all the men in her department were taking business trips, but she had never been on one. Finally, she asked her boss about it, and was told that it would cause too many problems for the men if she were allowed to travel with them. Another woman said her boss told her that he would take her along on a business trip if she promised never to breathe a word of it to his wife, because he would be in big trouble if she ever found out.

If you suspect that you are not getting your share of business travel, it probably is because of attitudes like those described above. Most of the time these attitudes will never be openly discussed with you unless you bring them up yourself. Confront the boss's wife, if you have to, and set her mind at ease with your honorable intentions. Business traveling can be critical to career growth, for it broadens your perspective and widens your exposure as a professional. Don't hamper your career horizons by allowing this kind of discrimination against you. The woman who told her prospective male employees, "This job requires traveling with me. Is this going to be a problem for your wife?" confronted the problem head-on, and you should too.

In all honesty, some wives *should* be concerned about the behavior of their husbands traveling with a businesswoman. Only the problem is his, and not yours. A man who would never dream of making a pass at you at the office can turn into an incorrigible monster once he gets away from his hometown. Some men think that because you are sleeping under the same roof they are, you should be sleeping with them. At least they are more apt to consider the possibilities on a business trip.

Most female executives have had similar experiences to this one: "I was traveling with a group of men. We were at the hotel, and I was in my room by myself. There was a knock at the door. I opened it, and one of my male colleagues walked right in, without saying a word. He started to close the door, and I said, 'Leave the door open, please,' which set the scene. He left in about thirty seconds."

But the most demeaning experience I ever heard of happened to the first woman sales representative for a major food manufacturer. The incident occurred at the first sales meeting she attended for the firm. These meetings were regular events, and the personnel department always handled the reservations, booking two sales reps to a room. Unknowingly, she was assigned to room with one of her male colleagues, who was well aware of the situation since her predecessor always used to room with him.

After dinner that night, she went up to her room, still unaware of her predicament. She knew all the men were meeting in the bar below, and even though no one had asked her to go along, she decided to join them. When she reached the bar, the room was dark, causing her to stop in the doorway until her eyes readjusted. She heard her name being bandied about by her colleagues over in the corner. But she couldn't believe what she saw. Her accidental roommate was auctioning the key off to the highest bidder. She said she fled to the ladies' room, composed herself, and went to the desk clerk and explained the predicament. He assigned her another room, and later that month she received an apology from the personnel department. She told me the experience so infuriated her she almost decided to quit right there on the spot. Fortunately, she didn't, and she is still with the firm, but she had to overcome that, as well as many minor annoyances, in order to survive.

When a group of people are traveling together, it is traditional for the group to have a night out on the town and charge it off on expense accounts. You can go along on these nights out with the boys, if you wish, but an executive from New York has some good advice on how you should handle yourself: "If I'm traveling with a group of male colleagues," she said, "I'll go out after work or out for dinner with them, or even sit and drink with them in a bar, but I refuse to get up and dance. If I'm asked, I politely refuse, and gloss it over. Dancing with them is just not something I would feel comfortable doing. There are a few of these situations I avoid getting involved with because I don't feel it would relate well to my business position."

Trade Shows and Conventions

Once or twice a year scattered members of a society herd together because of common professional interests for trade shows and conventions. These rituals often assume a carnival-like atmosphere where old friendships are renewed. The auditoriums echo with business gossip, and at least one-third of the attendees are there to look for another job. Pseudo-blasé executives complain about having to attend these functions, but they return to them like homing-pigeons, year after year, full of good-natured lies about their business achievements. Participating in these functions is all part of the game.

Jump at the opportunity to attend a trade show or convention, for they offer you a chance to broaden your professional perspective and learn the insides of your industry. At these functions, all aspects of the industry, from the trade publications to the suppliers that serve that business, are brought together in one place. There is no better arena to increase your knowledge of how business operates, and you should consider each gathering a learning experience.

The second benefit of attending trade shows and conventions is the valuable contacts you can make to help further your career. You will be exposed to the people who make things happen in your industry, and they are the people who can make things happen for you. Nowhere else will you have the opportunity to meet numbers of top executives, who are not only delightful to know, but could hold the key to a sensational career for you. Make all the contacts that you can, and renew the contacts every year thereafter. There's some truth to the addage, "It's not what you know, but who you know." Attending trade shows and conventions helps you get acquainted with the people you should know.

Freely exchange business cards, which is part of the ritual. If you have trouble remembering names or faces, make notations on the back of the card that will help remind you exactly who that person is. Then, before you attend the next year, review the cards. Be aggressive about greeting both people you would like to know and those with whom you wish to renew your acquaintance. Walk right up to them and introduce yourself. Or if you have met before say, "Hello. I'm Penny Goodbuy with International Corporation, and I believe we met last year. It's nice to see you again." The trade show or convention is one arena where aggressive behavior is acceptable.

"When I go to a trade show, I attempt to have dinner with the most influential people there," a successful sales rep told me. To further your own career, you should think in these kinds of terms. Status climbing is part of the corporate game, and having dinner with important people is the best way to do it. Here's where you have an advantage as a woman. As an advertising executive, I was often invited to dinner with a group of powerful publishing executives. I suspect the reason was that I offered female

companionship, although without my business credentials,
I would not have been there in the first place. But neither
was I there just for decoration, for I always participated in
talking business, and I learned valuable inside information.
I was frequently invited along, and I loved every minute
of it. Not once did any of my hosts make any sexual overtures toward me, nor did I anticipate that they would.

Another advantage of being a female executive is that,
because you are in the minority, you are more apt to be
remembered. You will have an easier time making an impression on people. Of course, the kind of impression that
you make depends on how you handle yourself.

There are some situations that can occur at trade shows
and conventions that make being a woman a disadvantage.
Here's one such situation, described by a San Francisco
executive:

> You get the big customer who is intent on dinner
> or cocktails, and the last thing you want to do is go
> out with him. You explain very kindly that there are
> dozens of your company's customers at the show, it is
> your job to see all the customers, and consequently
> your schedule is very tight. Sometimes they can't ac-
> cept that. I've actually had a man go to my boss and
> say, "That little broad over there refuses to go out
> with me, and I'm your biggest customer," and he puts
> the manager on the spot. I've been in enough of these
> situations to know how to politely get out of them.
> Instead of blatantly turning them down, I say, "If
> possible, perhaps we can have lunch together tomor-
> row," but I never make a firm date. Then if I really
> don't want to go out with him, I will tell him some-
> thing has come up, or hopefully, I will not see him
> again. It's better to leave him with the thought that
> you would have liked to have had dinner with him,
> rather than just refusing him and possibly insulting
> his ego.

Another woman had this story to tell:

> During my first week on a new job I was running a
> showroom in New York City, and the buyer's trade
> there is very tough. I was taken to a reception, where

there were only three women out of four hundred people. Obviously, I had more offers than I could handle.

There was only one guy who got out of line, and he was one of the biggest customers the company had. He asked me to dinner several times, but each time I politely refused. But he got drunk and obnoxious, figured I was a hooker, and thought nobody could refuse the prices he was offering. He got up to $1,000 for the evening. Finally, to shut him up, I told him that if he could collect $1,000 in five minutes, he was on. I didn't think he could do it, but he came up with $897, and an IOU for the rest. He came running over to me with the money, and for a moment, I panicked. I told him $1,000 or nothing, and my heart was pounding. I marched out of that room, and up to my hotel room, and stayed there for the rest of the night.

You know, it didn't matter that I was introduced as a manager to everyone in that room. I was cute in those days, and I'm sure they all thought I was just a cutey with a title who was there to entertain the customers.

Companies have been known to provide women for some of their customers to take advantage of while they are out of town. This occurs less frequently than it used to, but the memories linger on. Don't be surprised if you are mistaken for one of these women, especially at a trade show.

Companies often hire attractive young women to stand in front of their booths and pass out literature or promotional items. These women are procured through firms that rent out convention hostesses, as they are euphemistically called. You may be asked to do booth duty. Go ahead and do it, as long as they don't expect you to act like one of these "models," dressed in hot pants and halter. Absolutely refuse to put yourself on display like that. If you work in a booth, it should be in the same capacity as your male peers, or you should refuse to do it at all. Don't let your company turn you into a sex object. From there on in, everyone will see you that way.

If at trade shows you may be mistaken for a hooker, at

conventions you may be mistaken for someone's wife. Business executives are more apt to bring spouses to conventions than to trade shows. Often the sponsoring association offers "wives' programs" to keep the women occupied with fashion shows and shopping expeditions while the men get down to business. If you attend a convention that offers one, you will have a difficult time staying out of it.

The first time I registered for such a convention, I waited for almost an hour while the committee searched for my advance registration record. After checking every conceivable place, or almost, one of the harried lookers thought to ask a simple question, "Are you attending the convention?" "Of course I am. What do you think I'm doing here?" I replied. "Well that explains everything," she sighed. "We naturally assumed you were part of the wives' program."

A New York woman said she was actually told at a convention last year that women could only register for the wives' program. She called the program manager over and said, "Do you know there's a law against discriminating against women?" She got the registration. I asked her if she always dealt with chauvinism that directly. "That's the last resort to get what I want," she said. "Very rarely will I use force on anyone that I know, like inside my company or customers. But in that situation, the threat of legal action was the only recourse I had."

If the male executives bring their wives to a convention, should you bring your husband? It's better to leave him at home, unless he happens to already know a lot of the people attending. You can't shuffle him off to the wives' program, and your concern over making him feel comfortable could detract from your ability to make viable contacts. My husband attended one convention with me but spent the whole time playing tennis and looking uncomfortable. One journalist said she brought her husband with her to a company-sponsored conference in the Caribbean. "Husbands and wives were invited, so I thought I should bring him along," she recalled. "He felt awkward because he was the only 'husband' there. He played tennis with the wife of one of the men there, and in the afternoon he would play golf with me. At night, we'd all go out to dinner, and he'd feel uncomfortable. Since then we have both decided that it is better if he stays home for these events. It's an extremely awkward area to handle."

Whether or not you bring your husband, be prepared to feel isolated at these conventions. The men are reluctant to be friendly toward you, especially with their wives around, and the wives will dislike you because you are not one of them, and you pose a potential threat to their structure. Consequently, the quality of contacts that you make at a spouse-attended convention are apt to be less than those at trade shows, where wives usually stay at home. That's not to say that you shouldn't attend, but view it primarily as a learning experience. Expect to feel left out for a while, floating on the periphery of the social interaction. Eventually, you'll become part of a group and will be accepted, but the first few times you attend, it might be rough.

❧ 13 ❧

Dressing for Success

As noted earlier, one of women's greatest obstacles to success at executive levels is our lack of role models—other people that we can observe to know how we should behave. Nowhere is this lack felt more than in the matter of dress. Fashion and grooming have always been important to women, but the importance of proper attire increases tenfold for the striving executive woman. Many people will argue that fine feathers don't make fine birds, but in practice a business person is greatly judged by appearance. To be considered a proper candidate for promotions and top jobs, the executive must look like an executive. This is simple enough for men, because they have a plethora of role models everywhere. Stores such as Brooks Brothers cater to the business executive striving to create an image and help him create it.

So what is the proper image for a female executive? This presents an interesting problem, compounded by the variety of garments available to choose from. Also, styles of women's clothing change more frequently than men's, so the selection of clothes can become a perplexing problem, as fashion is in a constant state of flux.

As I traveled across the country interviewing executives, I documented how each woman was dressed, her hair style, make-up, skirt length, etc., hoping that I would arrive at a composite model of dress that I could share with you. From here on in, you would presumably know exactly how to dress. But I could not establish a set pattern of dress among women business executives. The styles of dress varied considerably, and when I asked them about their wardrobes, most of them were curious about what other women were wearing. *Everyone* is confused about dress.

The styles differed according to individual personality, industry, profession, specific job, geography, and climate. Some of the taller women wore styles that would be unflattering to a shorter woman; older women tended to be less fashion-oriented than the younger ones. Women in banking dressed more conservatively than those in publishing or advertising. Geography and climate were also considerations. East Coast women, especially New Yorkers, were more formal in their appearance than were Midwesterners or West Coast ladies, yet San Francisco dwellers were more formal than those in Los Angeles. Proper attire for East Coast winters would be unsuitable for moderate climates.

So it is impossible, unfortunately, to provide absolute information on the correct way to dress. But I can discuss with authority the looks these executive women achieved with their clothing, the kind of image they conveyed, and how they went about achieving it.

Creating an Executive Image

How you dress communicates how you feel about yourself and who you are. Everything from your blue jeans to your evening gowns is a reflection of you. Each time you dress, you say something about yourself that indicates how you wish to be seen. This is both an advantage and a disadvantage to the executive woman. It is a disadvantage because you do not benefit from the inherent assumption of power that is enjoyed by males. You do not look like an executive, because you are a woman. It is very difficult for a woman to create a powerful image. But the proper selection of clothes can help you build an executive image, and you should do your clothes buying accordingly.

Business has long carried the banner of traditional clothing. Men learned a long time ago that they were more effective as business people if they donned traditional dress, and studies have proved this to be true. With the exception of the creative industries, such as show business or advertising, conservative clothes have become the uniform of the majority of the business community, if for no other reason than they do not detract from the business at hand. Businesswomen should also convey a conservative image. Consequently, conservativeness is the keynote when you select clothes for business.

The degree of conservatism you adopt depends on your particular industry. Look to your male colleagues and see how they dress. If your peers are ultraconservative (dark blue or gray suit, white or blue long-sleeved shirt, subtle tie), then you should dress in outfits where the jackets and pants or skirts are of matching material. If the men wear sports coats with contrasting slacks, then you can mix and match your wardrobe, too. If the men wear leisure or denim suits, then you can be casual also. If you are unsure of the parameters permitted by your profession, dress more conservatively than you think is probably necessary. Having a conservative image in business can rarely hurt you, and, in fact it is mandatory for any notable career climb.

Perhaps the conservative image is incongruent with your personality. Nevertheless, you should adopt it if you wish to succeed. "My goal is to make money," one woman told me. "I don't like to give up any of me to do it, but I'll compromise certain things, like how I dress, during the work day in order to meet my goal. In the long run, I don't feel like I am compromising myself. It's all part of the game."

Especially if you are younger, you need to set yourself apart from the typical woman found in business, the secretary. Secretaries tend to dress alike, and you should differentiate yourself from them by adopting your own style. A little snobby perhaps, but it's all part of establishing your image as an executive type. Secretaries tend toward faddish clothes, and you can set yourself apart by avoiding fads. The fashion industry is built on the concept of constant change, and today's fresh styles are tomorrow's leftovers. Never buy fad clothing until the style has survived at least two years and only buy styles that are conservative to begin with, styles that reflect your executive image.

Although you should look toward the men in your profession to set guidelines about your dress, you should never attempt to emulate them exactly. Hoping to keep pace with the times, the fashion industry has offered suits and ties for women that were tailored identically to men's suits. On the surface, these suits would appear to be the ideal apparel for female executives assuming a typically male role. However, successful women have discovered that they are more readily accepted if they maintain a degree of femininity in their dress. As explained in Chapter 2, "The Power of Femininity," successful women have learned to mask their internal toughness (generally thought a masculine trait) with a soft veneer of femininity that lets men know we are not out to usurp their masculinity. A bit of femininity in your clothes that are seemingly suitable for the corporate environment but are too mannish somehow make men feel uncomfortable. The quest to be accepted because you try to "fit in" backfires. Clothes that are too mannish convey an inappropriate image.

So the clothes that you wear for business should fall into the category of conservative, but mildly feminine. You do have some latitude in the degree of femininity depending upon your personal preference, as long as you don't overdo it. Avoid lacy, frilly looks. You may be slightly tempted to don high fashion, especially since the stores that you shop in will carry the latest and best, but you should be cautious with it. As long as the style is not too outrageous or out of step with current fashions, go ahead and wear it. Your clothes should be pleasing but never distracting.

There are two basic looks that are suitable for female executives: the classic tailored, and what I call the gently tailored look. These styles can be intermixed. You can take the same basic suit, and how you use accessories with it creates your look. If you wear a tailored blouse and perhaps a single gold necklace with a suit, you are achieving the classic tailored look. Add a silk scarf or a blouse with neckties for a soft, floppy bow and you look gently tailored. Buy a three-piece suit and wear the vest on the days you are classic tailored, and leave it home on days you wish to appear soft and feminine. Women's clothes offer more variety than men's.

Although you can never go wrong wearing a suit, many one- and two-piece dresses are acceptable for executive wear. Since there are so many variations of dress styles from which to choose, I cannot possibly describe those which are suitable. You must use your own discretion. For this, there is no substitute for good taste and a trustworthy sales clerk.

Dressing conservatively means being covered up. Long sleeves are preferable. In the summer, you can get away with cap sleeves, but never wear garments that are sleeveless. Mini skirts, which are now out of style anyway, are forbidden. Find a flattering skirt length below your knee, and have all your clothes hemmed to the same length. Avoid low-cut necklines or blouses unbuttoned so low as to expose your cleavage.

The color of your clothing should be conservative, too. Camel, gray, black, navy, white, or beige in a solid color are most acceptable. You can wear a subtle pattern or plaid providing you are not overweight and the pattern is repeated many times on the fabric. Randomly patterned or bright splashy fabrics are too casual for executive women. Avoid purples, lavenders, hot pinks, oranges, and reds. You can add a dash of color with a bright silk scarf, but even that should be a repeated pattern rather than a random one.

The most sophisticated look is a neutral-colored outfit worn with tasteful gold or silver jewelry, very expensive, of course. Appropriate jewelry for female executives has smooth, clean lines, and is elegantly understated. Save the bangles and beads for a luau. In business, the simpler your jewelry, the better. The richest look is always understated. Your jewelry should be impeccably tasteful and not distracting in any way.

Pantsuits vs. Skirts

A few years ago a big issue in corporate America was whether women should be allowed to wear pantsuits to work. As you might expect, the financial institutions were the last to allow it, but eventually pantsuits were acceptable garb for women, and many adopted wearing them. The women I interviewed were equally divided on the issue of pantsuits. Only about half of them wore them to the office; the rest had made a conscious decision not to.

I started wearing pantsuits when they were still controversial, and I discovered they were a great way to help position myself as an executive, for the secretaries were still wearing mini skirts. Once secretaries adopted pantsuits as their uniform, I stopped wearing them and returned to skirts and dresses.

Very tailored pantsuits are still acceptable for female executives, but they are fading. If you are considering a new purchase, buy a skirt instead of pants. You'll get more wear out of it, and a suit with a skirt is now a more sophisticated look than pants.

Men have hated pantsuits from the beginning, and would much prefer to see a woman in a skirt. Wearing skirts will help you gain the power of femininity over men. I realized this some time ago when I switched back to skirts. I sensed that men were more receptive toward me if I wore skirts, and I became conscious of the effect I was having on others by what I wore. I discovered that I was more apt to gain a positive reaction from men while wearing a skirt.

I am not the only person who discovered this. A woman recently told me, "After I invested a fortune in pantsuits, I found out that men really liked dresses. I probably have twenty or twenty-five pantsuits, and if someone poured a bottle of bleach over them, they all would look alike. So now I'm stuck with all these pantsuits when I know I am more effective wearing dresses."

This same woman had an interesting comment about the application of wearing dresses. She said, "If I am going to call on a customer, and the meeting is with a man, I'll wear a dress. If the meeting is with a woman, I'll wear pants." She learned that women prefer to see women in pants, whereas men prefer to see them in skirts. Use this knowledge to your advantage.

To Bra or Not

Many of the women I interviewed confessed they went braless at home, but they all wore them to work. Even though going braless is a symbol of liberation, its symbolism is incongruous with the conservative image you wish to project. To many in our society, going braless is a suggestion of sexuality rather than independence. You have enough problems not being seen as a sex object without adding to the image. Going braless in business is in bad taste.

A secretary who worked for a company that I was with adopted the braless look, despite her well-endowed thirty-eight-inch bustline. She was causing quite a furor among the clients and other employees. The man she worked for was too embarrassed to speak to her about it, so he asked me to do it for him. I agreed to do it, but even I felt reluctant to speak to her about such a personal matter. Imagine how embarrassing it would be for a man to do so.

"I never used to wear a bra," an executive who started out as a secretary told me. "But when I interviewed for my present position, the man that interviewed me started hemming and hawing around, until I knew what the problem was. I said to him, 'If you are worried about me wearing a bra, I'm going to go out and buy some.' And he said, 'Oh, thank goodness. That was the only thing about you we were unsure how to handle.'" Don't place anyone in the position of having to ask you.

Investing in Your Success

When I landed my first management job, I borrowed $2,000 from the bank to buy a new wardrobe. Up until then, my clothes had been inexpensive and casual. But I decided it was necessary I change my image, so I went for a tailored, conservative look, and only bought from the better stores. It turned out to be the best investment I could have made. I know that wearing the right clothes helped me get to where I am today, if for no other reason than the clothes helped my self-confidence. If I felt I looked good, I was more apt to confront an employee or my boss, something that was always hard for me to do. I feel that buying that expensive wardrobe was one of the keys to my success.

This corporate vice-president discovered a secret of corporate success: quality clothes help make the executive. Observe top corporation men, and you will never see a group of better dressers than they. Then look at the junior executives who are still climbing. The ones that already look like the affluent top executives are more apt to be promoted, because in management's eyes they better fit the image of what an executive should be. In your case, you will have a more difficult time looking like an executive under the old male rules, but you can help overcome this stigma by wearing expensive clothes. It is one of those inexplicable quirks of human nature: the more successful you look, the more successful you are apt to be. You must look affluent before you can become affluent. Wearing expensive clothes will help position you as an executive.

As part of your executive training, you should develop a discerning eye for quality in clothes. If you can't see the difference between a $20 blouse, and a $50 blouse, then look again. There is a difference, and a big one, in the quality of the garment. Those who are conscious of the difference and value well-made clothes—and all executives do—will be able to look at you and immediately judge your clothes taste. Just as shop clerks favor those who dress well, so will the people making the decisions regarding your career. If you wish to be a success in business, it is mandatory that you dress well, even at lower managerial levels.

Although the cost of the garment doesn't always reflect its quality, often it does. Go for the most expensive clothes you can afford, and you'll always feel proud of the way you look. It's better to have a few good outfits than a multitude of cheap ones that will do nothing to enhance your executive image. Don't feel bad about wearing a basic suit twice in the same week. You can change the look with a different blouse or scarf, and still convey an image of financial well-being. The important thing is that it reek of quiet elegance and sophistication and reflect your good taste. This is proper attire for the executive woman.

When all is said and done, inexpensive clothes are rarely a bargain anyway. Consider the durability of the clothing. You will get more than twice as much wear out of a garment that is twice as well-made, and you will do a world of good for your image in the process. Inexpensive clothes tend to look tired after just a few cleanings, whereas quality clothes beautifully withstand the years. You can buy a lot of "cute" clothes at moderate prices, but they reflect neither class nor taste.

Styles for conservative clothes, such as the popular

vested suits perfect for female executives, tend to be less faddish than inexpensive clothes, which is another reason why you can wear them longer. As I said earlier, many secretaries wear faddish and inexpensive clothes, female executives do not. If you avoid faddish clothes and buy only classic styles, the life of the item is greatly increased, and you can easily justify the expense.

Don't be a polyester princess. To achieve an upper-class look, wear clothes made from fabrics such as silk, cotton, or wool; fine wool blends are also acceptable, as long as the store or label is one that you can trust. I have a particular dislike for polyesters since so many cheaper clothes are made from it, although I agree that they are great for traveling. If you are on the road a lot, it might be wise to invest in a polyester suit or two, but other than that I would avoid them, and insist that the bulk of your wardrobe consist of pure fibers. The type of fabric you select also contributes to your classy act.

Shopping

Achieving a well-dressed, put-together look does not just happen. It takes hours of pavement pounding, searching through endless stores for just the right shoes or blouse, and then finally reaching a decision on the best item for your needs. Because you spend more than the average person on clothes, each decision that you make is more important, for you cannot afford to make costly mistakes.

Shopping can be fun if you have the time to devote to it, but the busy executive, especially if she has a family, has little time for leisurely browsing through shops. Finding the time to shop is one of your biggest problems. Some women, who do not have the kind of job that requires business lunches, shop on their lunch hour. This is one solution to the time dilemma, although you should use your lunch hour as a relaxing breather from the pressures of the business day.

Because of your limited time, you can alleviate a lot of wasted motion by developing a relationship with several stores that specialize in tailored clothes. Properly trained sales clerks in better stores know how to put together outfits, and once they get to know your preferences, they can be a godsend in helping you select clothes. Call them before you plan to visit the store, and give them an idea of the kind of thing for which you are looking. They can have several outfits ready for you to try on once you get there, and this alone can save you valuable time.

Sales clerks will also call you when they receive a new shipment of clothes that they think will match your tastes. And I've had them call me to give me advance notice of a big sale, and even hold items for me until I have a chance to stop by and look at them. If you are a good customer of the store, they are happy to provide these extra services for you.

Do the majority of your shopping in large cities. If you do not live near one, then plan several trips a year for the sole purpose of buying. Although most Midwest executives go to Chicago, I know a Minnesota executive who buys all her clothes in London. On the West Coast, I prefer San Francisco to Los Angeles for buying business clothes, because San Francisco caters more to the sophisticate, while Los Angeles features the chic and bizarre. But there's nowhere like New York. Fashion is the city's biggest industry, and nowhere can you find a better selection or more reasonable prices than in the Big Apple. A Chicago executive said her business took her to New York several times a year, and each time she would stay another day for the sole purpose of shopping. She picked up the extra tab at the hotel herself, and said it was more than worth it because of the money she saved. She found the same items less expensive in New York than in Chicago, and always at least a year ahead of their styles.

Besides knowing where to shop, there are some other tips that will help you become an expert shopper. Wear the same undergarments and shoe height that you wear to work. When you try on clothes, sit down in them, and move about. Make sure the garment doesn't bind or pucker awkwardly. Check the mirror when you are sitting down, and observe how you look, for you will be spending a great deal of time seated. Make sure that the fabric doesn't wrinkle too badly. Crinkle a bunch of it in your hand and test how it springs back to shape. If it wrinkles too badly, it's not for you. Incidentally, a well-lined garment always hangs better and will retain its shape longer. Check the inside of the item for detailing and its interior construction. The way the seams are finished and the way that it is lined will tell you much about the quality of the garment.

If your blouse is too tight, the buttons on your bustline will continually pop open—a most embarrassing happening. Try to touch your elbows behind your back, and if the buttons burst open, it's too small. If the garment seems a little bit tight, it's better to buy a larger size and have it tailored down. The fit of the clothes is almost as important as the quality. A beautiful suit that doesn't hang well looks tacky, no matter how superb the quality of the garment.

Something women often overlook is the length of their sleeves. Long-sleeved blouses or shirts look best under jackets, and the blouse sleeve should be a half-inch longer than the jacket sleeve. If one or the other is too long, it is a simple alteration to have it shortened.

Cosmetics

Along with the braless look and unisex clothes, the trend of the 1970s is away from make-up, a practice considered silly and frivolous by some feminists. But the completely natural look is unacceptable for life in the executive suite. The glary fluorescent lighting found in most offices is unflattering, and you should wear make-up to compensate for its harsh effects.

Properly applied make-up improves your looks. Can you think of a better reason than that to wear it? Too much make-up is always tacky, but the appropriate amount of skillfully applied cosmetics gives you a sophisticated air and makes a dramatic statement that you care about yourself. Women who don't wear make-up tend to look sloppy.

There have been volumes written on the appropriate use of cosmetics, so I am not going to get into that here, but I would like to raise some observations that I have made during the years. Some women will don a $300 outfit, and then use dime store cosmetics on their face. You can always buy a new dress, but you can't buy a new face. Treat your skin as a valuable commodity. Pamper yourself with quality cosmetics. They'll last all day, won't rub off or streak, and will make you feel better about yourself. Nothing looks worse or is more apparent than shoddy make-up.

Styles in make-up tend to be faddish, just like clothes.

Every time you turn around there is a new line of cosmetics on the market. But don't get caught up in the cosmetics marketing games. You'll find that even though the package and name may vary, in reality little has changed. Don't succumb to all those advertising gimmicks cosmetics manufacturers employ. Find shades and brands that suit you and then stick to them. If you feel bewildered about which shades and applications are right for you, go to a cosmetics salon and have a professional assist you. You will probably spent over $100 by the time you are through, but from there on in you are set. You can simply replace the make-up as needed.

An area that seems to confuse many women is eye shadow. You should wear shades that match your outfits, not your eyes. Blue-eyed women are especially guilty of this. Many wear blue eye shadow with everything they wear, where in reality they should be matching the shades in their clothes. Mascara should always be dark brown or black, no matter what color your clothes.

Hair and Nails

Nothing is more attractive and sexy than long, free-swinging hair. But in the office, a flowing mane can be distracting and could be a detractor in your power over people. Hair for female executives should be no longer than shoulder length, and relatively simple to maintain.

Short, geometric styles work best with tailored clothes. If you tend toward more feminine attire, curlier styles are best. Your hair should never be so long or combed toward your face so that it is distracting when you work over a desk. If you have to keep pushing it out of your face, it will get dirtier faster and can be a source of annoyance. If you are short, hair piled on top of your head or cut to expose your neck will make you look taller. As you get older, softer hair around your face is more flattering.

Coloring your hair is acceptable (even Gloria Steinem streaks hers), but always have it done professionally by a name salon. Don't chance those raccoon-striped tresses that are often the result of home jobs, and have your roots touched up on a regular basis.

Everytime I wear a wig, I have an uncontrollable desire to take the nearest sharp object, place it under the wig, and scratch my head with it. Wigs drive me crazy. But, for a busy woman, they are a salvation. For office use, only wear wigs that are close to the color and style of your hair. You don't want to call too much attention to yourself. And once you develop your look, you should stick with it.

Manicured nails are a must. Have them done professionally if you can afford the time. If not, you can do an adequate job at home. The biggest problem with fingernail polish is that it chips after a day or two. When this happens to me, I become so self-conscious about it that I find myself spending the rest of the day keeping my fingers rolled up in tight little balls. I discovered that if I apply a clear topcoat every evening, it prevents the chipping. By the end of the week, you may be sporting ten coats of fingernail polish, but you can bet it won't chip off.

Jewelry

As in the case of clothes, the jewelry that you wear should be tailored and expensive. Simple, classic designs in gold or silver are best. Save the sparkly jewels for evening wear.

Clip earrings are a pain in the lobe if you have to spend much time on the phone. Those who do usually end up spending the day with an earring dangling from only one ear. Pierced ears are a matter of personal preference, but they certainly eliminate the phone problem and are also a more secure way to keep earrings fastened.

Bracelets always bang around on the desk, and since most of the time you will be wearing long sleeves anyway, I recommend not wearing them to work. As for necklaces, elegant but understated gold or silver chains are always in good taste and will work well with your style of dress.

Glasses

Avoid wearing glasses with ornate frames, or one bespeckled with rhinestones. Save the flashy specs for night. Frames that match your hair color are always flattering and will blend well with any color of garment that looks good on you.

Always wear sunglasses when it's bright outdoors for

you want to avoid squinting, which causes premature crow's-feet. Indoors, a very subtle tint to your glasses is fashionable, but if you go this route, you should invest in several pairs with hues to blend with your entire wardrobe. Never wear glasses indoors that are so dark others cannot see your eyes. This makes you appear as if you have something to hide.

Shoes, Purses, and Briefcases

Shoes that go best with tailored clothes are clean, classic lines in black, navy, or tan leather. Boots are a fashion trend which emphasize the covered-up look you wish to achieve, and are acceptable.

You are not going to have time to change your purse every morning, so don't worry about it exactly matching your shoes. If you use a briefcase on a regular basis, use those thin clutch bags that you can easily slip into your briefcase so you will only have one item to carry. You will look more put together that way. When you need just your purse, you can take it out of the briefcase. Too large a purse looks awkward.

On the subject of briefcases, you can get a standard style in a lighter color than a man would use. A more feminine-looking version is preferred, however. The right quality of briefcase is an executive status symbol: buy leather or suede in a chic, slim design. Manufacturers are just beginning to design cases for women, and several companies now have them on the market. The size that you get really depends on your needs. You can't go too wrong on your selection as long as you stick to a high-class store. A Gucci briefcase is always in good taste.

Health

You are not the bionic woman. Take care of yourself. Work-a-holics tend to let their health suffer for the sake of the company. You are not doing anybody any favors, least of all the company, by letting yourself get run down. No job demands are so great that you have to sacrifice your health for them. Keep yourself fit.

❧ 14 ❧

The Great
Dual-Career Divide

The alarm rings at six-thirty. They both bolt out of bed in silence and head for their separate bathrooms, trying to shake the grogginess they feel after only six hours sleep. The woman hears her baby daughter stirring in the nursery and dashes into the room while removing cold cream from her face. She gives the child a quick kiss and hurriedly puts her on the changing table to dress her so she can take her to the baby-sitter.

She finishes dressing her daughter and races to the seven-year-old's room, where she wakes him up and gets out his clothes for school. She is relieved the boy woke up in a good mood but finds herself feeling impatient with him when he wants to recount what happened at school the day before. He didn't have a chance to tell her last night because he was already sleeping when she finished up at work. She tells her son that she will hear all about it that evening, but right now she doesn't have time to talk.

In the meantime, the man is hurriedly going about his morning responsibilities, thinking about an important client meeting he has in an hour. He cuts himself twice while shaving. He takes his last white shirt out of the drawer, and swears angrily under his breath when he sees the laundry had failed to sew on a missing button. He stops to sew the button on himself, which puts him behind in starting the children's breakfast, one of his many household duties.

The woman takes both the children to the kitchen to deposit them with her husband while she finishes putting on her make-up. But her husband is not there, and she calls to him to hurry up, that she doesn't have time to waste this morning. He yells back that he will be there in a minute, and to just leave the kids in the kitchen.

She returns to her bathroom to finish her make-up and do her hair. She hears her youngest crying, probably from hunger, and the woman sighs, feeling guilty that she cannot run to her child's side and fulfill her needs. The woman hopes her husband can cope by himself, for she has to catch her train in twenty minutes. She finishes applying her make-up, and nervously checks her watch. She absolutely cannot afford to miss her train, for she has an early morning meeting, with her compulsively punctual boss. She had better hurry if she expects to get there on time.

Into the kitchen again she goes, this time to pick up the baby. But her husband is late with breakfast, and the children have not yet been fed. She tells her husband that he will have to take their daughter to the baby-sitter himself, that she hasn't the time. But he says that he has a breakfast meeting with an important client, and he cannot be late either. They compromise. He will drive both her and the baby to the baby-sitter if she will feed her in the car on the way. In the car they both sit in stony silence, both already frustrated and angry at the day's events before they reach their offices. They had agreed to share the burden of a dual-career marriage, for in theory it sounded like the civilized, chic thing to do, but they both harbor secret resentment toward it. She resents feeling guilty about leaving the children, and feels society has given her unfair responsibilities. He wishes his wife would stay at home like other women for it would relieve him of the responsibility for tending to family needs. His job keeps him busy enough without additional burdens. Yet so does hers.

And the conflict rages on.

Coping with marriage and family responsibilities is the single biggest problem facing you as an executive. And guilt can be your biggest enemy.

The shackles of a male chauvinistic society are firmly

entrenched in the woman's role as wife and mother, and these are the most difficult roles to escape. Career women may also seek the security and social conformity of a marriage relationship, but under a new set of rules where the husband shares in the responsibility of the family. If a woman enters a traditional relationship, she usually has the energy to cope with family pressures. But once she begins depleting her energy sources elsewhere, she is limited in what she can give. The family, especially the husband, must assume a greater share of the responsibilities.

Finding a man who will agree to the new set of rules is difficult. Men have been the ruling class of our society, and many of them are reluctant to relinquish their status. We are asking them to change a system that benefits them, so it is no wonder many of them resist. As an ambitious woman, you must find an enlightened man who is willing to share in the family responsibilities, plus have an ego strong enough to withstand the assaults that you will make on it. He must possess a tremendous sense of self-esteem. Because such men are rare, I have reached the conclusion that those executive women who have successful marriages are very lucky indeed.

Many executives have eliminated the problem by remaining single. More than half the women I interviewed were single at the time of our conversation, not because they were necessarily against marriage in general, but because they felt being married was a detriment to their careers. Here is a typical response I received when I asked why these women had chosen to remain single: "Being single has made it easier for me because I don't have to run home at night and take care of a family. I need to travel on my job. I can go out of town without a single thought, and not have to worry about someone else. I'm lucky because I'm in a profession that I love. I get up in the morning and I'm glad to go to work. And at night, I can come home and only worry about me."

Some women chose to stay single for other reasons. There is an interesting phenomenon that has bothered many women executives, and that is in the area of role-playing. After spending the day making decisions and exercising authority, many find it difficult to relinquish this role and be submissive when they go home. One woman who was contemplating marriage to a man with whom she was living said she broke off the relationship because she could not deftly interchange roles:

> My work situation was so draining that when I got home, and I had to step into a personal relationship, I was ineffective. After playing boss all day, it was too hard for me to adjust to a personal relationship and play the feminine, hausfrau role in the evening. Besides that, I didn't have the energy left to give any more. It wasn't that I didn't want the relationship to work out, but I didn't have the energy to be receptive. I have a hard time just plain relating to anyone else after I've put out so much during the day. Right now, my priority is work. I thoroughly enjoy what I'm doing, and my social relationships are secondary.

Her attitude was reflected by many. This is not to say, however, that the women executives that I interviewed had never tried marriage. Over one-third of them were divorced, and the majority of them gave the identical reason for their separations: their husbands could not cope with their wives' careers. Most of these women—there was only one exception—had married early in life, before they had reached any level of business success. Once they started their career climb, many passed their husbands by. They eventually reached a turning point where they knew they would either have to sacrifice their career or their marriage. These women chose the career route. (Of course, I did not talk with the women who had opted to stay home.)

A New York chemicals executive told me about the break-up of her marriage:

> If I had decided to stay home and have babies and give up my job, I still would be married. But I wouldn't be happy because that wouldn't have been what I wanted to do. The more I succeeded, the less he felt the leader. The last two years of our marriage I definitely achieved more than he did. It was clear that we were going in opposite directions, and that my work came first in my life. I was living the way I wanted, and he didn't like it.
>
> I never wanted children and he said he didn't care

one way or the other. But he was raised in a traditional mode, and I knew the day would come when he would want kids. When my salary got past his, when I worked late and would go in on Saturdays, and as my business trips began taking more time, it was clear our relationship was going two different ways. There was no fight or hassle, but our relationship gradually became nothing. My career definitely had priority over my husband. Now I have no plans to remarry, and it's not something I would ever actively pursue. My career is enough for me.

Another woman talked about the effort she devoted to her marriage to save it:

The reason for the break-up was that I progressed faster than he did. The widening gap between us reared its ugly head in the form of jealousy. I worked very hard to save it. I went to extremes. I never went to a night meeting unless it was absolutely necessary. If I worked overtime at the office, I would make sure that he knew where I was, and I would call him regularly.

He was an aerospace engineer, and he could not accept what he called my "social butterfly" role at a company function. When a woman would not stand one step behind the man and be the charming wife, he didn't know how to handle the role. It was very difficult for him. But it's also very difficult to work until ten and then go home and explain yourself. The guilt becomes too great. I had to reach a decision.

Unlike many single career women, this woman was planning to remarry and, in fact, was marrying one of her former employees. (She had left the company; he was still there.) Since she already had one marriage break-up over ego problems, I was curious about why she thought her new marriage would survive. She felt that since her second marriage relationship had begun when she was an executive, her fiance already knew her in that role. Her former husband had married her when she was a teenager, and she barely knew who she was herself. She was very confident her second marriage would survive. "Tom fully understands that my career is me, and that I'm going to work," she said. "That's the package he bought. There will never be a choice between the two like there was in my first marriage."

The one divorced executive who had *not* married very young before her career was established, was a brilliant executive in her fifties. She had waited until late in life to marry, but even then it didn't work out:

> I think being so independent handicapped my marriage. I did marry late, but it wasn't successful. I did know I would have to wait until I found someone who was secure enough in his own ego so that I could have one of my own. I waited so long to marry because I discovered the kind of man I wanted married young, and stayed married. The one that I chose I thought was very strong and very successful. But he ended up having a very fragile ego. We were in the same field, and he couldn't handle my successes. I discovered that marriage is too confining for me. I might marry again, but chances are good that I won't. But this doesn't bother me.

If you're stuck with a husband who is hampering your career growth and you are serious about your endeavors, it's simply better to cast him off rather than fight it out all day at the office and then at home too. Your home life must be in reasonably good shape so as not to distract you from the business at hand. Your only other alternative is to discard your career or be willing to compromise your goals. The choice is up to you.

The Option to Bear Children

The issue of mixing career and child-raising is so loaded with implications for our family and social structure that I cannot possibly discuss them all here. My personal belief is that both are full-time jobs, and assuming dual responsibilities places impossible demands on the mother. Attempting to do both seems to me a chaotic way to live one's life, but I know some women who have combined both very successfully.

But many executive women have opted to remain

childfree. I noticed a common factor among the women I interviewed: of the women who had been married, more than half remained childfree because they felt children would be a detriment to their careers. One woman explaind her decision this way: "Having children places tremendous demands on both parents. As an adult in a marriage—even if you have no children—you recognize that you are putting demands on your spouse beyond his or her capability to give, so you try to understand those limits. Children don't recognize or understand that."

The decision to have children is a difficult one, for unlike the decision to marry, it cannot be undone. The woman just quoted said that it had taken her husband and her twelve years to reach a decision to remain childfree, and even then, they remade the decision several times. "There were times when I wanted children," she said, "and there were times when he wanted them, but our timing was never together. We decided that it is possible to have both children and careers, but we felt neither of us possessed the tremendous stamina that it requires. So we decided not to, and it is the hardest decision we have ever made."

A Minneapolis executive admitted to wondering about her decision to forsake husband and family to pursue a career:

> Sometimes I'm concerned about not having children. But I look at all the working mothers around here who really have two full-time jobs, and it's hard on them. When the kids are sick, one parent has to stay home, and it's a detriment to their career. But there's no way around it. When you have young children, you have great responsibilities, and I admire anyone who wants to give both a try. I simply do not have the energy.
>
> I know that I am missing something not having the warmth and closeness of a husband and family, but I have so many other things that I enjoy doing that it is not on my mind. I've got a great life. I love my job, the people that I meet, my apartment, the vacations that I take. I don't think a great many housewives would be as happy if you asked them the same question.

Because of the natural role of the mother in the rearing of the child, the burden of responsibility falls on the woman whether she has a career or not. For career women, with that burden comes a sense of guilt—that we as mothers with careers are neglecting our children. No matter how much of the burden they claim to bear, men will never feel the degree of responsibility and guilt that comes from having both children and career. The only responsibilities most men will assume is to do well in their careers and to be an ample breadwinner. Family units, including wives, are there to be supportive of them. No matter how much help men claim they are willing to give, women continue to bear the brunt of family responsibilities.

The years that usually demand the greatest from you as a mother—your twenties and thirties—are also the years when you can most accelerate your career climb. Business problems are often as seemingly pressing as family ones. You must resolve this internal tug-of-war, and you're apt to become frustrated and exhausted in the process. A research team from the University of Michigan recently studied the comparative marital happiness and satisfaction of working wives (they were not necessarily executives), husbands of working wives, housewives, and husbands of housewives. They found that "the least happy and satisfied person was the working wife, particularly if she had young children."

The optimum solution for the conflict between children and career for executive women who are intent on success is to not have any children. The women who have reached that decision say that their careers are fulfilling them, that they derive their satisfaction from their work, and that children would just get in the way. It is this kind of woman with singular determination and drive who is representative of the new woman executive. She has set her priorities.

The Lady Is a Juggler

Having both career and family can be a difficult life-style to maintain. But you can have both if you are a special type of woman with seemingly limitless energy and a penchant for attempting the nearly impossible. You should be like the executive who told me, "I don't feel like I have neglected my family for my career, but I have an incredible amount of energy. I only need six hours' sleep a night, and I also run two miles every day." You must possess the additional resources necessary to cope with your multitude of responsibilities.

Listen to the schedule of this divorced finance executive with five children. "I come home on Friday night and take everyone out to dinner. On Saturday, the children and I go through the house room by room and clean and do the laundry. In the afternoon we go to the beach or the zoo. On Sunday, I iron from six until ten, and then start getting my clothes ready for the week. I do my shopping on my lunch hour."

Some executive women proudly boast of their Wonder Woman abilities to successfully juggle career, husband, children, social life, exercise and beauty regimes, and then have time left over for themselves. But I am not blessed with limitless energy, and I doubt that most women are, nor should we be expected to be. Our male equivalents are allowed to come home from the office tired, but we can't. Your additional responsibilities put you at a disadvantage when competing with men.

If you attempt a dual career as mother and executive, you must possess the ability to deftly interchange roles. You should know the difference between mothering and managing. You should not treat your children as adults, nor should you treat your employees like children. Often, when a woman has a problem in either area, it is because she cannot quickly change roles from one to the other, and she applies identical tactics in both situations. You must wear a variety of hats.

The executive with five children explained how she coped with this. "I played my role as manager as a 'with it,' well-dressed businesswoman—with a bit of mystery added. You have to play roles, but you must not lose sight of who you are. But I could not have been both a mother and businesswoman without putting myself into two distinct roles."

Displaying a consistently positive attitude about herself and her life-style (another trait of a successful executive), this ambitious lady felt having five children was an advantage to her. "Being married and having five children was an advantage because men never looked at me as competitively. There still had to be something very feminine about a woman with five kids. Everyone would say, 'My goodness, she has five kids,' and that would immediately make me safe. To them, if you were a mother, you couldn't be competition. I succeeded in business because men never considered me a threat—at least until it was too late."

Obviously, this woman had been willing to sacrifice a part of her career to raise her children. If you wish to do likewise, you will indeed make many sacrifices for the sake of the children. And you can't have children and work without wanting to devote your spare time to your family. Forget about free time for yourself. There just won't be any.

Many times the company's needs will have to wait, whereas those of small children won't. You will be inclined to meet your family's needs first, and rightly you should, but each time you do so you're taking something away from your efforts toward your career. You will be competing with men who do not have the additional role responsibilities that you have, and your progress will be impeded because of it. Again, it's all a matter of priorities.

If you are attempting motherhood and management, you should come to grips with your guilt about leaving the children. Learn to think in terms of the quality, and not the quantity, of time that you spend with them. This could turn out to be a benefit to you. Studies have indicated that a woman who spends less time with her children than the typical housewife is apt to enjoy her children more, and the time is more apt to mean more to the children.

One of the ways that you can feel more relaxed about leaving the children is to have dependable, quality child care. If you are secure about whomever is watching over your brood, you will not feel anxious about leaving your children there. Hiring live-in help is desirable, if you can afford it, because you can regulate the quality and consistency of the care, and you don't have to worry about picking the child up at a specified time. This affords you some much-needed flexibility in your schedule. Several businesswomen who had children said they never would have attempted it without full-time, live-in help. Day-care centers are an alternative, but most of them insist on regular hours, and they are no help at all if you must travel. Men who are willing to be househusbands are a rarity, and the concept of bringing children to a nursery at work, although a sound and practical solution, is still a pipe dream. (By the way, you will find the services of a weekly housekeeper mandatory.)

After the children reach a certain age, they should be willing to assume some responsibility for themselves. This should not put impossible demands on you, and you should learn to delegate responsibility to them. Although she kept her managing and mothering roles distinct, the finance executive and mother of five felt the delegation of responsibility was common to both: "Having children is the best training in the world to be a manager. You stroke their egos, you hand them some responsibility, and they develop the ability to make their own decisions. I found that as my management skills increased at the office, I was also a better manager at home. I trained my children to be self-sufficient, just like I do my employees." Running a household and a department both require managerial skills, and both of them will be easier for you as you develop those skills, but unless you have a supportive husband, successfully combining children and career is virtually impossible.

The Corporate Husband

Although I am dubious about the merits of mixing children and career, I think marriage and career can blend harmoniously. Almost half of the executive women I interviewed are married. This seems to prove that marriage and career can work for some people. The key to marriage success is to find the proper sort of man who appreciates your zest for business life instead of feeling threatened by it. You need a man who is understanding and supportive, and if you can find such a mate, he can be an asset to your career.

Corporations have been known to openly evaluate the wives of male job candidates to determine if the applicant's wife would be supportive in his career. This includes being understanding when he would work late and being an asset to him socially. Books have been written on the proper behavior for wives of corporate executives. Having the right kind of wife and an appropriate number of children is still considered an asset for a man applying for a job.

Corporations may not evaluate your husband to see if he would be a suitable mate for an executive, but *you* should. You cannot successfully merge career and marriage unless you have a supportive husband who takes your career as seriously as you do. As a University of Michigan study said, "The major problem in a dual-career marriage is that men do not take their wives' careers seriously." If you do not have the right kind of husband, you will reach a point in your relationship where one or the other will have to be sacrificed.

Getting the man in your life to be helpful and supportive can be a gradual process of education or it can be one of the basic tenets of the marriage. But one thing is for sure. He cannot be a male chauvinist. Your career will not allow you to live up to a sexist husband's expectations of your role in the marriage. You cannot peacefully cohabitate with a person who is intrinsically opposed to the lifestyle you have chosen.

The man in your life should possess a multitude of qualities. He should strive to fit the model of the ideal "Corporate Husband."

1. The Corporate Husband has an ego like Muhammed Ali.

He is not threatened by your success, and he is proud of you if you make more money than he does. He sees every career move you make as a reflection on his good judgment in picking a mate, and he considers himself lucky to be paired with such an ambitious and successful woman.

2. The Corporate Husband does not expect you to be home whenever he is.

He does not expect you to be there every night waiting for him, and he doesn't mind starting dinner if he arrives first. If you attend a business meeting in the evening, he understands and does not hassle you if you come home later than anticipated.

3. The Corporate Husband shares in the housework.

And you don't feel guilty about asking him to do it, ei-

ther. He does not expect you to pick up after him. You
can't have a husband who nags you because the bureau
needs dusting or he's out of clean socks. If he's truly bothered, he'll simply have to do it himself.

4. The Corporate Husband is not overly jealous.

He understands that you must spend time with other
men. If you are having dinner with a male associate, he
will accept that it is just business, and he won't interrogate
you when you arrive home.

**5. The Corporate Husband understands that your job re-
quires you to travel.**

Indeed, he will make a special effort to be helpful
around the house while you are gone.

**6. The Corporate Husband sympathizes with your struggle
for equality.**

If he is offered a promotion that would require your
moving, he puts your job in front of his. But if you were
offered a promotion out of state, he would gladly move
because he knows how much more difficult it is for you to
get a job than for him.

**7. The Corporate Husband understands that you can't al-
ways accompany him when he entertains clients.**

He realizes that you have other things to do and that if
he insisted you go he would be placing undue hardships on
you.

8. The Corporate Husband isn't on his own power trip.

The Ivy League study conducted by David Winter,
Abigail Stewart, and David McClelland concluded that
power-motivated men are a poor risk for career women.
The study found that the higher his wife rose in her
career, the worse a power-motivated man felt.

Solutions to Conquering the Divide

The best solution to conquering the "great dual-career
divide" is to find a man who fits the profile of the ideal
Corporate Husband. But such a person is easy to create on
paper, yet in reality he is virtually impossible to find. How

to make dual-career marriages work is not only a constant topic at dinner tables, in bedrooms, and in magazine articles, but it's a growing concern of psychological and sociological studies. At a time when society is in transition, so is marriage. Unfortunately, there is no magic solution to the problem.

Establishing priorities is the first step, however. If you expect your relationship to work, your marriage must share equal importance with your career—for both of you. Sometimes you'll need to put your work in the drawer and devote some special attention to him. And he should do the same for you. Sometimes you must give your relationship first priority.

The task before your man and you is to find new solutions, new terms of agreement, new arrangements. Your expectations of your marriage will change, and you will have to refashion your expectations of each other, too. Your only chance for a successful dual-career marriage is through compromise and communication. Without this, underlying currents of resentment and jealousy will slowly erode your relationship until it is eventually destroyed. I know of no way to avoid this unless it is through frank and honest communication, with much giving on both sides.

To keep your marriage healthy, you and your partner cannot be competitive with each other. Dr. Irene Kassorla, in her book *Putting It All Together* (New York: Hawthorn Books, 1975), says that the partnership of competitive people is almost certain to fail.

Couples who have arrived at dual-career solutions have done so by devising unique agreements that are practical for their individual situation. You must also approach the dilemma creatively. Here's how a transportation executive and her husband did it:

> A few times in my career Jack has put pressure on me to drop out. But most of the time he is very supportive. But there's pressure on both of us at all times. He's under pressure with his career to travel often, and he would like me to go with him. And there's tremendous pressure on me with my job.
>
> I'm a morning person, so I get up at four to read my mail, and by seven I'm having my first meeting.

I'm usually at the office until seven. Jack is a night person. He gets up about nine or so, and this is right for his career. He's in the sports entertainment field, so he works during the day and attends sporting events at night. But I'm exhausted by ten. We've had conflict over the schedules, but we're learning to work it out.

Now I will go out at night only for Jack's business. I just recently learned how to get up and excuse myself from a basketball game or tennis match. When I get really tired, I leave. I make arrangements to have my own car there so I can. This way I can be with Jack for some of the time. At first I felt guilty about leaving. I thought my role was to be there. But I fell asleep on his shoulder during a Warrior's playoff game with 40,000 screaming people in the stands, which didn't please him much. You learn by mistakes, and I decided I was never going to go through that again. I told him that either I would stay home in the evenings, or we have an understanding that I could leave when I became too tired. So far this has worked out, but we are constantly readjusting to meet each other's needs.

This same ambitious lady was previously vice-president for a Los Angeles-based airline. Since her husband's business was in San Francisco, they kept a home at each place. They would commute to one or the other on the weekends. By innovative thinking, they have arrived at solutions that are workable for them.

If you are one of the lucky ones who finds a satisfactory relationship, it can be a wonderful enrichment in your life. Having the right kind of husband can be a great help to you in your career. Moreover, you won't stay married out of economic need, but from choice. So what you'll receive from marriage is companionship and comfort, love and security. Isn't that what it's all about?

❧ 15 ❧

Strategies for Success

If you were going to be an actress or a model, you almost certainly would hire a manager who, for a percentage of your income, would chart your career path. Your manager would give you advice on how to approach getting jobs, where to look, and how you should behave. As your career progressed, your manager would steer you in the right direction, help you evaluate opportunities, and help negotiate a salary for you.

As a business executive, you have no one but yourself to rely on to determine what is the best career path for you. You are your own manager. You must make decisions about changing job responsibilities or employers, requesting a higher salary or more authority, and, in general, keeping yourself upwardly mobile. You must be able to analyze yourself to determine where you have your strongest capabilities, and which of these skills are marketable on the executive scene.

There is no set path that works for everybody regarding career planning. You have many alternatives, and the path that you choose depends on your background, your experience, your education, your particular talents, whether they be verbal or numerical, and the kind of industry that you select. But no matter how you go about accomplishing it, you should have a goal in mind. After you have taken inventory of yourself, you should set your objectives realistically so that they are attainable, but not so low that they are limiting. As a woman, you may still have a problem seeing yourself in a position of authority. Don't assume that just because a woman has never done a particular job, that it is beyond your reach. If you expect to get anywhere, you must think big. You are in control of your own career path. View the business world as your arena, and not just a man's world. Don't be afraid to shoot for the stars.

Charting Your Career Path

There are advantages to starting your career in a large company. There are also advantages in a small company. Large companies usually have management training programs, formal or informal, and they hire trainees right out of school. A college education is a prerequisite for most of these programs, and having a master's degree in business administration is preferable. The larger the company, the more competition you face for jobs, and playing a good game of office politics is mandatory for success.

If you start your career at a smaller company, the threat of inter-departmental politics is less. As the company grows, you can grow with it. Once you feel confident of your job skills and have earned a certain degree of responsibility, you can move on to a larger company, where the potential is greater. You can work your way up through a smaller company faster than in the large firm, but you are apt to earn less. Nevertheless, once you gain experience at a smaller firm, you can make a lateral move to a larger corporation, and keep the same title with an increase in salary.

Any kind of career building takes time. Be prepared to pay your dues, especially in the first few years. But if you regard each job as a stepping stone to a higher position, and not an end unto itself, and if you consider the time you spend on menial jobs as an investment, your receptive attitude will make those first few years worthwhile. How you handle the opportunities that are afforded you is up to you.

Another part of your career strategy is deciding when you should change jobs. Many male executives escalate their career climb by job-hopping, staying at each company only a few years, and moving on to a better job at a new place. During my interviews, I discovered that the women who had progressed the fastest were those who had changed jobs a number of times. Their credentials were impressive enough, both in work experience and college, to make them a valuable commodity on the job market. A certain amount of job-hopping can indicate aggressiveness and drive, two positive traits of successful executives, and if you possess the self-confidence to pull it off, it can be a good strategy for you.

The prevailing attitude among the women I interviewed, however, was that job-hopping for them was unacceptable. One said, "I think job-hopping to extremes is dangerous for a man or a woman because you get an unreliable work history. It's even more dangerous for a woman because there's already enough prejudice against women, and the chance of getting into a prejudiced situation somewhere else is greater. I would rather remain and work my way up through my company than risk it somewhere else."

Since women traditionally do not enjoy the benefit of doubt that men automatically receive in starting a new job (men are expected to succeed whereas women are expected to fail at management jobs), the advantage of staying with one company is that you don't need to constantly reprove yourself. Male chauvinistic management may agree to give women executive jobs, but many are reluctant to bring a woman in from the outside. Since she is an unknown, they are unsure of whether or not she might be a "troublemaker." There is reason to believe that management is more inclined to promote women from within, that is, women who are familiar to them, rather than strangers.

One way to get promoted from within is to get management to create a new job for you. I know of one enterprising lady who, when a secretary, saw a need for a new managerial slot in the department, suggested it to her boss, and asked for the job herself. He agreed with her, and gave her the job immediately. And since she was the first person to hold the new position, she gained visibility to higher-ups. The first person to hold a new job has a good chance of being seen. Remember this strategy.

Having a job with visibility is important for career climbing. Some jobs allow for more visibility than others.

Routine jobs, which, unfortunately, many women have, are nonvisible. If you have a humdrum job, try to do something out of the ordinary, like suggesting the reorganization of your department, or recommending a new system, or even proposing a new product.

When women are passed over for promotions, it is often because they don't make their desire to be promoted known. They sit around waiting to be asked, and then wonder why they are continually passed by. A successful journalist told me the best advice she had ever received was from a boss who told her, "Figure out what you want to do, and then ask for it. At least, on a short-term basis, always have a goal." If you wish to accelerate your career climb, you must always be thinking in terms of reaching the next step on the ladder. You should be preparing yourself for the next step, and you should alert management that you are doing so. Be aggressive about making your ambitions known. To be promoted from within, you must be your own publicity agent. Be certain that those in power are aware of your contributions and your capabilities.

It is essential that you maintain career visibility outside your company if you plan to accelerate your career by changing jobs. That means attending trade shows and conventions, belonging to professional societies, writing articles for professional journals, and maintaining ties with former colleagues. Job-hopping is only possible if you know the kind of work available and maintain connections that will inform you of opportunities as they arise. Successful job-hoppers are social types who have friends at every company.

For many reasons, successful job-hoppers don't burn bridges when they leave a job. They may end up back at the original company or work for the same person at another company. This happened to me. I left a secretarial position to take my first nonclerical job writing promotional copy for a magazine publisher. I took the new job at nearly the same salary because it was an opportunity to escape the secretarial slot. Less than a year later I was hired back by the original company to be their advertising manager at twice the salary I was receiving when I left. If I had not made that decision to leave (and it was a tough one because I liked the firm and enjoyed working there), I might still have been sitting there typing letters and filing.

Whichever avenue you choose for career advancement, the best one depends on your unique situation. As your own manager, it is up to you to make things happen for yourself, and you can do this by keeping your wits about you.

Here is a delightful story told to me by a San Francisco executive on how she got to be a manager.

> My first job when I arrived in San Francisco was working as an assistant to a man who was a sales rep for a company that sold radio time. After I had been there about a year, another company called looking for my boss to offer him a job. He was in Europe at the time, so I told them I would like to interview for the job. Since the job entailed starting a new office for the firm, I convinced them if they hired me, they wouldn't have to hire a secretary. I told them I could do all the typing and filing, and they would save money.
>
> Well, they hired me, and I was here about a year when they decided to hire a man to come in and run the office. I wasn't going to be his secretary. We were both going to sell, but my boss made it very clear that I would work for the new man. He had worked for big, important companies and had much more experience than I, so I accepted the arrangement reluctantly.
>
> The first day he came we had lunch together and I told him where I was at. I told him that my ego was hurt by his coming in and taking over the office, but I knew he had a lot of experience and could teach me a lot about the business, so I was looking forward to the education. I told him that as long as we kept everything split down the middle like we had agreed, everything would work out fine. That meant he was going to do his own typing, and we'd split the filing.
>
> Doing his own typing and filing was demeaning to this man in his forties who had always worked with large companies, and had always had secretaries do that for him. But I soon realized that I knew more about the business than he did, that he had only

worked for large companies where he didn't have to sell very hard. I ended up teaching him how to read a rating book. I told my boss what a loser he was, but he told me I was just nursing a hurt ego, and that I should mind my own business.

Well, the new guy lasted about three months. I ended up covering for him all the time. I was on tranquilizers the whole time because it upset me so much. I really cared about the company, and to him it was just another job, and he couldn't have cared less. He finally got fired. After it was all over, my boss came to me and complimented me on not trying to bad-mouth the other guy. He told me that he would have defended him anyway, and not listened to me. As a businesswoman, you must constantly re-establish your credibility.

Today she is undisputed manager of the firm's San Francisco office. She got there by knowing when to speak up and knowing when to keep quiet. Keep this in mind when planning your own career path.

Tokenism

Hiring token women is a gesture by corporations to compensate for past injustices against women. An appropriate number of minorities in management positions salves the company's social conscience. In reality, tokenism is another form of discrimination, for the practice concedes that discrimination exists, but by giving a woman a token job, the company reinforces the myth that women are not capable of competing with men. Often, a token woman will be given a good title, respectable salary, and the fringe benefits that go along with executive life, but any real power will be withheld from her. She is put into a powerless position so that her supposed irrationality will not harm the company. Others on the same level will resent her.

But tokenism is better than nothing. Several women with whom I talked mentioned that they had started their careers with token jobs, but once inside the company, they were able to gain real power by performing well. One woman said she had a respectable title, but once she detected tokenism, she went to other firms in her industry and was given a real job with responsibility because of her experience working for the first firm. She claims that if she had not started out as a token, she would never be where she is today.

If a token job is the only kind that you can get, then you would be foolish to refuse it. Suppose you had a choice of starting out as a secretary or a token "manager." You would be better off starting out as a token in a management job, for once you secure your position, you can change the job from within. When a chauvinistic management learns that you can make contributions, they will be more than eager to utilize your talents in a real capacity. And even as a token, you will have more visibility than you will as a secretary, and if you maximize your opportunities, you can turn the job into something meaningful.

Traditional vs. Non-traditional Jobs

Now that the business community recognizes that women are on the job scene to stay, some of its inherent prejudices are melting away. These prejudices are a long way from disappearing altogether, but the business community is altering its attitudes toward businesswomen.

For example, many men have told me that it has been their experience that female executives are usually twice as good as their male counterparts. I've heard men say that they hate to sell against a woman, for a woman who has perfected selling techniques is much more persuasive than a man. And, in fact, there is some truth to this argument, not because women are naturally superior to men, but because the women who have succeeded have *had* to be twice as good as their male counterparts. This attitude can work in your favor. Once you have reached a certain level of success, some men will believe that you are better at your job than you actually are, merely because you are a woman.

The majority of men, unfortunately, don't feel this way, but even the die-hards among them are starting to soften their attitudes toward women. Expecting society to change its attitudes about women overnight is unrealistic. The business community is a society in transition. Men who a few years ago believed that women couldn't successfully compete have altered their viewpoints to believe that women can compete in certain select areas in certain job functions.

If you are looking for the easiest place to build your career, look toward job categories that take advantage of sexist assumptions. For example, look first to industries that cater to women, such as cosmetics, fashion, food, or housing. These are some of the biggest industries, and a male chauvinist management in these types of companies can justify to themselves why you would be an asset to them.

Women are thought to be naturally inclined toward writing and communication skills, which is why you find so many in advertising and public relations. Another assumption is that women have an intuition about people. This is why women have made in-roads in personnel departments. Women are being readily accepted as bookkeepers, purchasing agents, and media buyers, stat analysts and market researchers, because women are assumed to be good at detail. These are all sexist assumptions that you can use to your advantage, especially early in your career.

You may have aspirations to become plant manager in a manufacturing plant, but you will have an easier time securing a position if you apply to the marketing department. Once you get into the marketing or personnel department and develop some credibility there, then you have a better chance of reaching your first goal. This is certainly not the most efficient way to secure your goal, nevertheless, compromises may be necessary to overcome the prejudice against you.

Getting in initially is your primary objective. Obtaining that first job is the hardest part of all. Once you gain experience, credibility, and contacts, you can springboard yourself to other jobs that are still masculine domains. But you first need to get in the door.

I am not suggesting, however, that you should take the easiest route in charting your career. For one thing, you may want a non-traditional job because that is what you would like to do. Then by all means go after it.

But there's another reason why you should consider non-traditional occupations, and that is the matter of money. According to *Women's Work Book* by Karin Abarbanel and Gonnie McClung Siegel (New York: Praeger, 1975) you're more apt to get paid well in a non-traditional occupation where the pay scales haven't already been adjusted for women. But most executive jobs are non-traditional, which is why you're apt to be paid very well.

General vs. Specialized Management

There has long been a debate in corporate America over the virtues of general vs. specialized management for success in top executive jobs. *Dun's Review and Modern Industry,* which surveyed the 250 largest United States corporations, found that 18.5 percent of the companies were headed by men who had come up through general management rather than through a specialty. This was the largest single source of company presidents.

Although general management may be the best route for men, I believe that specialization is a better route for women. Having a specialized job skill, rather than only general management skill, is more apt to get *you* a job in today's business climate. And if the economy takes a downward turn, you are more apt to keep your job if you have a specialized skill. All the women I interviewed had a particular job skill, even though many of them now would fall into the general management category.

Business Week agrees with my findings. In a 1970 article, they say, "To a large extent, specialized expertise is the woman's trump card in many executive situations. The lawyer who wins most of her cases, the account executive whose advertising campaigns sell millions of products, the tax analyst who saves her company huge sums all have an advantage over the woman who merely 'manages' however well."

The Mentor Relationship

A mentor is a guide who counsels and teaches a younger person in a paternalistic fashion. Promising young executives are often taken under the wing of an older person who can give them valuable insights into business and act

206 *Strategies for Success*

as a sounding board for decision making. In one sense, the mentor relationship in business is equivalent to an informal apprenticeship. Both sides benefit from the arrangement. The mentor receives the satisfaction of watching the student grow, and the apprentice enjoys the benefits of the mentor's experience.

Behind many successful young business people is a mentor who has helped pave the way. This has always been true for men, and there is reason to believe that it is also true for women. Most of the women I interviewed acknowledged that there were one or more mentors who had assisted them in their careers. In her 1970 Harvard doctoral study of twenty-five high-level women executives, entitled "Career Development for Women Executives," Dr. Margaret Hennig discovered that early in their careers each woman had a male mentor who had guided her along.

Developing a mentor relationship with a person with influence is probably the most effective career strategy for anybody. The problem for women is that most of the available candidates are men. It is obvious that the older man receives satisfaction from nurturing a male because he sees something of himself in the younger man. He cannot as readily identify with you. The logical source for your mentor is another woman. However, if you can find one who is in a position to help you, you are lucky, for such women are few and far between.

In an article in *New York Magazine,* based on material in her book *Passages: Predictable Crises of Adult Life* (New York: E. P. Dutton, 1976), author Gail Sheehy claims that the problem with a male mentor to female apprentice relationship is the threat of sexual intentions on the man's part. She says, "When a man becomes interested in guiding and advising a younger woman, there is usually an erotic interest that goes along with it." But I, like so many women, have been fortunate to have had several male mentors who helped boost my career. I was never aware of any erotic interests from them, nor could I uncover any such problems with the women I interviewed.

One Midwest executive attributed her notable job success to a mentor, her boss. When I asked her if she had any problems with sexual overtones, she just laughed and said, "I do have a problem with my boss right now, but it has nothing to do with sex. The problem now is my next step is his job. In companies like this one, you must keep moving, and now I have nowhere to go unless he gets promoted, too."

At a certain period in your career, your mentor will finish his usefulness to you, and it may be necessary to discard him. Dr. Hennig found that the twenty-five women she studied had all remained dependent on their mentors until age thirty-five, at which point these women made other drastic changes in their lives.

Achieving a mentor relationship with an older person is like falling in love—you can't force it to happen, and it only works if the chemistry is right. You can, however, make yourself receptive to such a relationship by displaying a teachable attitude and an eagerness to learn. If you set about to find a mentor and you stumble across a suitable candidate, you need to bring out the paternal instincts in him. And you should practice the art of stroking the male business ego as outlined in Chapter 3.

But just like a doting parent, your mentor can be overprotective of you and try to save you from the harsh realities of business life. You do not need to be protected, but you do need to learn how to deal with problems. He can help you by teaching you how to solve them.

Up from Secretary

To those scores of capable and ambitious secretaries who are wondering if they can ever escape the bondage of the steno pad, the answer is unequivocally and joyfully YES! You can shake the shackles of the secretarial syndrome and rise toward the realm of executivedom. Over half the executive women I interviewed did it. So did I. Making the jump from secretary to manager is possible for you, too.

Your biggest handicap is the sexist business system which continues to typecast. You were hired to be a secretary. You are functioning as a secretary. And you will continue to be seen as a secretary unless you do something about it. The burden is on you to create an image for yourself which broadcasts that you have managerial capabilities and talents. You must take positive action on your own behalf.

Only a few enlightened bosses will search to discover your potential, and many more will fail to recognize it when it is demonstrated to them. Most just don't think of secretaries in management terms. Consequently, climbing from secretary to manager is seldom easy. Escaping a stereotype that is being constantly reinforced requires a diligent effort on your part. But I can offer some insights as to how other women accomplish it.

1. *Read what you type.*

Sitting right in front of you, in your typewriter, is the easiest way for you to gain some knowledge about the operations of your company. Merely understanding what you are typing is the obvious way to begin learning about your boss's job. I know from being a secretary myself that, especially on busy days, the temptation is to proofread for typing errors only, and then go on to the next assignment. But take a few minutes to read what you type for content. Try to understand why the document was issued, what it means, and what the expected results are. Most important communications in business are typed, and you'll have access to most of them. From this, you can begin learning what your boss actually does.

2. *Read your boss's mail.*

Again, the temptation is to skim the mail quickly so that it can be sorted and distributed efficiently. But take a few extra minutes to *read* the correspondence that comes across your desk. You'll see responses to letters and memos that you've typed, and you'll begin to understand their impact.

Circulating memos or copies of internal correspondence provide excellent sources for more intelligence about corporate goings-on. Read and ponder. Consider the implications of the communication. From this, determine how your boss's function fits into the scheme of the entire company and how the various departments interact. Understanding your department's function and how it contributes to the entire operation are keys to becoming a manager.

If you're new at a job and have managerial aspirations, you'd be wise to read correspondence files dating from prior to your arrival. You can get a flavor for what's been transpiring and accelerate your learning.

3. Ask questions. Observe. Absorb.

So many secretaries sit at their desk with blinders on, not taking advantage of all that is happening around them. You can begin to remove those blinders by paying attention to communications. Once you have a general view of what is going on and you have some basis for understanding (or at least knowing what you don't know), you can begin to ask intelligent questions.

The reason to ask questions, obviously, is to learn all you can. If you employ timing empathy, you'll be amazed at the receptiveness you'll encounter. But the advantage of asking questions goes beyond that. By asking intelligent, thoughtful questions, your boss will notice you as someone more than the typical secretary who only does what she's required, nothing more. You'll demonstrate an interest in your environment and a desire to learn more about it. More times than not, your teachers will be eager and delighted to impart such information. There's a whole education in your company that's available merely for the asking.

I was able to start an advertising agency at a young age because I possessed a specialized knowledge about the marketing of electronics and computers. I gained the basis of my knowledge when I was a secretary. I worked for the marketing department of an electronics company, and my tasks included typing lengthy technical proposals on the complex systems we manufactured. The technical jargon was all gibberish to me, and I had no idea if what I was typing was even a sentence—none of it made any sense. I was curious about the meaning behind all those strange words, but I didn't know even where to begin learning.

One afternoon I discovered that the engineers in systems assembly (the department that hooked all the magic boxes together) were regularly working overtime. So I began to spend time every day after work watching them assemble the equipment and asking them questions. They were flattered by the attention, and I received an education.

Once I began to understand the language and the basics of the technology, the activities of the marketing department all began to make sense. Because of my interest, my

boss made a point of discussing with me the strategies behind what was happening. The invaluable knowledge that I
gained as a secretary was the cornerstone of my career.

4. Learn all you can about your products and your indus-
try.

Besides assimilating all that is happening around you,
you should make an extra effort to gain knowledge about
your company's products and industry. Much printed
material is readily available to you. Obtain copies of your
company's annual reports. Ask to see your advertising and
brochures, and discover what the firm says about itself.
Read industry newspapers and trade journals. Attending
evening classes that are related to your job function offers
another opportunity to further prepare yourself. If you do
enroll in courses, be sure those in command are aware of
it and that records of your pursuits are placed in your personnel file.

By taking this initiative, you will prepare yourself for
managerial responsibilities. Inundate yourself with information. Those who can see how their function and
company fits into their industry and into the economy in
general are the most likely candidates for executive chambers.

5. Make your aspirations known.

From the day you interview for the job, you should
make your aspirations known. Management won't simply
assume you want something more. It's up to you to speak
up and ask for the opportunity for advancement. You
must be aggressive on your own behalf, and you must constantly remind them. An executive told me about how she
was promoted from secretary after she discovered the
secret of making her desires known:

I was secretary to a vice-president with whom I
had worked for some time. One day a resumé came
in to him from a woman who was a college graduate
in a certain field. He put a note in the margin to personnel that we could use people like this within the
organization, and that the company should talk with
her. He gave the application to me to pass along to

the personnel department. I read over the resumé and realized she had her degree in the same field as mine. I went to him and said, "Wait a minute, what about me? I have the same background as this woman." My boss said he had forgotten all about my college background, and that it had never occurred to him that I would be interested in a management job. I set him straight, and the next job opening that came up was offered to me.

6. See yourself as more than a secretary.

Throughout this book I have been preaching the necessity for a positive self-image as a prerequisite for executive success, and the message is doubly important for aspiring secretaries. You're a woman, so in management's eyes that's one strike against you. And you'll continue to be seen as a secretary unless you take aggressive steps toward altering your image.

But you can't convince others that you possess managerial capabilities unless you are convinced yourself. You must *believe* that you are a suitable candidate for advancement, and your positive attitude will eventually be reflected by others. Your career aspirations must fit comfortably with your self-image.

7. Be professional.

One executive woman told me that even when she was a secretary, she always dressed in a businesslike fashion, and that fact, she believed, helped propel her career climb. Maintain a degree of decorum in your dress and help create a professional image for yourself.

The importance of your professional demeanor carries over into other areas, too. Your actions will say a great deal about your management potential. Be willing to work extra hours when necessary, and demonstrate that you are a "team player." Be loyal to your boss and your company, and look out for their better interests, which, in turn, become yours. Keep confidential information to yourself, and avoid partaking in office gossip. Show management that you are on their side. You must demonstrate these qualities before they will allow you to enter the competition.

8. *Attach yourself to a fast-moving boss.*

The type of boss you have is crucial to your ability to progress through the company. If your boss works in a vital, growing area, you can seize upon the opportunity to advance with him, assuming more administrative and managerial duties as he progresses. After several years, he could continue moving upward, and leave you behind to fill a space he just vacated. Many women executives that I spoke with built their career in just that fashion.

The kind of boss that you *don't* want is the one who has you do all the work, and then takes credit for it himself. And since you are so invaluable, he selfishly won't let you move on. Or he's such a male chauvinist, he truly believes that women are suitable for nothing more than secretarial work, even though you have proven otherwise. Who your boss is plays a critical factor in your ability to escape the secretarial stereotype. Choose your boss as carefully as he chooses you.

If You Are Fired or Laid Off

Once you secure a management position, especially in a large company, the fact that you are a woman, and therefore needed for the firm to comply with government regulations, helps immunize you from company layoffs. Your being a woman might even save you from getting fired in some situations. But for the most part, you are subject to the corporate ax like any other executive, and you should be prepared to face the reality that one day it could happen to you. Getting fired or laid off is no disgrace and is all part of the normal ebb and flow of business. People come and people go, and the cycle of job changing continues.

Once you get over the initial shock of being terminated, your first concern might be, "What will everyone else think?" Don't let this attitude bog you down. Anybody with any business experience knows that people leave jobs for many reasons, including cut-backs and politics, internal reorganization, and the like. Incompetency is just one reason among many. Don't be ashamed to face your friends or colleagues, as they may be a great source of new job leads.

The minute you learn of your unplanned departure, immediately begin looking for another job, even if the company has given you a week or two notice. Chances are they will be very understanding of your search so don't delay it for reasons of "loyalty" to your former employer. It's important that you begin looking immediately. You'll eliminate a wad of needless worry by taking positive action on a potential problem (unemployment). The longer you procrastinate, the harder it will be for you to begin looking. The key is to start immediately.

A calming device on the unemployment blues is to have some money in the bank set aside for an emergency such as this. If you are too desperate, you can be tempted into grabbing the first opportunity that comes along rather than giving yourself a chance to consider all that is available. And during your interviews, your attitude should not be one of desperation, because it will affect the way you relate. Somehow, the less you seem to need the job, the more apt you are to get it. This is one of the idiosyncracies of corporate America that is hard to explain. But in any case, it is certainly true.

Leaving a Job

"I resigned four times from my job to get what I wanted," an assertive female executive told me. She had used the technique of threatening to leave in order to get what she wanted. In order for you to do this, however, you must be fairly secure within your position, or you might find yourself out on the street. Some companies will react negatively to this kind of manipulation.

It's a far better rule never to quit a job unless you have another one lined up. You should also never quit in anger. If you quit in a fit of temper, you might be sorry later. Give yourself at least one night to settle down and clear your head before you sever your employment ties. Another reason why you should not quit in a fit of anger is that during a period of uncontrollable rage you may say things that you will later regret. Remember that you need the company for a reference. You may even want to return there some day, as I did during my career climb. Avoid burning bridges behind you.

One way to resign is by letter. A brief, concise statement is all that is necessary. A few lines like "This letter is to inform you of my resignation from your employment effective (a future date)." It's good form to give at least two weeks' notice, although this can be difficult if your new employer wishes you to start immediately. There is a good chance that your former employer will ask you to leave as soon as it is practical. Having someone around who is leaving the firm can be bad on the morale of the other employees, and management knows it.

Looking for a Job

If you already have a job and are looking for another one, there are two ways you can go. You can either call a few of your contacts who can be relied upon to be discreet and ask them if they have any openings. You can also use employment agencies, called "head hunters." Head hunters are executive placement services that promise confidentiality. Their fees are paid by companies that hire them to find managers. Using head hunters or discreetly using a few personal contacts are the best ways to look for a job if you already have one.

When you look for a job, start with your business contacts or friends. They can furnish inside information about openings that you would not learn of through personnel departments. Often a friend can tell you of a job opening in his own company. That's why having friends throughout the industry is important. The contacts you make can be valuable assets when you are looking for a job.

Here's a job-finding approach that one Midwest executive told me about: "The longer I stay in business, the more I feel that employee selection is an irrational process. It's very helpful to know someone. Whenever a woman asks me about how she should apply for a job, I suggest that she write the president of the company rather than the personnel department. The president of the company will look at the application and send it down to the personnel department, but then it comes from the president, and not from her. I have seen this technique work."

If you do not get any response by going through the company president, then go ahead and send another letter to the personnel department. Each time you send a letter, include a copy of your resumé. The resumé can be duplicated, but each letter that you send should be personalized. State in your letter that you will be calling to see if the firm would be interested in setting up an interview. Indicate in your letter the specific day you plan to call, and then make a note to yourself to do it on that day. Demonstrate by this that you are good at following up, a desirable trait for managers.

Your resumé must emphasize your contributions and experience. If you have little experience, but do have a college degree and an outstanding grade point, put those at the top of the paper and bury your work experience toward the end. If you have worked before, give your job title and describe your responsibilities in full. A job title alone will not give a prospective employer enough information to determine what you actually did. If you don't have any notable job experience, emphasize your other involvements and interests. If you have worked on a political campaign or done some charity work, also give that, as at least it shows experience doing something. Take an inventory of your strongest points and put them on the resumé first.

Many experienced executives who have worked for only one or two companies have never written a resumé for themselves and are at a loss when circumstances require that they have one. Much information is available about how to write the resumé that will do the best sales job for you. If you don't know how to write one, go to the library and find out (there are several books available on management- and executive-level job-hunting) or get the help of a reputable executive placement service. Approach writing a resumé like you would advertising copy, but instead of selling a product, you are selling yourself. Your resumé is your brochure.

The Interview

The final decision to hire you will probably hinge upon your prospective employer's impressions of you during brief interviews. Usually you will be asked back for more than one session if the company is seriously interested in you. More care is taken in hiring employees in management jobs, so the higher the position, the longer it usually takes to make a decision. Thus you may have to endure several interviews before you land a management job.

Everyone experiences some nervousness before an interview, and your interviewer will take that into consideration. Nevertheless, you should appear as calm and self-confident as possible. As an executive, you must be able to withstand pressure, and how you conduct yourself during the interview gives insight into your personality. If you quiver at just the thought of an employment interview, it will help you to know that they become easier the more times you do them. I know a sales rep who says he actually looks forward to them for they give him an opportunity to demonstrate his sales ability. You may never reach a point where you eagerly anticipate job interviews, but at least you can learn not to dread them. Here are some tips on how to ease the pain of employment interviews.

The first rule is to allow plenty of time. Give yourself extra time in the morning so you can leisurely groom yourself to perfection. If you are interviewing for a new job during your normal work day and must invent a reason for time away, plan to be gone more hours than you think you'll need. Scheduling ample time will eliminate undue nervousness on your part in case you are caught in traffic or get lost. Instead, plan to arrive early. It makes a good impression and gives you a few minutes to catch your breath and collect your thoughts.

Dress conservatively for the interview and wear your best executive-type outfit (see Chapter 13, "Dressing for Success"). You will be judged on appearance. Whether you wear a pantsuit or a skirt is up to you, but you may want to follow the advice of one female executive who said, "When I interview with a woman I always wear pants. When the interview is with a man, I wear a skirt."

Practice answering typical questions that you might be asked before you get there. A typical question might be, "I've looked over your resumé, Ms. Fisher, but why don't you tell me a little about yourself?" When you answer this type of question, emphasize your contributions to profits and your achievements, e.g., "While at Whiz Manufacturing, I increased efficiency in my department by 20 percent while reducing the budget by 10 percent," or, "As a sales rep, I averaged 20 percent over quota for my territory," or, "As office manager, I headed the installation of a new computer system that cut bookkeeping costs in half." Cutting costs and increasing profits is music to corporate America's ears.

If you don't have much experience or achievements you can discuss, emphasize your willingness to learn and your desire to build a lifetime career. Especially if you are younger, you need to overcome an inherent prejudice against you, namely, that to you it is just a job and that as soon as you can afford it you will leave. Emphasize your career orientation and let them know you are serious about your endeavors.

Laws have been passed that protect women from being asked personal questions by job interviewers about marital status and childbearing plans. According to law, an employment interviewer may not solicit information regarding the applicant's marital status unless the inquiry "is made in good faith for non-discriminatory purposes." Nevertheless, you are wise to mention those topics yourself, as your assumed family responsibilities may be silent objections about hiring or promoting you.

If you are married, tell the interviewer that your husband is very supportive of your career, and he understands that you may have to work late. If the job requires traveling, mention that you have the arrangements for that worked out—provided that you do. If you have children, it's wise to mention that you have babysitting solved, as this may be a huge objection against you. Women with young children are considered the least desirable employees, for sick children can keep them home from work. To seriously pursue a career, you must make provisions for your home and child-rearing responsibilities, and you should let a future employer know what they are. Even though you may never get them to admit it, these are important considerations in hiring you.

I also think it is prudent to ask the interviewer if he sees any objections to a woman handling the job, especially if the position is non-traditional. The interviewer may be reluctant to mention it himself, but you can be sure he's thinking about it. Get him to raise his objections and then discuss them. If you ignore the issue, you have no way of overcoming the probable inherent objections toward you. Face the fact you must deal with these problems, and then deal with them positively.

Besides the special concerns you must respond to as a woman applicant, there are other areas of concern relevant to all job applicants, male and female. Research concerning decision making in employment interviews (see Battalia, O. William, and Tarrant, John J., *The Corporate Eunuch* [New York: Thomas Y. Crowell, 1973; Mentor paperback. The New American Library]) has isolated nine positive characteristics that interviewers look for in prospective employees. These are cooperativeness, ability to accept responsibility, dependability, trustworthiness, self-control, ability to get things done, conscientiousness, stability, and responsibility. Keep these characteristics in mind when you talk about yourself. Tell the interviewer what he wants to hear.

Usually salary is discussed toward the end of the interview. The interviewer may inquire about your salary requirements or your salary at your previous job. Answer him with a salary range and always speak in terms of annual salary, not monthly, weekly, or hourly wages. Executives always speak in terms of annual salaries. Don't be afraid to ask for a higher salary than you are currently earning, and, in fact, you should always at least try for more. But if the job appears to be a good step in your career climb, you might gain long-term benefits by taking a temporary salary cut.

If you don't get offered the salary you think you deserve, and you've reached an impasse in the negotiations with your interviewer, be willing to compromise on a lesser amount, to be reviewed, however, in ninety days. Demonstrate that you are willing to work with them, but be vocal about what your salary aspirations are. This ninety-day review procedure gives you an opportunity to prove yourself and does it without making your employer compromise his position.

When you are negotiating salary, fringe benefits should also be included in the discussion. Typical fringe benefits for executives include company cars, expense accounts, life insurance, health insurance, stock options, bonus or profit-sharing plans, and vacation time. At a higher level, executive demands include company airplanes, limousines, a multitude of assistants, country club memberships, and so on. These niceties serve as a tax advantage to you. After a certain salary bracket, the government takes a larger hunk of money. Fringe benefits are deductible for the company, and they are not taxed as income for you. They are a legal, tax-exempt way for the company to reward you. Negotiate fringe benefits as well as salary. (The law requires equality here, too!)

The interviewer may ask you if you have any questions about the company, and the kind of questions you ask will say something about you. After you have a clear understanding of what the job involves, make sure you know who you will report to and where you are on the ladder. Ask to see an organizational chart, and determine where you would fit in. Knowing where you fall among the chains of command will help you assess the prestige of the job.

You should be concerned about your long-term career potential at the company. Ask the interviewer about what kind of growth opportunities the company offers. Make sure you will not be stuck in a dead-end job. (Token jobs are often a dead end.) Tell the interviewer of your long-term career plans and discuss whether the company would be a desirable choice for you. By asking these types of questions, you are demonstrating your seriousness about pursuing a business life. You show your priorities are in order.

Also be concerned about the company as a whole—how profitable it is, what its future plans for expansion are, where the company expects to be in five years. Ask to see an annual report and see if the company is in a period of acceleration or of cutback. All companies go through these phases, and as a new hire, you should be wary of the company that appears to be on a downward slide, for you will be the first to be laid off. Investigate the company's potential, both as a vehicle for you and as an entity in the business world. You will go further if you join forces with a winner.

After all this discussion, ask the interviewer if he has any additional questions for you. Then ask when the firm plans to make a decision. He will probably tell you that he will get in touch with you in a few days, and then you must endure the agony of waiting. Seldom are you offered a job on the spot. But if you are, play it cool and act in control. Say that you would like to think about it for a few days, and then give your decision. Each career move that you make becomes part of your total career strategy. Carefully plot your path to maximize your potential. Make them anxious to hire you while giving yourself time to weigh your decision objectively. Playing a little hard to get will make you seem a little more valuable, human nature being what it is.

Above all in an interview, remember to relax. Take deep breaths or meditate, or do whatever you must to relax, but do it. The more self-confident and poised you appear, the better the impression you will make. If you are confident, you will look competent. It's as simple as that.

Asking for a Raise

In executive positions, salary reviews are usually done on an annual basis and are a formalized procedure within the company. There will be times, however, when you feel you merit more money, and you are assertive enough to do something about it. You have decided to ask for a raise.

To maximize your chances for an affirmative decision, you should develop timing empathy so you know when to ask for a raise. Plan your timing so it is just after some successful project you have completed and the memories of your recent victory are fresh in management's mind. Try to pick a time during the year when corporate earnings are doing well, increased profits or dividends have been announced, or a new product has been launched and sales are already over projection. These are the times management will be in a receptive state of mind. Approach them when they are thinking bullish about the company. Certain times during the business month or quarter will be more hectic than the rest. Avoid approaching your boss right before his monthly report is due or when you know he must make a presentation before the board of directors. It's better to hit him right after such a deadline is past, for he will be basking in the relief that he feels having the project over.

If you are going to ask for your raise in person, use the

techniques of timing empathy to determine when is the best part of the day to approach your boss. Your boss could be most receptive first thing in the morning, right after lunch, or after work hours when interruptions are at a minimum. Determine which is his best time. You should also practice timing empathy on yourself and gauge your own reactions. If you are groggy until noon, then approach your boss in the afternoon. You should also avoid any discussion right before or during your period or any other high stress time for you.

I feel the best method for asking for a raise is to write a confidential memo to your boss outlining your request, and then following up with a face-to-face discussion. Some people automatically say no if they are caught by surprise. Writing a memo gives your boss time to consider your request without your pushing his back up against the wall.

When you talk about a raise, you should speak in terms of your increased contributions to the company. The fact that your job skills have increased through experience is really not reason enough, because you will probably receive an automatic raise for that every year. For a merit raise, speak in terms of your increased responsibility. Describe how you have cut costs, increased efficiency, or any other profit-generating tactic that you have employed. Measure your worth by your own contributions.

Asking for a raise because someone else at your level is making more money than you falls into the category of a teenager trying to convince his parents to let him do something because someone else is allowed to. Although you do have legal recourse if a man doing your identical job is earning more money than you, never ask for a raise, initially anyway, for that reason. Instead emphasize the contributions that *you* have made, and you are apt to find management in a more receptive mood.

If you know you are being discriminated against because of your sex, then you have a legal problem to deal with. The Equal Pay Act of 1963 prohibits "discrimination on account of sex in the payment of wages by employers." But some pay differentials are considered legitimate under the act. These are based on bona fide seniority, merit systems, piecework rates, or any system in which sex is not a factor. Before you have a legal case, you must first establish a violation, and this is not an easy thing to do. Although it will certainly leave a bad taste in the mouths of management, you can contact the Labor Department if you think your case is one of sex discrimination. But be prepared for the potential ramifications if you choose such a route. Flexing your legal muscle should be your final recourse, but be thankful that you have it when you need it.

The Woman in Sales

Not too long ago a friend and I were discussing the potential for women in sales positions. He had been a professional sales rep for some time and had trained several women in the vocation. "I think that women could actually do better than men in sales," he confessed, "but most of them don't have enough self-confidence. Once they have gotten over their initial nervousness, though, they really start to produce. Since I've had such a positive experience with women sales reps, I've recommended that the company hire more. We think women can be great assets in sales."

Increasingly more women are cropping up in sales positions across the country, as increasingly more companies are recognizing their potential. Donald B. Miller, chairman of the board of Rumrill-Hoyt advertising agency, at a recent meeting of the American Business Press, issued a call for more women business publication space reps. He said, "The salesman, for better or worse, personifies the publication for us. . . . From personal experience, I can tell you that women media reps are often far better prepared, far more organized, do a far better follow-up job, and think a lot faster on their feet than many of their male counterparts. To women, a sales call is an opportunity, not a duty. They come in with ideas, not just numbers and comparisons. They want to talk first about the client and his marketing opportunity and how their publications fits in, rather than simply talking about the publication itself."

A position in sales is an ideal springboard to other executive positions within the company, especially in marketing management. If you wish a job there, sales is practically the only way to go. A large percentage of top management have had sales jobs somewhere along the way. Working in sales also gives you a fantastic opportunity to grow. You gain an intimate knowledge of your company's products and markets while also learning about those of your customers, you escape the ennui connected with a desk job, and you enhance your circle of contacts by continually meeting new people. As a sales rep, you usually receive a company car and expense account, and often you travel.

One sales rep told me the reason she liked sales so much was that it offered complete accountability of results. Her previous job had been in a large department where her individual achievements did not shine. And often her boss took credit for her contributions. So she applied for a job in sales. "Each month our sales figures are reported to the sales manager. As my sales have increased, so has my prestige with the company. My contributions are highly visible, and I like it that way. No one can question my abilities," she said. She had discovered one rule of sales: your accomplishments are highly visible. But this can work either way. Your failures are also apparent. However, if you do well, you will be grateful for the accountability. If you are the right kind of person for sales, your results will sparkle, and so will your earnings. Successful sales reps are extremely well paid.

Not all women possess the right personality for sales. Unfair as it may seem, good looks are an asset. An extroverted, enthusiastic personality is desirable. Poise and good communication skills are essential. You must be a disciplined self-starter and enjoy working independently. These attributes describe the ideal sales personality. If you possess these qualities, you should seriously consider sales as a starting point for your career.

You go about getting a job in sales the same way you approach other positions. Often you will be placed in a sales training program sponsored by the company, especially if it is large. In a small firm, you will probably be trained by another person. Professional sales skills take training.

Many of the executives that I interviewed had sales experience, and several had started as secretaries in sales departments. As a San Francisco lady told me:

> I went to college for three years, majoring in physical education. The only job I could get was working

as a clerk in a camera shop, so I went to secretarial school. I worked as a secretary for several New York ad agencies before moving to San Francisco.

I took a secretarial job in San Francisco with the hopes of getting in sales. I worked for a sales rep, and I learned everything I could from him. He started letting me make sales calls on my own. The first year I wasn't even on commission, but my boss gave me a commission out of his own pocket for what I had sold. Now I have a salary, commission, and expense account of my own.

That is a typical example of how women have landed well-paid jobs by going through the secretarial route.

Although many people, including the salesman quoted at the beginning of this section, think that women can make better sales reps than men, I am still not convinced that any worthwhile job in business is easier for a woman. I spoke with each sales rep that I interviewed about her feelings on the subject. The conclusion to be drawn from their comments is this: it is easier for a woman to get an appointment or get through to a prospect on the telephone because of the curiosity factor, but it is harder to command respect once you get in. Because of your uniqueness, however, you are more apt to be remembered, and this gives you an advantage in sales. But as a woman, you must continually prove yourself. You do not receive the same benefit of doubt that a man earns just by being a man. So there is no real advantage being a woman, but then there is no real disadvantage either. In sales, your performance is up to you.

Your Best Strategy for Success: Initiative

I promised confidentiality to the women with whom I spoke, as many were concerned about the possible repercussions of their comments. With her permission, however, I do want to tell you about Beverly Kees, assistant managing editor of the *Minneapolis Tribune*, who at age thirty-five has been named a judge on the Pulitzer Prize panel. Her attitudes and initiative exemplify the type of woman who is successful in today's business climate. She is "opportunity prone." Here is the story of her career.

I went to the University of Minnesota as an English major. I began working on the *Minnesota Daily* as a freshman and soon decided to change my major to journalism. My senior year I became editor of the newspaper. I went to a luncheon sponsored by the *Minneapolis Star*. Although journalism students attended, I was the only person to ask them about job possibilities and the only one to actually land a job with the paper. My first job was in the women's department covering society and fashion.

Most women in business sit there like Lana Turner on a drugstore stool waiting to be discovered. But, as a veteran editor pointed out to me, if I wanted change, I'd have to do something about it. So, since I wanted a job in the business department, I took the initiative and turned in ten story ideas to the editor. He chose three, which I wrote. Then I applied for a job as business reporter and went on vacation. When I came back, I discovered that one of the business writers had quit and I had his job. If I hadn't taken the initiative, they would never have thought of me.

As a woman, I found I could ask basic questions about business and get away with it. Sometimes they would treat me like a child in their explanations, but I didn't mind as long as someone wasn't conning me. I learned a lot that way.

My first big break was when I was given the opportunity to head up the first special section on the newspaper, except it was about food. I took the job even though I was concerned about ending up back in the women's section. But things turned out well for me, and my section earned national recognition.

One day the publisher of the *Star* and *Tribune* called me into his office and said that they had decided to take certain people within the organization and move them into other departments for nine months or a year to learn other sides of the business. Frankly, I wasn't interested because I loved what I was doing. But I was no dummy either, and I knew that they were giving me an opportunity. The next day I was called in and told I was going to be assigned to the research and planning department.

It turned out to be a fascinating experience. I

learned how all the other departments in the paper operated and interacted. From that I was offered my present job as assistant managing editor of the *Minneapolis Tribune*.

I asked Beverly what she thought was the key to her success. "I am almost embarrassed to talk about success," she told me. "I don't feel I have achieved all that much. I still have a long way to go. I do have feelings that I should be doing more than I have, that I should be doing some more writing or something. I deliberately put myself into an insecure position so that I'll work harder," says this woman who has already been nationally recognized by her peers. But she does confide one key to her success. "I work hard, but most of the women who have made it around here have worked more and hard, too. I have always learned everything that I could, even though it wasn't my job. A lot of people are afraid to learn other skills, especially clerical functions, because they are afraid they will have to do them some day. You must take risks," she continued, "and women have been trained not to take them. We've been told that it's not feminine. We're taught to be good listeners, so rather than contribute, we listen to others."

I asked Beverly if she thought the women's movement had helped her in her career. "Oh yes," she replied. "When I started here in 1963, there was not one woman who wanted to be an editor. A few years later a woman with aspirations to the managing editor's position did join the paper, and everyone was appalled that she could be so brazen. I confess that I was a little shocked by it myself. Women simply didn't do that. Women didn't say they want to be president of the company some day, because that simply is not feminine. But now the women's movement has made these kinds of desires respectable. We're being told that it's now all right to be ambitious, and to want to achieve."

Many of the executives with whom I've spoken had as inspirational a story to tell as Beverly Kees', but I chose her story because she is so representative of the kind of woman who makes it in business—the woman who has the vision to see an opportunity and the assertiveness to do something about it. Indeed, Beverly Kees is "opportunity prone," but the opportunities did not just happen to her, she made them happen for herself. Let's review some of the reasons why Beverly Kees is a success, and maybe you can apply some of the same tactics toward your own career:

• When she was in college and attended a meeting held by a potential employer, she was the only person to actually ask for a job. She spoke up, and when she did, she positioned herself as a person serious about pursuing a career.

• She started in a traditional area, the women's section. But once she had a chance to prove herself on that job, she seized the opportunity to place herself in a non-traditional section—business. She did it on her own initiative.

• From there, she headed up a new project, one that gave her a vehicle to gain visibility in a large organization. As noted earlier, being the first person to head up something new is a great career strategy.

• She agreed to change her job responsibilities, and she kept flexible, even though she really didn't want to. She took risks, but she understood the opportunity that was afforded her.

• And her life-style says something about her dedication and drive. She has remained single so as to devote herself to her career. She understood what she wanted in life, a career, and she made it happen for herself. Like Beverly Kees, you can make it happen for you.

A Note on Starting Your Own Business

One of the simplest, yet most complex, ways to become an executive is to start your own business. It's simple because you become instant executive, and it's complex because running a business is a difficult task. But it's an alternative you might consider.

To start your own business, you need scads of financial backing and an extraordinary amount of courage. And to succeed, you need a heaping measure of good luck, because four out of five new businesses fail. The main reason for their failure is undercapitalization. The cliché that you need money to make money is certainly true in

business. You must possess financial resources if you expect to survive.

Banks, with their antiquated discriminatory policies, are
sluggishly beginning to consider lending business money to
women. The trouble is that most lending institutions don't
make what they consider high risk loans to people with
unproven track records. So unless you've had experience
running a business or have been operating your present
business for several years, your chances of getting money
through them are slight. You might consider other money
sources such as private investors, friends, other companies,
or your own savings. Whichever avenue you choose, be
sure to start with plenty of capital.

Starting your own business and watching it grow is an
incredible thrill, but it places tremendous demands on you.
Your life will have little room for anything else, and
sometimes the responsibilities can be staggering. I speak
from experience, for I started an advertising agency and
operated it for many years. I learned so much in the
process that I would not trade the experience for anything.

There's a wonderful headiness that comes from operating your own business, and you receive the loveliest
sense of satisfaction. It's magnificent to feel in control of
your own destiny and to make your efforts pay off for
yourself. But you must be willing to sacrifice yourself. Often I would come home at night so tired it was all I could
do to get undressed and go to bed. Socializing during the
work week was almost impossible, and my husband and I
took to writing notes to communicate with each other. The
business took all that I had to give, but the rewards out-
weighed the difficulties.

If you have entrepreneurial yearnings, don't be afraid to
start your own business, especially if you enjoy the element of risk. Those people who have succeeded most in
the corporate world are those who have been willing to
gamble. But you're playing where the stakes are high.

~§ 16 §~

A Dozen Dos for Executive Success

Here are a dozen items that are particularly pertinent to your role as an executive. I have listed them in this manner at the end of the book so that they leave a lasting impression on you. They are areas that you should be concerned with if you are truly intent on executive success.

1. Establish your priorities.

If you wish to become an executive, that goal must be the most important commitment in your life. You are competing with others who have made the quest for executive power the overriding factor in their lives. To compete with them, you must devote equal time and attention to your goal, if not more, as most executive women believe. Often you will be required to sacrifice your weekends or evenings, and you may have to curtail some of your other interests. Preparing to be an executive means establishing your priorities. Your career ambitions must come first.

This may mean adjusting your and your mate's expectations of your relationship, and you may lose it in the process. It may mean deciding to forgo a family for sake of a career, or coping with endless guilt if you choose to be a parent. Establishing your priorities may mean refusing a date from one of your company colleagues whom you find fascinating, because such an involvement would be a detriment to your career.

These are just a few of the ramifications of opting for a career, and ones that you should willingly accept. Building a career requires immense personal sacrifice.

2. Be assertive.

Being assertive is a prerequisite for gaining executive power. This may mean reprogramming yourself. Stanlee Phelps and Nancy Austin have written an excellent book called *The Assertive Woman* (San Luis Obispo, Calif.: Impact Pubs., 1975), and I suggest you read it if you have a chance. Assertiveness is vital.

You must be assertive in the supervision of your employees, and you will be respected for it. At all times you must maintain the upper hand with them. You must be assertive in standing up for your rights and demanding equality. To management, you must be assertive about letting your demands be known. In all aspects of your life, you must know how to say no. You cannot be the self-effacing stereotype of the submissive woman.

You must be assertive on your own behalf. Make certain that your accomplishments and aspirations are known by the powers that be. Don't expect that others will do this for you.

3. Speak up.

Speaking up falls into the category of being assertive, but it deserves special attention. Your executive skills must include the ability to speak before others. As long as you sit in a business meeting being seen and not heard, you are doing nothing to further your executive image. If you want to be noticed for more than your legs, you should be able to speak out and express your opinions, and you should do so at every available opportunity.

You may not look like an executive, but you sure can sound like one. Don't be afraid to voice your opinion or ask an intelligent question. Speak up. By doing so, you'll help carve an executive image of yourself.

4. Take risks.

Women have been culturally trained away from taking risks, and we tend to be more cautious than our male counterparts. However, taking calculated risks is an important element in executive decision making, and top executives are judged on their willingness to do so. If you're ever going to score big in business, you must have the courage to gamble. In fact, you should enjoy it.

A sure way to gain notice in a large corporation is to propose something out of the ordinary—shuffling a department or marketing a new product, that kind of thing. To be considered an innovative manager, you must be something of a risk taker. Indeed, you are gambling on the outcome of your proposal, and you are vulnerable to failure. But if you fail to ever do something out of the ordinary, if you never take risks, chances are you will be stuck in the same routine job year after year. Executives who are willing to take risks are the ones who receive the big promotions because they are the ones that are noticed.

5. Maintain career visibility.

Taking a risk is one way to gain visibility within your organization. Being the first person to hold a new job will also help you get noticed. And just being a woman helps. As a minority member of the executive ranks, you are more apt to be noticed than a man, and you should augment this advantage by participating in other activities that will enhance your career visibility.

I know an airlines executive who volunteered to become program chairman for his company's monthly management meeting. A seemingly thankless job that no one else wanted, he jumped at the opportunity. It was his responsibility to introduce the speaker every month, and he had a chance to appear before the top execs. He's been promoted twice since he assumed the task, and he partially attributes his success to this exposure.

A good way to maintain career visibility within your company and your industry is to join a professional organization and become active within it. I started out writing a newsletter for an advertising association, and I used it as a vehicle through which to demonstrate my abilities. Four years later I was elected president of the chapter—the first woman to hold that position. Although it involved devoting extra time, my outside activities did wonders for my career visibility.

A great strategy for exposure to your entire industry is

to attend trade shows and conventions, especially if you can somehow be on the program or assume a minor responsibility in the arrangements so you can sit at the head table. Sometimes if you attend these functions as an observer, you will be mistaken for someone's wife. Be concerned about letting others know that you are a professional, for these functions play a significant role in providing an interface for the old boys network, and if you are lucky, you may be able to become a part of it.

6. *Focus on the relevant.*

The necessity for relevancy applies to two distinct areas. The first is within your job tasks. You will always have more to do than you seemingly have time for. If this weren't the case, your company wouldn't need you to begin with. Only a portion of these duties are truly important. The rest may be the traditional busywork. You must isolate the matters which are pressing and relevant from those that can wait. To accomplish this, you must understand how your job fits into the scheme and what the true function is that management expects you to fulfill. To be a successful executive, you must perceive which tasks are relevant to your job and which are not.

The second need for relevancy centers upon your job as a whole. Are your responsibilities vital to the continuing success of the firm, or are they nonessential? If you are stuck in a routine, busywork job, you are less apt to be noticed in a favorable light by management, and you will be overlooked when it comes time for promotions. Having relevant responsibilities is a way to gain power within organizations, and it is also a method to gain career visibility.

7. *Accept responsibility for your actions.*

I'm sure you've heard the story about Harry S. Truman keeping a sign on his desk that said, "The buck stops here." There's a point to be made here about effectual leadership. If you are going to be an executive, you must be master of your destiny. If you make a mistake, excuses are unacceptable. And you must shoulder the responsibility for your subordinates as well. These are the traits of a strong leader. Management and your subordinates will be watching you to see if you display the strength of character to accept full responsibility for your actions.

In business, you must make things happen for yourself. No one is going to do it for you. If your career climb is sputtering, you might be tempted to blame your lack of progress on male chauvinism (which conceivably could be the cause). Nevertheless, you must assume responsibility for yourself. Don't let male chauvinism become a psychological roadblock to your growth.

8. *Learn to live with trial and error.*

I once heard a business lecturer say that if an executive makes just 50 percent of her decisions correctly, she can be successful. The key is to make them. Often, we tend to procrastinate for fear of making the wrong decision, but in doing so we often make the worst decision of all—no decision. No one expects you to be perfect. Part of your learning process involves trial and error. Accept it, and don't let your mistakes become a source of frustration. So much of management is educated guesswork that trial and error is about the only method you have to improve your job skills.

Learn from your mistakes, and then forget them. Don't allow a few errors in judgment to erode your self-confidence. Expect to live with trial and error learning.

9. *Be patient.*

The new executive woman is the glamour symbol of our time. But don't expect it instantly. The really glamorous jobs are few and far between, and the competition is keen. Seniority is often a factor, and women are just beginning to gain the experience that will qualify them for the top jobs.

Many younger women have come into business expecting too much too soon and have been disappointed at their seemingly slow progress. We must pay our dues too. It takes from fifteen to twenty-five years for a manager to become a top executive. Establish high goals, but be realistically patient about achieving them. Business success rarely happens overnight.

10. *Be strong.*

Being an executive requires an inordinate amount of

courage and a strong sense of self-confidence. Moreover, as a woman, you are pursuing a life-style that is contrary to the norm, and the price you pay is partial non-acceptance. Often you will experience loneliness and frustration, resentment and prejudice, and sometimes you will question whether it is all worth it. Men share those feelings, too. Some of this is the price you pay to be a woman, and the rest is the price of executive life.

If you are going to survive, you must possess great internal strength and fortitude. The harsh demands of executive life require it. The saying "When the going gets tough, the tough get going" should apply to you.

11. Look out for yourself.

Corporations can indeed be jungles full of predatory monsters eager to wipe you out. To survive, you must be savvy to the politics transpiring around you, and, most important, you must learn to look out for yourself. Don't naively assume that everyone can be trusted or that everyone is your friend. The competitive spirit is the catalyst for the business system. But often it brings out the worst in people. As a woman, you may have to fight it out alone. Your rule of survival: watch out for yourself. Other women are depending on you to succeed.

12. Help other women.

I believe the business system can change from within if women will help other women. In the long run, it will be easier for you if women executives are not a rarity. By helping other women, you are helping yourself.

You need to help create a women's job network that can compete and counterbalance the old boys network that has helped men so much. If men will not let us become a part of theirs, we must create one of our own.

You don't have to always hire a woman to help her. You can alert her to job openings within your company or on the outside. Executives frequently gossip about job openings; you can pass that information along or you can recommend her. And when you're looking for a job, others will reciprocate and assist you. Experts estimate that at least half the jobs in business are landed this way. Help establish a network where you can benefit, too.

❧ 17 ❧

Now It's Up to You

I've covered a lot of ground in this book, and I trust you've found its contents useful. I've offered suggestions on how to handle passes and problem employees, wives and secretaries, supervisors and subordinates, and everything in between. I've explained how the businessman thinks and behaves, how he's apt to relate to you, and some strategies to combat sexism and stereotyping. I've given rules of etiquette to follow, and laws of survival you should obey. I have portrayed a composite role model of the new executive woman, and I've suggested how you can become like her.

I've attempted to be impeccably realistic about the problems and frustrations you will face as an executive. I have warned of the pitfalls and pressures, the politics and prejudices that you'll encounter. I've described what a difficult and lonely pursuit executive life can be. I've told of the sacrifices you must make. I've given you the truth.

But now I want to give you one last thing. Encouragement. Encouragement about the future of women in general, and encouragement about your own future.

Ambition is no longer a dirty word. The women's movement has made you and your desires to seek wealth and power socially acceptable. You can say you want to become president of the company and not be considered aberrant, and yet stay feminine in the process.

You have a chance to be independent, to fulfill an ambition of your own, to work at top capacity, to have a sense of achievement, to discover talents you never knew you had, to experience personal growth, and to earn a sizeable income. Pity the woman who must pin all her aspirations on her subservient nature, her looks, her husband, or her children. You have a chance to gain recognition by being intelligent and resourceful, innovative and informed. And you'll feel wonderful about yourself in the process.

We are not the only ones who will benefit. Women have something special to offer, and business will benefit too.

Although many skeptics have tried, no one has been able to establish that any differences exist between the intellectual abilities of men and women as they apply to business. However, there are differences in our emotional compositions. Moreover, we have been culturally trained to respond differently to similar stimuli. A woman tends to be more sensitive to her own feelings, and she is therefore more sensitive toward the needs and feelings of others. A typically feminine personality trait, this inclination can be an asset for the business executive.

I am not claiming that women are better managers than men. But I do think that women, given the opportunity, will excel in certain distinct areas that could potentially make us better managers than men. Women as managers are more likely to become people-oriented, and this can become an important asset indeed. Once the male establishment is freed from the shackles of chauvinism, they will recognize this and capitalize on it. Women executives will become desired commodities because of their special people-handling skills.

Chester Burger in his book *Survival in the Executive Jungle* (New York: Macmillan, 1964) says, "Of all an executive does, getting along with people is the most important." In another place he says, "Researchers have confirmed that the executive who concentrates on production instead of on the people doing the production will fail." Most women, by nature, will concentrate on the people.

Corporations claim that people are their most important asset, and then move the plant out of state because labor is cheaper elsewhere. They claim they care about their employees, and then create unsafe or adverse working conditions for them. But the truth remains that people are business's most important asset. The infusion of women into corporate chambers will alter the character and texture of business. Women's natural inclination toward humaneness and their special skills in dealing with others will help business realign its priorities and be more people-oriented. And business will benefit from it in terms of dollars and cents, too.

I believe women will eventually become a hot commodity on the job market. Up until now, we're virtually unproven. But now that we have an opportunity to gain seniority and power by working through the system, we will have a chance to demonstrate what we can do. Industry will welcome women once it sees us for what we are—an untapped resource that can and will make valuable contributions. I'm enthusiastic about the future.

As David J. Mahoney, chairman and president of the Norton Simon Corporation, said at a conference on equal opportunity for women in business, "The women's movement has been good for America, and it will be good for business." Other bright, far-seeing corporate leaders are recognizing women's potential and are just beginning to realize its possibilities.

There is a great deal of pessimism within the women's movement about the real opportunities for women. Social change is at best a painfully slow process. Progress is being made, especially at entry management levels where there is little visibility. Ten or twenty years from now the effects will be more apparent. In the process, some necessary changes will be made. I expect more tolerance and flexibility by management regarding work schedules and home responsibilities. Men will become more active in the raising of children. Both men and women will restructure their expectations of marriage. The next generation of children may possess entirely different attitudes and values than those passed along in previous generations. And all this restructuring of business and society will benefit you.

Business is indeed making room for the new executive woman, however slow the progress may seem. It's not an equal world yet, but the extra effort you must devote is worth the satisfaction, as women everywhere are discovering. Corporate doors are being unlocked. Increasing opportunities exist. Now it's up to you.

Index